"I've known Dr. Smith for over thirty years, and throughout those years he and I shared the ups and downs of our institutional journeys. Evidently institutional intelligence was not always present! I'm thrilled that Dr. Smith has written this book in which he was able to reflect creatively on what constitutes the right building blocks for a healthy institution. In doing so, he amazingly succeeded in weaving in crucial themes from the nonprofit world, connecting them to Christian values and offering down-to-earth insights on how to implement them. The 'Individual and Group' exercises at the end of each chapter provide a helpful tool to make this book a workbook. I highly recommend this book to all church, seminary, and nonprofit leaders."

Riad Kassis, international director, Langham Scholars Ministry

"This book engages one of the most important and yet inadequately addressed changes unfolding all around us: widespread disillusionment with, if not outright rejection of, institutions. And this disillusionment is characteristic of both the larger cultural context and the subcultural context of churches and parachurch organizations. Gordon Smith addresses the challenge head-on with the insight of a theologian, the experience of an organizational leader, and the realistic hopefulness of a thoughtful Christian. Supposed 'reflective practitioners' too often disappoint. Smith does not. He provides both richly insightful analysis and constructive, applicable principles and practices with which institutions may thrive. Not just identified 'leaders,' but both friends and foes of institutions, along with the people they serve (which is all of us), would do well to learn from this book."

W. David Buschart, associate dean, Denver Seminary

"We can be walking among ruins without realizing it. Our buildings might stand tall, with shimmering glass or towering spires, but the institutions they house are eroding. Whether it's our cynicism or our fixation on individual 'authenticity,' our commitment to institutional maintenance has suffered. And as a result, mission suffers, because institutions are how we channel energies and sustain common work. This is why Gordon Smith's book is so important. Drawing on rich theoretical insight and years of lived investment in institutions, Smith has written a veritable handbook for the future of faithful work. I can't imagine anyone who shouldn't read this."

James K. A. Smith, professor, author, editor of *Comment* magazine

INSTITUTIONAL INTELLIGENCE

HOW TO BUILD AN EFFECTIVE ORGANIZATION

GORDON T. SMITH

IVP Academic

An imprint of InterVarsity Press
Downers Grove, Illinois

InterVarsity Press
P.O. Box 1400, Downers Grove, IL 60515-1426
ivpress.com
email@ivpress.com

InterVarsity Press® is the book-publishing division of InterVarsity Christian Fellowship/USA®, a movement of
students and faculty active on campus at hundreds of universities, colleges, and schools of nursing in the United
States of America, and a member movement of the International Fellowship of Evangelical Students. For
information about local and regional activities, visit intervarsity.org.

Scripture quotations, unless otherwise noted, are from the New Revised Standard Version of the Bible, copyright
1989 by the Division of Christian Education of the National Council of the Churches of Christ in the USA. Used
by permission. All rights reserved.

While any stories in this book are true, some names and identifying information may have been changed to
protect the privacy of individuals.

Cover design: Cindy Kiple
Interior design: Daniel van Loon
Images: © Vjom/iStockphoto

ISBN 978-0-8308-4485-2 (print)
ISBN 978-0-8308-9180-1 (digital)

Printed in the United States of America ∞

Library of Congress Cataloging-in-Publication Data
https://lccn.loc.gov/2017010362
Smith, Gordon T., 1953- author. Institutional intelligence : how to build an effective
organization / Gordon T. Smith. Downers Grove : InterVarsity Press, 2017.
   pages cm
   ISBN: 9780830844852 (hardcover : alk. paper)

P	25	24	23	22	21	20	19	18	17	16	15	14	13	12	11	10	9	8	7	6	5	4	3	2	1
Y		34	33	32	31	30	29	28	27	26	25	24	23	22	21	20	19		18		17				

for joella

CONTENTS

1 The Meaning of Institutions   1

2 Mission Clarity, Part 1   19
Affirming the Institutional Charism

3 Mission Clarity, Part 2   35
Discerning Institutional Identity and Purpose

4 Governance That Works, Part 1   53
Making the Right Things Happen

5 Governance That Works, Part 2   74
Finding Wisdom, Making Decisions

6 The Right People   89
Recruiting, Developing, Empowering

7 A Generative Institutional Culture   107
Fostering Hopeful Realism

8 Financial Equilibrium   131
Making Economic Sustainability a Priority

9 A Place to Be   151
Creating Built Space

10 Strategic Partnerships   174
The Synergy of Collaboration

Conclusion   192

Appendix A   197
Boards and Presidents

Appendix B   207
Institutions Are Good for the Soul

Appendix C   223
An Institutional Intelligence Essential Reading List

THE MEANING OF INSTITUTIONS

Institutions matter. Vibrant institutions—effective organizations—are essential to our personal lives and to the common good. Thus they merit our time and attention. And because institutions matter, we need to learn how to work with them and work within them. If organizations are going to be effective and if we are going to thrive within them, we need to foster institutional intelligence.

But we live in an era with a pervasive ambivalence about institutions. This might not be as much the case in the East—in Asia, for example—but in the West the very word *institution* has a negative ring to it for so many. It is not a happy day, for example, when someone is "institutionalized." It is often assumed that institutions and institutional thinking are at cross-purposes with dynamic communities, with personal vocational calling, and with core human values. Thus Jean Vanier, the esteemed founder of an organization that provides homes for the mentally handicapped, insisted in an interview that it was his original vision to establish communities rather than institutions. I have huge regard for Jean Vanier, but I was struck that this comment reflects a common assumption: institutions don't foster community; institutional thinking, he suggests, is contrary to communal values and commitments.

Similarly, faculty in academic institutions tend to view the institutional character of their colleges and universities somewhat cynically—as, perhaps, a necessary evil. They might accept that there is an institutional character to the place in which they work, but often they view it as essential to their own vocations to actually polarize the work and calling of the faculty from the infrastructure that is the "institution" and, by definition, those who exercise authority within the academy, particularly the so-called bureaucrats. They tend to speak somewhat tongue-in-cheek of colleagues who have become administrators as having gone over to the "dark side."

Then also, church leaders often look upon the administrative side of their work—essentially the organizational and institutional dimensions of congregational life—as a distraction from true spiritual leadership and ministry. Here too the language of "community" is often viewed as the defining vision of what it means to be a church: religious leadership should focus on teaching, preaching, presiding, and offering spiritual direction. Sometimes what it typically called *administration* is viewed as a problem, an obstacle to true religious leadership and pastoral care. The most influential pastoral theologian of our generation, Eugene Petersen—as just one example, but an influential example—does not at any point in his key contributions to the vocation of pastoral ministry consider or speak to what it means to work with the board, the denominational bodies, the finances and the budget, and the other institutional aspects of congregational life.

And yet for so many pastors, the biggest challenges and greatest source of stress will come precisely at this point: the institutional character of congregations, particularly matters of governance, board effectiveness, and their working relationship with the board. Yes, of course, a congregation is not merely an institution. But could it be that a local church will never thrive without attention to the institutional dimension of congregational life?

Then also, those who work in nonprofit agencies often stress the need for flat organizational structures that, it is argued, foster collaboration and personal empowerment, all with a view of downplaying the institutional or organizational character of the agency. Again, all this assumes that institutional identity and character is somehow inherently suspect and by its very nature, contra good work and what it means to live and work in community. And the word *institution* is often linked with the word *power* with the assumption that power and organizational hierarchy are somehow contrary to vital and effective organizations.

And in this context, it is not uncommon for religious communities to stress the need for servant leadership as though this means that no one exercises authority and that there is no executive decision making. Vital organizations, it is suggested, are flat—no hierarchy, no boss, no executive—where decisions are made by consensus because the organization is more like a family than an institution.

But is there another way to think about institutions? Can we perhaps actually recognize that institutions are essential to human flourishing? Rather than see them as a problem or as a necessary evil, can we appreciate instead that institutions are the very means by which communities thrive, individual vocations are fulfilled, and society is changed for the good? Can we consider that we are all enriched and we all flourish when we invest in sustainable institutions? And more, could it not be that we all need to learn how to work effectively within an institution and that we can view this capacity as a good thing—as vital part of our personal development? Could it be that institutional intelligence—the wisdom of working effectively within an organization—is an essential vocational capacity for each of us?

Many of us who think this way about institutions have at some point come across the little classic by Hugh Heclo, *On Thinking Institutionally*. Heclo observes this:

> Humans flourish through attachments to authoritative communities, not as totally unencumbered selves. Because institutional thinking goes beyond merely contingent, instrumental attachments, it takes daily life down to a deeper level than some passing parade of personal moods and feelings. By its nature, institutional thinking tends to cultivate belonging and a common life.[1]

In like fashion, James Davison Hunter insists that ideas are just ideas until institutions are established; he stresses that to change history, one has to get beyond ideas to institutions.[2] Ideas—even great ideas—are only going to make a difference when they are embodied, given a social structure,

---

[1]Hugh Heclo, *On Thinking Institutionally* (Boulder, CO: Paradigm Publishers, 2008), 189.
[2]James Davison Hunter, *To Change the World: The Irony, Tragedy, and Possibility of Christianity in the Late Modern World* (Oxford: Oxford University Press, 2010), 78.

within a dynamic and effective institution.[3] Thus Hunter insists that we need to find ways "to create conditions in the structures of social life we inhabit that are conducive to the flourishing of all."[4] He speaks of how "in each occupation, vocation, or profession, leaders need to look for opportunities to form networks and mobilize resources including symbolic capital, financial capital, social capital, and administrative capital in common purposes, . . . creating structures that incarnate blessing, beauty, meaningfulness, and purpose not just for the benefit of believers but for the good of all."[5]

In other words, institutions give us an opportunity and a mechanism, a means, to invest in something much larger than ourselves and to make a contribution that we would never be able to make individually and on our own. We invest in something—a means, a system, an entity—that will outlast us. When we invest in institutions and learn to work with institutions in partnership and in synergy with others—committing time, energy, and resources into something that matters to us and to others, working together with others to create the conditions in which institutions can flourish—the opportunity emerges for something very important to us to happen.

THE CHARACTER OF INSTITUTIONS

An institution is a social structure that leverages wisdom, talent and resources toward a common cause or purpose. More specifically, it is a means, an architecture—specifically a social architecture—by which we can pursue a shared and greater good together. Just as a soul cannot exist except as embodied, there is no community, no vision, no mission without institutions. The idea, the vision, will not happen, will not make a difference until and unless it is housed in an institution.

Thus James K. A. Smith suggests that while we do not need to romanticize institutions—we can and do recognize their limits—we also do not need to demonize them.[6] Rather, we tend them—and his use of the word

---

[3]Ibid., 44.
[4]Ibid., 278.
[5]Ibid., 270.
[6]James K. A. Smith, interview with James Davison Hunter, "The Backdrop of Reality," *Comment*, Fall 2013, 36.

tend is so apt—we tend them with all their limitations, for they are the means by which we do something significant together. Smith words it well when he writes this:

> Institutions are durable, communal ways that we can act in concert with our neighbors to achieve penultimate goods. So, instead of thinking about institutions as big, hulking, static behemoths, think of institutions as dynamic, social *enactment.* Try to imagine "institutions" as spheres of action. Institutions are not just something that we build; they're something that we *do.*[7]

The point at issue, then, is not whether we have institutions or not. Rather, the question is whether we will invest in them and know how to make them effective. They are always imperfect because people are imperfect. And yet they outlive us, and to the degree that we get them right, good things—indeed, very good things—happen.

If you want to address matters of poverty, invest time and energy in an institution that gets at the underlying causes and responds deeply and effectively to the problem. If you have a dream to educate a generation, dream on, I say, if you are not willing to invest in an academic institution that will actually make the dream happen. If as a church you want to have a long-term impact on the lives of individuals, families, a community, and the lives of those in that community, then you must consider the institutional character of congregational life. Do not be naive or utopian about your dream; rather, attend to the nitty-gritty of what makes the church an effective agency of substantive change. If you want to deeply affect the way that a community or a city think about and understand and embrace the arts, then it will be schools of art and art galleries and studios and artists' guilds—institutions, each of them—that ultimately alter the social landscape. And when I am taken into the ER with a crisis, I want a dynamic, powerful, and effective institution that is able to respond to my immediate and very urgent need. At that point, I am not wanting creative and critical thinking about great medical care. Rather, like many others in such situations, we are looking for a hospital—an institution—

---

[7]James K. A. Smith, "Editorial: We Believe in Institutions," *Comment*, Fall 2013, 3-4.

made up of people who do not merely have good ideas and are very competent at responding to medical crises. I am looking to be admitted into a hospital with a vision for excellence in health care that has been translated into effective systems transcending the ideas or competence of any one person. I am not saying that good ideas do not matter. Of course not. I am not saying that critical thinking and creative thinking are not crucial. Rather, we need clear and creative thinking that is housed within institutions that deliver on the very best of this clear and creative thinking.

We need institutions that protect communities: police forces, fire departments, and the military. We need institutions by which we are governed, civic institutions on a municipal and national level. It is stunningly naive to be anti-government; without government institutions civilization does not happen. It would be "every man" for himself or herself. To govern a society—a city, a province, or a nation-state—you need institutions that work. And then also there is no great art, learning, or human achievement—commercial, religious, intellectual, or otherwise—without institutions. If you want to hear Beethoven's Ninth Symphony in all of its power, wonder, and grandeur, the only way will be if an orchestra—an institution—mounts it.

In none of these cases do we merely need someone with a good idea. We need people who have invested in and know how to sustain effective, vital institutions made up of people, at all levels of the institution, who know how to think institutionally. They get it; they know what it takes for a good idea to actually make a difference. They have institutional intelligence.

As a university president, I live with the daily awareness of the potential of institutions of higher education. And I am convinced that we need such institutions—public and private, including those such as the one I lead, that embody the core values of the Christian intellectual and spiritual tradition. Since the Christian intellectual and spiritual tradition matters to me, I am eager to see it lived out within an institution. As a reader you no doubt have your own defining values and commitments, a vision for what matters to you. The only way this will find concrete, tangible, and long-term expression in society or community—in our world—is if you learn how to work with others and form a society—a guild, a school, a hospital, an art gallery, a church, that is, an institution—that will bring together the strengths and abilities of a variety of people who can work together over a sustained period of time toward a common end.

In this regard, we need to persuade a younger generation of Christian leaders that investing in institutions makes sense. They can be creative, strategic, and even revolutionary and not assume that in so doing, they have to be anti-institutional. Indeed, if they are going to have a lasting impact on the church and on society, they need to think institutionally and invest time and energy in institutions, especially institutions they believe in. But for that, two things are needed: to affirm that institutions matter and, further, to identify what it means to think and act with institutional intelligence.

I say to those in their twenties and thirties, you can try to make it on your own, as a freelance worker or contractor, as a stand-alone agent. And those who make such attempt as often as not do so because they have become cynical about institutions, and perhaps have been hurt by institutions. And there might be good reasons for us to appreciate their circumstances.

We might be impressed by the pioneer missionary, not part of a mission agency, perhaps, independently striving to change the world. Or we might be taken with the individual blogger who is valiantly profiling some recurring wrong, a prophet alone in the wilderness. Or we might be moved by the clever entrepreneurs or inventors who emerge from their back rooms with revolutionary ideas. And yet if the impact of the blogger is going to take and truly alter our society—the church, the community, the politics that shape our shared lives—eventually those ideas need to find expression within the core values of an institution if they are going to make a difference and truly come up against the very thing the blogger is protesting. And the inventor? Here as well, the brilliant idea, if it is going to go anywhere at all, needs to be housed. Otherwise it is merely a distant and perhaps clever idea or invention that does not ultimately make a difference in the lives of communities, churches, societies, and countries.

In academic institutions, faculty are invited into something larger than themselves. They flourish, with others, when they foster an institutional intelligence to work effectively within those institutions.

Pastors need to be encouraged to view the work of administration not as a necessary evil, a distraction, but as rather an integral part of what it means to provide congregational leadership. Indeed, if their vision for a vital community of faith is going to happen, they will need to attend to the institutional dimensions of church life—the administrative, financial, personnel issues of what it means to be the church. Their theological vision for what it means to be the church will be housed within particular practices, institutional practices that embody that vision.

Those who work within a nonprofit agency need to appreciate that the organization is not merely a platform for their own vocational aspirations. Rather, the organization of which they are a part reflects a potential, a possibility for making a difference, that merits focused attention not merely on the individual calling but on the shared calling reflected in the organizational mission.

If you are violin player or a flute player, you can be a soloist for sure. But there are few things so powerful as an orchestra, a symphony orchestra, and you cannot be part of an orchestra unless you learn to work with, to play with, others as part of an authoritative community—that is, a community that has a structure, a form, a system that is governed toward a common objective. There is no orchestra without a script, without a common plan and objective, and without a conductor. We defer, as musicians, to the composer and the conductor; we listen to another—attentive to those around us—committed to a common objective. We defer our own egos to the mission of the greater whole.

So much great talent and opportunity is missed simply because we do not give adequate attention to the institutions that could leverage our shared potential toward a greater good. Taking this personally I say to you, the reader: if you want to make a difference—with all the talent, vision, and wisdom that God has given you—then learn to work with and in institutions. Your impact will be exponentially greater if your calling or vocation can be leveraged against the calling and potential of others toward a common goal, a shared vision.

It will mean fostering institutional intelligence: learning to work with others, within institutions. It means understanding how institutions work, how they can be most effective, and how you can contribute to a greater whole by learning to work within institutional systems. It means growing in your capacity to appreciate how institutions are founded, how they work, how they grow and adapt, and how they are governed.

THE PROBLEM AND THE POTENTIAL OF INSTITUTIONS

In saying all this about institutions, we are certainly not sentimentalizing them. They can be a problem. Some, of course, are bent on evil outcomes—whether it is systems that foster human trafficking, or the drug trade, or the casino industry. There are indeed evil institutions that violate our core human values. Then also, institutions are a problem when we fail to distinguish between means and ends. All too easily institutions can take on a life of their own, lacking any clear sense of mission. This distinction is so very important. An institution is always a means to an end—the end, of course, being the mission. Jesus used the image of wineskins and distinguished this from the actual wine, and this image helps when we think about the character of an institution. Institutions are wineskins—systems and structures that hold in trust sacred values and commitments. They are not ends but means to an end.

We have all met them: people who live and dream and work to make the institution strong but lose sight of the mission and values that the institution is meant to foster. They get caught up in the bureaucracy rather than fostering the institution's capacity to achieve its mission. They lose a sense of the reason for which the institution actually exists. Or, perhaps most common, they work toward the financial sustainability of the organization but do so in a way that actually undercuts the mission and core values of the institution.

And those whose lives are affected by these people are understandably put off by such thinking and assume that the problem is institutional thinking. To the contrary, this is actually not true institutional intelligence. True institutional intelligence will distinguish means and ends. If you want a glass of water, you need a glass; if you want a good meal, you need the stove, the grill, the plates, the cutlery, spices, and the chair and table. But we do not confuse the table with the meal or the plates with the appetizer. When someone confuses the means and the end—they are more taken with the glass than the water—the solution is not to dismiss the glass but to understand and appreciate that the glass is a means to the end: a refreshing drink of water.

And then also, in speaking of the problem with institutions, there is no avoiding the reality that institutions are never perfect. For starters, they are populated by people. And often when we feel let down by institutions, in actual fact we were let down by a person—someone who used the system or the structures of the institution to their own personal ends. We blame institutions, but a person was at fault.

Then also, without doubt, sometimes institutions are often poorly designed—lacking missional clarity, appropriate governance structures, and qualified leadership. As a rule, if institutions do not work, it is because people have not attended to what it is that makes organizations effective. Thus the solution is not to dismiss institutions, but rather to realize two things. First, they will fail; they will not be perfect. And second, individuals in institutions will abuse power, will act in inhumane and inconsiderate ways, and the net result is that people will be hurt. Institutions fail when they are poorly conceived or poorly designed, or when the shared purposes are not honored. And yet for all their imperfections and the imperfections of the people who populate them, they still merit the investment of our time and energy. The solution is to invest ever more so in institutions, to understand how they work—develop institutional intelligence—and to be patient with others who are also trying to make institutions work.

WHO NEEDS INSTITUTIONAL INTELLIGENCE?

Those in the for-profit world without doubt need institutional intelligence as much as anyone. But the focus in the chapters that follow will be the nonprofit sphere. And it will be evident that this kind of thinking—institutional intelligence—is essential for the presidents and chief executive officers and executive leaders of nonprofit organizations. They are responsible at the most senior level for the viability and vitality of the institutions for which they are immediately responsible. And they need to be aware of the leverage points, the zones or spheres of energy investment that will foster the capacity of this organization to be effective. Nonprofit presidents and CEOs, along with their senior leadership team, need a guide to institutional thinking: how and where to leverage their time and energy toward mission effectiveness. Sure, the CFO will focus on finances, but a truly good CFO—along with other senior administrators—will think institutionally, will think and operate in light of the whole of the institution's well-being.

Those who are external constituents—be these donors, board members, or others who are not employees—also have a stake in the success of a nonprofit organization. They need a guide to help them assess an organization for which they may be a trustee or a donor. If you are invested in an organization, you will want to have in hand a way to respond to this question: How do I know if this is an institution that is vital and effective? What are the key indicators of organizational vitality and effectiveness?

Faculty members of colleges and universities will find it helpful to foster an attentiveness to the institution in which they are teaching, meaning that they consider not only their own research and academic responsibilities but also the dynamics of what makes for a vital institution.

As I have indicated, pastors and other church staff can come to a greater appreciation of the need for two things: the organizational and institutional character of their congregations and also the potential significance of denominational structures and judicatory bodies. And congregational pastors would do well to appreciate how they can function effectively in both spheres—both the local church and the denominational entity of which they are a part. The authors of *The Trellis and the Vine*, in speaking of pastoral ministry, make a very helpful and necessary distinction between the basic work of the ministry—the proclamation of the gospel and the care for people—and what they speak of as the "framework" that is so crucial if the ministry is to grow. Marshall and Payne put it this way:

> As the ministry grows, the trellis also needs attention. Management, finances, infrastructure, organization, governance—these all become more important and more complex as the vine grows.[8]

Their point is that the institutional character of congregational life is vital to the ministry of the church. Pastors long to make a difference, to be catalysts for substantive change in their congregations not merely

---

[8]Colin Marshall and Tony Payne, *The Trellis and the Vine* (Kingsford, NSW: Matthias Media, 2009), 3.

in numbers, but also in the emotional, spiritual vitality of their faith communities and their missional impact within their neighborhoods and communities. But this very kind of impact requires institutional intelligence, to appreciate the capacity to leverage the institutional strengths of the congregation—which includes a whole range of elements that will be addressed in this book—but also the capacity to manage their own anxiety as they work effectively with human systems and organizations.

Finally, I will highlight another group—perhaps, in some respects, one of the most crucial groups—that needs to consider what it means to have institutional intelligence: department heads, directors, and team leaders.

In many organizations—not all, perhaps, but many—there is a role or sphere of responsibility that is particularly crucial to the implementation of the mission. And the effectiveness of the organization pivots on the effectiveness of these particular leadership roles. I am thinking of three in particular. In academic institutions, these are departmental heads or chairs. The future of the college or the university depends on their capacity to lead, to build a department, to recruit potential faculty, to foster good conversation about curriculum, and to maintain a positive tone or outlook for the faculty and students within that department.

Then also, in most nonprofits, there is a role designated "director": thus, for example, in a university, you might have a director of communication, a director of enrollment management, a director of information technology, and others who direct campus operations, the residences, the athletic programs, the development and fundraising agenda, along with those who are the directors for alumni relations or government relations.

And then we need to keep in mind what is typically called a team leader, comparable to a department head in that the leader here is coordinating a team that has an active role in the field—perhaps, the lead person in a response team to a crisis. This is not the president of the organization or a board member but the person on the ground who has a team of anywhere from four or five to as many as twenty. In military terms, these are platoon leaders, those who lead a team that delivers very specific and measurable results.

These roles are pivotal. Typically, they report to a vice president or, on a pastoral staff, the director for children's ministry, youth, family, or outreach might report to the senior pastor or an executive pastor in larger congregations. And the role of the vice president or the senior person is essentially to recruit and appoint the most capable directors possible—or, in a university, department heads. Each of these needs to be a person of consummate institutional intelligence.

THE ELEMENTS OF AN EFFECTIVE ORGANIZATION

What does it take to be a dynamic organization that can deliver great results over time in a changing environment, an organization that knows that problems, setbacks, and difficulties will without doubt come but that these can truly be opportunities for institutional growth and development? Elinor Ostrom raises the question this way: "Can we dig below the immense diversity of regularized social interactions in markets, hierarchies, families, sports, legislatures, elections, and other situations to identify universal building blocks used in crafting such structured situations?"[9]

What are the essential organizational "building blocks," to use the language of Ostrom? The literature on institutions and management and organizational leadership is extensive, and from this literature it is possible to identify what makes organizations effective. Yes, each organization is unique. And yet there are some universal building blocks—the essential elements we need to attend to if we are going to have institutional intelligence, an appreciation of how organizations actually work.

In my own journey with institutions, I have not only been in a senior administrative role within a number of academic institutions both in Asia and in North America, I have also had the opportunity through an extended chapter of my career to work with academic institutions in the global south—everywhere from Vietnam to Romania to Cuba and points in between. And what is clear is that when institutions work, when organizations are effective, it is not merely a matter of good fortune or divine providence. It was clear why it was happening: these institutions did what it takes to have an effective organization. But also, if they were not effective,

[9]Elinor Ostrom, *Understanding Institutional Diversity* (Princeton, NJ: Princeton University Press, 2005), 5.

it was equally evident that one or more of the essential elements of an organization were either being ignored or creating significant operational drag. In leaning into the rich body of literature on the topic and in conversation with leaders globally, I increasingly concluded that vital institutions foster some very specific capacities, elements of an effective organization. The strength of effective institutions comes from the dynamic interplay of seven distinctive features or characteristics—each an essential building block:

1. mission clarity: functioning in light of a well-defined institutional identity and purpose

2. appropriate governance structures that leverage wisdom and power effectively

3. quality personnel appointments: hiring well, developing people effectively, and managing exiting transitions with grace

4. a vibrant institutional culture marked by hopeful realism

5. financial resilience, evident in a well-managed approaches to revenue and expenses

6. generative built spaces

7. strategic alliances and collaborative partnerships

None of these can be addressed in isolation from the other six; each is part of an integrated whole. And yet neglecting any one of these seven will cripple an institution. Therefore, those with institutional intelligence need to be attentive to each of them, like an engineer working with design elements of a bridge, attending to each element, each aspect of bridge construction, connecting all the essential parts, dimensions, and elements so that the end product is a span that serves vehicular traffic brilliantly.

Of course, no two institutions are alike; there are no generic institutions and for each organization there will be a unique configuration of these seven elements. There is not, in other words, one set approach to good governance. And yet there are elements, working principles, and considerations that have universal application such that we can actually say the following:

1. People with institutional intelligence will have an intimate appreciation of the purpose—the identity and mission—of the organization of which they are a part, will believe in that mission, and will know how their role or responsibility contributes to that mission.

2. People with institutional intelligence will understand how governance works within the institution and will contribute to the process, constructively and collaboratively, by which decisions are made and implemented in a way that is consistent with their role within the organization. (Thus, for example, a faculty member will understand the role of faculty in governance, a congregational member the role of the congregation as a whole, while also appreciating the role of others in governance.)

3. People with institutional intelligence will recognize that personal talent and commitment are critical to the organization's success and, if they have a role in hiring, will be committed to hiring well, developing staff effectively, and learning how to transition out of the organization in a way that is both timely and constructive when that time comes.

4. People with institutional intelligence will have an appreciation for the power of institutional culture and will do their part, consistent with their role in the organization, to foster a healthy and dynamic spirit of hopeful realism.

5. People with institutional intelligence will recognize that the financial health and vitality of the organization, while the particular responsibility of some, is owned by all and that in some form or other, everyone knows what it takes to have an organization that has financial viability and resilience.

6. People with institutional intelligence will appreciate the significance of built space; they will know how to read and work effectively within a building that houses the institution in a way that fosters their capacity to flourish within the institution and contribute to the fulfillment of the institutional mission.

7. People with institutional intelligence will contribute to effective and strategic partnerships and alliances with other agencies in a way that

is consistent with their role within the institution, recognizing that the fulfillment of institutional mission necessitates these kinds of collaborative arrangements.

Having identified earlier in this introduction those who need to cultivate institutional intelligence, not all chapters are going to be equally relevant to each reader. The following might be helpful as a guide for those who might want to read selective chapters.

Some chapters are simply basic: chapter three, on mission and institutional purpose; chapters four and five, on governance; chapter six, on how institutions are ultimately about *people* on mission together; chapter seven, on organizational culture; and chapter ten, on strategic alliances.

Chapter two, on institutional charism and its implications for mission, will be of particular interest to those who want to ask theological questions about institutions and who, particularly as CEOs—presidents, executive directors, senior pastors—and board members, need to see how institutional mission is located within the organization's history.

Chapter eight on finance is essential for all who have direct responsibility for the financial health of the institution, including board members and all those who serve as directors or department heads.

Finally, chapter nine will be of particular interest for those who want to reflect more extensively on how institutions are located within appropriate built spaces.

INSTITUTIONAL INTELLIGENCE AND STRATEGIC THINKING

What will be noteworthy to some is that strategic planning is not on the list of seven essential elements of an effective organization. It is a common assumption or conventional wisdom that effective institutions are effective precisely because they know how to do strategic planning and then in a disciplined fashion, throughout the institution, put a strategic plan into effect. We live in an organizational world and climate fascinated with the "art" of strategic planning, despite the publication of Henry Mintzberg's classic, *The Rise and Fall of Strategic Planning*. Nonprofits are known for having a senior leadership team head to the hills do to strategic planning—for a two-day retreat, perhaps—and return to present the outcome of their deliberations to the governing board and eventually roll out the plan for the whole organization and, sooner than later, move toward implementation.

And when all is said and done, the plan is published. And then is it shelved. Why? Because it does not work; it is borderline useless. The reason for this is that by the time you finish the entire exercise, the environment has changed, the key variables on which you did your planning have changed, perhaps some of the key players have changed. In other words, our environments are fluid, not stable. Some contexts and settings are even chaotic. But the word *fluid* is likely a more helpful image: we live in a world where we simply cannot make assumptions about our environment or make any confident assertions about the future. We only see as far as the next bend in the road; we do not know what lies around that bend.

Thus vital and strong institutions are not so much those that have a great strategic plan as those who are able to think strategically and respond strategically with creativity, innovation, and agility to the unexpected, the unforeseen. Some things can be anticipated, no doubt: downturns in the economy are likely to happen. University enrollment managers can get good data on the number of high school students in their region and thus get a read on how many college students there are likely to be one, two, three years down the road. A pastor can get data from city hall on anticipated growth in the sector of the city in which they are located—city plans that might affect the demographics of a congregation in the years to come.

I am not questioning the need for planning and for thinking and acting strategically. Of course not. I am merely challenging the preeminence of strategic planning as that which, ostensibly, makes for organizational effectiveness. I am agreeing with Patrick Lencioni, who in his book *The Advantage: Why Organizational Health Trumps Everything Else in Business* makes the case that institutional health, vitality, and resilience are the truly crucial elements of organizational effectiveness.[10] We need to consider what it takes for organizations to adapt, to be innovative and nimble—without melodrama or fear of the future but able to respond with institutional agility in the midst of fluid environment.

---

[10]Patrick Lencioni, *The Advantage: Why Organizational Health Trumps Everything Else in Business* (San Francisco: Jossey-Bass, 2012).

Dynamic organizations are masters of what in chess we call the "middle game." A chess player has control over most of her opening moves: set up the preferred pawn structure, castle the king, perhaps; move the knights into their strategic positions. There are a variety of opening moves—gambits—but they are all fairly basic. Further, a good chess player knows when it is time to move toward the endgame. And as a rule, these moves are rather straightforward. Often it never happens; a losing player recognizes that checkmate is just a matter of time and thus concedes.

What makes for a good game is not the opening, which is basic, or the endgame, which often does not even happen, but rather the "middle game." The magic of chess is precisely that no two games are alike; and the middle game is where the energy and heart of the match is found. As a player, you do not know what the middle game will look like till you get there because you do not know what your opponent will do by way of her opening moves. So the essential thing is this: Can you in your opening moves establish yourself on the board in a way that does two things? First, can you position yourself to defend your king? And can you also open up enough lines of mobility so that you can attack your opponent's king? And there is a tricky balance: if you emphasize defense, you will limit your mobility; if you are too aggressive, you become vulnerable to attack.

This book is about positioning your organization for the middle game—to move the pawns, castle the king, and open up the lines of attack for your bishops and eventually for your queen. Great organizations foster the capacity of their institution to be responsible, nimble, creative, and courageous in response to the unknown, to that which lies around the bend in the road.

And this means attending to the essential elements—the building blocks—of effective organizations.

MISSION CLARITY, PART 1

Affirming the Institutional Charism

There is no such thing as a generic institution. Each organization has a unique identity, calling, and purpose—a reason for being. Institutional vitality depends on finding and living with clarity precisely at this point: Who are we, and what is *our* purpose, *our* mission, *our* calling?

This means that the organization has a mission statement, of course, but clarity on mission is much more than just having some kind of statement in place and published. Missional clarity is about a distinctive sense of the vocation of the institution: a deep and nuanced understanding of what *this* organization is called to do, at this time and place, within this economic, social, political demographic. Many organizations have mission statements but still have ambiguity and uncertainty about their actual purpose or vocation. Yes, we need to do the due diligence necessary to craft a statement of mission; this is an important exercise. But this is only a part of what it means to have a compelling, defining, and animating mission. A single statement can never capture the essence of identity, purpose, vision, and meaning of this particular organization.

One can review the mission statements on the websites of Christian universities, for example, and find them to be remarkably similar. But when you get on the ground and breathe the air on campus—talk to the leaders and sit in classes where faculty are engaging students—a sense of a distinctive identity, a way of being, and a sense of purpose will be evident.

You can visit many churches that will likely have similar mission statements on their websites and reference the same biblical verses to justify these mission statements. But when you gather on Sunday with them, it is clear that every congregation is unique. Denominational affiliation and heritage, geographic and cultural location, and the accumulation of shared experiences, in this time and place, reflect a particular way of being and a particular calling or vocation.

You can be on the ground in a disaster zone and encounter two different relief agencies, and both can perhaps speak of the need to respond to this crisis effectively, be it a typhoon or an earthquake or a major fire. But when you are back at base camp and listen to their leadership, it becomes clear that while they may look very similar in the field, in fact here too there is a prevailing uniqueness—again, a distinctive way of being, reflected in core values, commitments, and a sense of purpose.

Having this clarity about identity and purpose is essential for organizational effectiveness. Vital institutions cultivate missional clarity; women and men with institutional intelligence know and work with the mission of the institution of which they are a part. To get clarity about mission, it is helpful to approach the question in two stages or steps. First, we ask about the founding vision or charism; this will be the focus of this chapter. And then second, the focus of the next chapter, we spell out the key questions that help an institution come to clarity about organizational identity and purpose.

A THEOLOGICAL VISION FOR INSTITUTIONS: IDENTIFYING THE INSTITUTIONAL DNA

One helpful way to approach the mission question is through the principle— the theological perspective—of seeing institutions as having a distinctive charism. By *charism* we mean a gift, a contribution, very specifically a gift from God—something that reflects the way in which the Spirit, thus the language of "charism," is gifting and making a difference in the church and in the world.

This way of viewing institutions emerged during Vatican II, the great 1960s renewal council within the Roman Catholic Church. Pope Paul VI observed that this was a potentially significant way to think about religious communities—notably religious orders, including the Franciscans, the Jesuits, the Benedictines, and more. It was the pope's way of signaling that what defines and sustains a religious community is not, in the end, strategic plans or brilliant leadership but rather the enabling of the Spirit, who is at work in the church and in the world and at work through such institutions and communities. The charism of the religious order typically reflected the way that the Spirit, through the founder, had gifted—graced, "charismed"—the church and the world. Typically this means looking at the particular giftings and vision of the founder of the religious order. Thus, for example, deep in the DNA of the Franciscans is a call to attend to the poor. The Dominicans are the order of preachers with their commitment to learning and teaching. And the Jesuits are known for their unique synthesis of scholarship, contemplative prayer, and apostolic service.

What I am suggesting is that this way of thinking about Catholic religious orders is transferable, providing us with a way to think about the vocation of all institutions. This is so for a number of reasons.

First, the language of "charism" gives us a *theological* vision for institutions. We see them—regardless of how significant the person, the individual founder, or any other individuals who succeeded them—as the work of God. In the final analysis, the organization is a means by which God is doing God's work in the world. We should always maintain a gracious humility about our organizations; it can be a little presumptuous to always assume that our organizations are God's instrument for God's purposes in the mission of God. And yet there is a sense in which institutions do have this quality; they are bigger than any of us and they potentially have a vocation in their own right.

We rightly think this way about congregations, and we immediately recognize the violation of a faith community when someone or some group assumes that they somehow own the church and expresses the entitlement that they assume goes with this. But the language of "charism" gives us a way to think in similar ways about the organizations that reflect our collective efforts—as vehicles by which the Spirit of God is gracing the church and the world. We are reminded that these institutions do not ultimately belong to us, even if we were involved in the startup or founding

CHAPTER 2

of the school or agency or church. They belong to God. And we are but stewards of the organization in that we are stewards of the charism, the means by which this organization is a gift of God to the church and to the world.

Second, the language of charism implies diversity. Though there is one Spirit, that same Spirit is the giver of many and diverse gifts that reflect the diverse beauty and the whole gospel of Christ Jesus in the world. When we compare and contrast other institutions that are our sister agencies—other universities, or other churches, or other relief or mission agencies—there will no doubt be many deep points of commonality. And yet the language of "charism" helps us consider the distinct manner in which the Spirit graces the world through each particular institution, meaning that there can be much diversity as particular individual institutions reflect a distinct embodiment of a particular grace or charism.

And the perspective of "charism" means that we can accept, affirm, and celebrate these differences. Franciscans are different from the Jesuits. This is as it should be. Diversity is not a problem but part of the wealth by which God graces the world.

G. K. Chesterton has done a couple of wonderfully nuanced studies—biographical reflections and observations—on St. Francis and St. Thomas Aquinas, a Dominican. For Chesterton, Thomas is clearly the great son of St. Dominic, the embodiment of the Dominican vision or charism. And his point is that both St. Francis and St. Thomas, while different, are both vital and essential means by which God was working in the life of the church in their respective eras. In other words, neither is the standard by which the other is judged; they each have a distinct calling or purpose. They represent a different charism.[1] Thus, Thomas Aquinas would not have been a good Franciscan monk. His calling belonged—needed to be housed, one might say—in a different order, with a different charism. And I will be pressing this point as we consider what it means to speak of institutional intelligence: we will thrive or flourish if and as we can find ourselves within an institution that fits us, that has a deep congruence with our own calling or vocation.

---

[1]G. K. Chesterton, *Saint Thomas Aquinas* (1933; repr., New York: Image Books, 1956), 26-29.

But the main point here is that institutions can, without apology, accept differences. Moreover, we can actually view this diversity as a point of strength, not weakness. We let others be who they have been called to be and embrace the particularity of our own lives, our own circumstances, and our own calling. And this perhaps cuts against the trend and the temptation to franchise—the proclivity of some institutions or churches to find a model that has worked elsewhere and then try to reproduce this model in their own context and setting.

Third, the lens of institutional charism gives us a way to recognize and appreciate the full breadth and depth of our institutional identity, a way to think of the whole: the mission, the values, the particular network of relationships with diverse constituencies, and the geography (the sense of place). This whole is bigger than any one of us, leader or staff person, and our contribution to the institution is but a contribution to the whole, a part that we play wherein there is no person who is the embodiment of the whole. Rather, we all participate in and foster or cultivate the charism. In other words, just as we can speak of the diversity of charisms or gifts of the Spirit that are given to the church, with each essential to the whole and each a distinct contribution to the whole (see 1 Corinthians 12), even so we can speak of institutions as diverse and distinct in the way that they participate in the purposes of God in the world.

Fourth, when we speak of charism, we affirm that history matters. A theological vision for institutions takes account of the past, of the occasion and circumstances that brought an organization into existence and to this point in time. We tell our story: Where did we come from, and who and what brought us into being? What was the original purpose for which this organization was established? What was the vision of the founders? The current institution has deep continuity with its past. It did not arise out of a vacuum; there was a genesis to the organization that inevitably is part of what it is today. And so we ask the question that gets us back to institutional origins.

We can without hesitation use God-language and ask, how did God bring this organization or institution into being? And, as best as we can tell, to what end did God gift the church and the world with this organization? What occasioned the establishing of this institution? What need did it respond to—what gap, you might say, did it seek to fill? What innovation or new beginning did the establishing of this organization represent? Was there a crisis that marked the identity of this institution at the beginning, when it was first organized?

When we tell the story, we tell the good, the bad, and the ugly. We speak of those elements in our history that might not be so pretty. There is no nostalgia, no sentimentality. We do not idolize the founder or the past or "the good old times." We are freed to name the challenges and difficulties that may have shaped our organizational history.

This does not mean that we live mired in a toxic past—if indeed there are elements of the history that are not so good. Rather, we name that past so that it can keep the present from being victimized by that past. We name it so that we can put it behind us—or, perhaps better said, we locate this segment of our past and keep it from defining our present. History, then, does not mean nostalgia. It means that we name reality— telling the story not as we wish it was but as it has actually happened. No sentimentality. And then we discern how that past can best inform the present. It the case of a congregation, it might mean naming the reality of a church split, perhaps two or three decades ago, that has left a scar in the institutional memory.

Fifth, the language of charism opens up reflections on how the past finds expression in the current situation—the present. We begin with history. We recognize, for example, that there is no avoiding that a founder significantly shaped if not actually embodied the vision in particular ways— St. Francis for the Franciscans, Ignatius Loyola for the Jesuits.

We begin here, but this is not the whole story. History is not just about the original vision and the original founder. When we use the language of charism we recognize that the institutional identity is ultimately larger than even these founders: it grows and matures, it has to adapt to changing circumstances—sometimes necessary changes that the original founder or original community could not anticipate. The institution itself has a history beyond its founding. It is now located in a new context and setting. Sometimes founders of movements or institutions become their own worst enemies when they refuse to accommodate and adapt to new circumstances and contexts. And so easily, also, they forget that they are not owners of the vision but merely stewards of something that is even bigger than themselves, even if they are the founders.

So we recognize that at this point in our history, as an organization, we are—"merely," one might say—living out one chapter in the history of this organization, this school, this church. And to get a sense of our calling, we need to appreciate the variables and factors, the history and story that got us here. But then we need to ask the here-and-now question: Who are we called to be—in light of our history, but now in a different time and place?

We still stress that each such community or institution is a gift of the Spirit to the church and the world, a gift given at the time of the founding or initial formation, perhaps to the founder or founders. But the charism is always bigger than the founder. And it is always something larger or bigger than the collective at any time in their history, so that at any point, those who are part of the collective are but stewards of that charism. But more, they are the *current* stewards of the vision, the charism.

Or, to put it differently, we do not reduce the vision and capacity of an organization to the vision and capacity of the founder. We might begin with the founder. We will recognize the extraordinary contribution of the founder in launching a particular institutional entity. But then we will also insist that the institution grows and matures and expands its horizons and adapts to new circumstances and developments that the founder could not have anticipated. The Jesuits of today, for example, look very different than they did when they were founded in the sixteenth century, and rightly so. This is so because this order, this institution, now fulfills its mission in a very different set of circumstances.

Thus we work with essentially two questions: What is our past—our history, the character of our founding—as an organization? And what is our present? How does our charism find unique expression in this time— indeed, to use the great line from the book of Esther, "for such a time as this" (Esther 4:14)?

The lens of charism frees us to grow and change—and adapt, as indicated already, to new circumstances. The institutional charism can serve as a guiding light or referent for the life of the community or institution. But—and this is crucial—it is not to stay the same; it is, rather, a guide for actually responding to and engaging change. The language of charism provides us with a dynamic way to process change, adapt to new circumstances, and embrace new possibilities. Institutions change with much difficulty and often assume that with change they are betraying their original founder and mission. But the language of charism suggests that the gift of the Spirit can and indeed must find expression in new wineskins. We can be very affirming of the past but then also recognize that given the change in the context or setting, it is essential that we respond to and adapt to new circumstances. And this is where we deeply need discernment to identify the charism at its very core, the DNA, so that we can with grace and courage, with creativity and a capacity for innovation, choose and embrace a new future.

Sixth, while the charism of an organization is bigger than its founder and without doubt bigger than any one person within the organization, it is helpful to consider if there is a sense in which there is an embodiment of the charism in the particular institution of which you are a part. In an academic institution, I would suggest that the faculty embody the charism: they are the mission of the college or university or seminary; they are its reason for being. They are why students enroll; they are those who deliver the mission. That is, typically, those who embody the mission are those who actually deliver on its mission, who actually implement the mission. They do what the organization is created to do. A university, for example, is established so that teaching-learning happens. And it is the faculty who actually do this; everything else—including the office of the president—is infrastructure, platform, the support network so that those who do the mission can do the mission.

For a hospital, it would surely be the medical staff: both the doctors and the nurses. They are those who deliver on the mission; when you and I go to the hospital, they are those whom I hope to see and have attend to me. Everything else, from the admitting staff to the cleaning staff to the board of trustees is infrastructure for the medical staff, the social architecture that allows them to deliver on the mission of the hospital.

When I go to a hockey game, I know full well that there is a whole infrastructure of managers, coaches, trainers, and many others who are essential to the "institution." But we go to the game to watch the players on the ice. They are what it's is all about: the players are the game—this game, this sixty minutes of action on the ice.

For a relief and development agency, surely those in the field embody the organization's charism: those on the ground who are responding to an earthquake or the remnants of a war-torn region, or, in development, those who work directly with community leaders in a developing region to accomplish the mission of the agency. Everything else is the supporting infrastructure that allows them to do what this agency says it is doing, its mission.

This has significant implications for how an institution is governed and to what end is it governed. To use the example of a college or university, the faculty are the primary (not sole, but primary) purveyors of the mission and vision of an academic institution. They are living representations of the charism of the university or college; they are why the students come to this school. Everything else is infrastructure, housing, support—the skeleton. And everything else exists to enable the faculty to do what the institution is called to do. The faculty are the heart and soul of the school. This in no way discounts or downplays the critical place of academic administration, trustees, clerical staff, and maintenance staff, all of whom are integral to an academic institution. This does not for a moment justify a culture of entitlement for faculty. Rather, it is a way of understanding what it means to be a university.

This has implications for governance, which I will address in the next chapter. But for now, let me just highlight that there may not be a one-to-one link between the embodiment of vision and the exercise of authority. The hockey players are the essence—the embodiment—of the team. But when they are on the ice, the coach has complete authority, and between seasons, the general manager oversees the team.

Same with an orchestra: clearly the embodiment of the charism is the players, the musicians themselves. But in the actual performance, they all defer to the conductor.

While I will be suggesting in chapter four that as a rule those who embody the vision and charism need to have a distinctive role in the governance of the institution, we should not assume a one-to-one connection.

A hockey team without a coach exercising authority is nothing but a pick-up game. It is not an institution; it will not be a winning team.

Surely with the church, the essence of the charism is the congregation itself. This means that governance is ordered so that the congregation flourishes and, collectively, is empowered to be the people of God. But that does not mean that authority is necessarily vested with the congregation. It is rather to make a different point: that the church only flourishes if and as the members of the congregation are encouraged, empowered, and equipped to be what they are called to be.

And then, seventh and finally, when we use the language of "charism" we are, in effect, insisting that we do not reduce an organization to its various practices. Yes, a charism and institutional mission is in the end about what we do, but it is also about who we are. It is about identity. Charism finds expression in particular practices, no doubt: all universities have academic programs; all hospitals have ER facilities; all churches conduct services, typically on a Sunday morning. But charism is not merely about practices; it concerns how those practices are expressed and nuanced in a way that reflects the particular identity—the particular way of being—of *this* institution.

All institutions, of course, must ask, what do we need to do? What are the practices that we need to engage in order to fulfill our mission? But organizations must first plumb and explore a prior and foundational question: *Who* are we and how will this find expression in what we do and how we do it? What particular way of being will be consistent with our identity? This will mean while those practices will look similar to outsiders—each hospital is a hospital and looks like one, each university or college looks to casual visitors like just about any other university or college they have visited—discerning eyes, and those who attend to the particular dynamics of this hospital or this university, find that there is indeed a nuanced expression of these practices that is particular to this school, this hospital, this church, this institution.

For many readers, all of these reflections are just another way of getting at the idea of the "brand" of the institution—the way in which the organization positions itself and differentiates itself from its peer institutions. And in many respects, this is accurate, the only difference being that the language of "charism" gives us a more theological lens through which to see and manage institutional identity.

As a side note, it merits observing that a theological vision for institutions includes an acknowledgment that sometimes there is a pathology that runs through the very heart, even the DNA of the organization—whether that be a college or university, a congregation, or a relief and development agency. Sometimes this pathology reflects the shadow side of the personality or character of the founder. At other times, it is a reflection of the religious ethos, for example, in a university, a service agency, or a denominational body with which the agency is affiliated: the congregation that has a profound distrust of any newcomer or any outside voice or authority; the academic institution that has a seemingly neurotic fear of anyone in authority; the obsessive work habits of the development agency staff that an outsider can easily see as nothing more than a reflection of the compulsive workaholism of the founder.

Each of these propensities—pathological propensities, I stress—might be easily explainable, given history or other factors. But they are still pathologies, and they need to be named lest they have undue power and influence on the organization. Sometimes a pathology is covered up by an appeal to a "core value" when in actual fact the supposed core value is nothing but a flaw in the system that cuts against the capacity of the organization to flourish. Beware of those organizations or churches that actually appeal to history or "our way of doing things" or even their charism to justify what are essentially pathological forms of internal governance—ways of being that marginalize voices or foster less than transparent approaches to decision making. I make this point to stress the following: we do not confuse charism with what is actually pathological. We do not appeal to a core value as a way to cover up fear, dysfunction, and ineptitude.

When we speak of charism we call forth our best; we open rather than close windows; we empower and animate rather than cutting the nerve of innovation and creativity. The language of charism fosters clarity about good governance that frees each entity within the institution to fulfill its function.

Finally, on charism, one more point—not as an eighth point per se, but as an aside. Everyone is special. Avoid as much as possible the overbearing presumption of thinking that your organization is uniquely special, one of a kind; your church is such a special church; your college is somehow uniquely favored by God; or your development agency is, by virtue of its history, the ultimate embodiment of how God is at work in the world. The perspective of institutional charism helps in this regard.

I remember sitting in a home in Manila, Philippines, visiting with a Russian broadcaster who was producing religious programming that would be aired into Russia with the Far East Broadcasting Company (FEBC). He spoke at length about how significant his ministry was—how his hearers were able to get the "pure" gospel, untainted by actual people, just voices through the air waves. I left bewildered by such presumption, wondering why he felt he needed to justify his work in this way rather than merely speaking of his contribution as but one contribution, one way in which—in partnership and as a complement to what others were doing—he did his part. And naturally, I wondered if he did this to get financial support.

Either no one is special or we're all special. We get on with the hard work of identifying what defines our identity and gives clarity to our mission. But we do this with humility. Any comparisons are only as a means of clarifying our charism or our mission, and we do so with a deep respect for peer agencies and institutions or churches whose mission and vision will have many similar features to our own or be a complement to our own vision and contribution. Beware of advertising—to potential donors, or to potential students if you are a college—in a way that subtly implies superiority. Rather, speak to your particular calling and perhaps to the specific things you are seeking to accomplish. And leave it at that.

FROM CHARISM TO MISSION

These reflections on charism are all to a particular end: (1) to stress the importance of mission—on the conviction that effective organizations have mission clarity—and (2) to foster good thinking about mission.

Effective institutions have mission clarity. They know who they are and they know what they are seeking to accomplish. All who think this way and stress this principle are indebted to management guru Peter Drucker, who insists that "mission come first" and that "the first task of a leader is to make sure that everybody sees the mission, hears it, lives it."[2]

Everyone has a stake in the conversation about the mission. But there are three entities that are indispensable to this process: the president or lead executive or, in a church, the senior pastor; second, the trustees; and then those who embody the institutional charism and actually deliver on the mission.

The president, executive director, senior pastor—whoever it is that carries the key senior executive role in the organization—is crucial in two respects: first, to foster and moderate good conversation about the mission, helping the organization come to missional clarity and second, to keeping the organization on mission. In many respects this is the most crucial aspect of the senior leader's role: clarify the mission, keep the institution on mission, and assure that all new personnel believe in the mission.

William F. Frame, speaking of college and university presidents, insists "that the primary responsibility of the president is to foster institutional vocational discernment."[3] Frame urges college presidents—but in a way that clearly has application to all who are in senior roles—to attend to "the traditions of the college to find among its founders and progenitors the seeds of a mission especially fit for modern circumstance . . . so that one has a 'single story' . . . a rhetorically reconstructed version of the school's natal identity."[4]

The president unavoidably carries the weight of rhetoric, articulating the mission again and again in distinct contexts and settings, in a way that is clear and compelling, and more, in a way that then locates and justifies the key activities of the institution. And, very specifically, a president anchors this sense of identity and mission in the charism, or what Frame calls the "natal identity."

---

[2]Peter F. Drucker, *Managing the Non-Profit Organization: Principles and Practices* (New York: HarperBusiness, 1990), 45.
[3]William V. Frame, *The American College Presidency as Vocation: Easing the Burden, Enhancing the Joy* (Abilene, TX: Abilene Christian University Press, 2013), 80.
[4]Ibid., 97.

One must affirm and indeed insist that presidents do not impose a vision on the institution—something that is their personal drive or something that they import and force on the institution to which they have been called. Thus when it comes to the appointment of a new president, unless the newly appointed president is an internal candidate, the board does not ask the new president to articulate her or his vision for the institution. That would be premature: a candidate for president or for a senior pastoral role can only speak generally to the values that might inform the process, but the articulation of mission takes time. And a new president needs to listen, to get a feel on the ground, to attend to what key constituents are saying, and then to test if he or she has a feel for what is indeed the mission of the agency.

The president asks questions. What is the history? What are the diverse constituencies that have a stake in the mission of this institution? Who are the customers and what are they seeing and experiencing and how have their needs changed? Who are the stakeholders who need to have buy-in to support the mission? Who are those who are actually delivering on the mission—the faculty, for example, of the university, or the members of the orchestra, or those in the field of a poverty-reduction agency—and what are they saying about what they see as imperative when it comes to defining the mission?

The president needs to be a good listener because vision emerges from being attentive to what is already there, those elements of institutional identity inherent and implicit that now need to be clarified, defined, and articulated.

Through this process, the institution is encouraged and animated as it discovers or rediscovers its identity, purpose, and ethos. At some point, the president puts a stake in the ground and calls the institution to live and function with a faithfulness to this mission. Indeed, the president's authority—very specifically the political authority to lead—arises from the rhetoric that emerges from the envisioning process. But this will only be the case if the mission makes sense, if it fits this institution at this time and place, and further, if it is compelling, calling the community to its highest potential—meaning that it captures the imagination of the key stakeholders.

Presidents are uniquely positioned to and responsible to foster good conversation about mission and calling, to profile the mission—to preach it, sustain clarity about that mission and work with others to keep the institution on mission. They are positioned to equip the trustees both to see and to understand the mission and know what it will take to be trustees of that mission. And they are positioned to communicate that mission to those external constituencies and to potential employees and volunteers.

The board of the organization are, in effect, the trustees of the mission— that is, they are stewards of the institutional charism. In a nutshell, their role within the organization is to monitor and be sure that the identified mission is the right mission for the organization and that the organization is on mission.

This means, of course, that board members join the board because they believe in the mission. And it is the mission of the agency that elicits and inspires their personal engagement and support for the agency. You serve on the board because the mission matters to you.

Thus the president ultimately has responsibility to the board, and it is thus to the board that the president is accountable for the mission. And it makes full sense that every board meeting should have at least some part of the agenda—perhaps no more than part of the report of the president—that affirms afresh and gives profile to some aspect of the mission of the institution.

And then, as mentioned, there is always some entity that actually delivers the mission: the musicians in the orchestra, the field workers in the development agency, the medical staff of the hospital, or the faculty of a university. They have to be on mission. No amount of rhetoric from the president and eager trusteeship from the board will make any difference if those who are responsible to deliver the mission don't actually get it. Faculty in an academic institution teach for the mission. They know the mission, and when they are recruited to join the faculty, mission alignment is a key part of the recruitment process. And this same principle applies to all nonprofits.

CONCLUSION

Charism—institutional history and founding and essence—is terribly important. And we need to be very clear about who embodies the mission, who has trusteeship for the mission, and who is responsible to keep the institution clear about and on mission. But there is more work to be done: we must do our due diligence in asking the questions that will help the institution foster clarity about it mission and institutional purpose.

MISSION CLARITY, PART 2

Discerning Institutional Identity and Purpose

Effective institutions are clear about their mission. And this is evident, in part, in that they are talking about it all the time. Dynamic institutions foster good conversation about mission—asking the right questions, addressing points of tension and diversity with courage, looking back to their history but also asking, what is our calling, our vocation, for this time and in this place? What follows is a guide to good conversation about mission, the specific questions and issues that need to be raised and discussed if an institution is to truly have clarity about the mission. What will be clear very soon is that mission clarity is not (merely) about crafting a mission statement. It is about understanding and living with a deep appreciation of one's institutional identity and purpose.

When we define and clarify the mission of an institution, here are the variables that need to be taken into account. These are the questions we need to ask:

- What is our industry—that is, what business are we in?

- Who are the primary beneficiaries of our work—the customer—and who are the key stakeholders?

- What is our particular niche within our industry?

- What is our particular context—our demographic, economic, religious, and cultural setting?

- How can we be both inspired by the mission but also very practical when it comes to actually implementing the mission?

IDENTIFY YOUR INDUSTRY

We begin by asking something that is simply basic: What business are we in? This fundamental question will guide so much moving forward. The answer needs to be stated clearly and often. It cannot be taken for granted or merely assumed.

In the world of higher education, for example, it is hugely significant if you are teaching at a community college in contrast to a comprehensive university. In Canada, the designation "primarily undergraduate" is used to specify universities where the focus is on excellence in teaching, often in contrast with comprehensive universities where the focus is on research. Research and teaching happen at both, of course, but they are weighted differently.

And this point needs to be pressed because in a university this has implications for professional development and promotion. One is evaluated on one's contribution to the mission of this particular institution. In a primary undergraduate university, you must develop competency in the classroom.

In my case, I serve as the president of a university that has a history—a heritage—in the Bible college movement. This is good; we value this heritage and affirm the strengths from that movement that inform and must inform our current mission. But now we are a university, and so we ask, what is a university? In its very essence, what does it mean to be a university? We are in the business of "university"; that is our industry. And we need to understand what this means for mission. What *did* it mean to be a Bible college; what *does* it mean to be a university? There will be continuities, of course. But still, "university" is now the industry we are in.

Now some might insist that if they are a religious institution—perhaps a Christian university—that is the industry: a *Christian* university. In response I would press them to hold that qualifier for the moment, suggesting that it is premature to bring this religious identity into the conversation. We will qualify; we will perhaps insist on the Christian identity. But first, we specify that it is a university and the Christian identity does not make it more or less a university. It is still a university. That is its industry.

Further, this very question will come back to us at more than one point in the upcoming chapters. For example, when it comes to finances, we will assume that the finances of the institution are congruent with the question, What business are we in? It is potentially problematic when a major source of revenue is not related to the fundamental mission or purpose of the organization. There is always the risk that something else—because it is a source of desperately needed revenue—will drive or even undermine mission.

Thus we come back to this again and again: What business are we in?

Churches ask the same thing: What does it mean to be a church? Are we merely a purveyor of religious products or a gathering point for people to come together for religious activities? Do we have a theology of what it means to be a church that actually informs how we do this work that we call being the church? This is essential because we will innovate and adapt and do things differently, but all of this innovation is highly questionable if we first do not have clarity about what it means to be the church.

Two or more congregations may have very different understandings of what it means to be a church, of course. But still, this is a baseline conversation that guides the institution through the inevitable times of change. In other words, the industry is not "Presbyterian church." In due time, the qualifier can be added. But both the Baptist and the Presbyterian are in the same business, so to speak, the same industry.

In the medical world, are we a clinic or a hospital? And if so, what difference does it make?

Are we a relief agency or a development agency, or both? And if both, where do we feel that we can express our primary strength or capacity?

Mission is about much more than just the mission statement. But at the very least the mission statement should make this point clear: What business are you in? And the statement should not be so vague that someone who reads the statement feels nice warm thoughts about good intentions but wonders what activities define your mission. If you are an academic institution—school or university or seminary—then it should be clear that this is what you are doing and intend to be doing.

I often come across vague mission statements that are not clear, on their own, what industry the organization represents. They speak of leadership training but are they actually a post-secondary college. They speak of patient care, but are they actually a hospital? They speak very broadly of theological education, but it is not at all clear who they are called to serve. Why not be clear and ask, what service will we provide? What product will we produce? What particular outcomes should emerge from the investment of our time and energy?

BENEFICIARIES AND STAKEHOLDERS

Mission is to a particular end: the agency, the institution, provides a benefit, a service to someone. The wisdom and insight of several voices, but particularly that of Peter Drucker, suggest that we really do not have clarity about our mission until and unless we are able to identify who is that primary beneficiary—what Drucker speaks of as the "customer"— and who are the key stakeholders. He rightly insists that this distinction is crucial.[1]

We begin with the primary beneficiaries—the customers—asking who is the principle objective of our mission, or, putting it differently, who is the primary and fundamental beneficiary of the work that we do as an organization? Indeed, Peter Drucker stresses, if you do not know your customer, you do not know your business and thus your mission.[2]

And yet the insights of Drucker lead to an important distinction, in that there may be multiple beneficiaries to the work of an organization. Thus the distinction needs to be made between the primary beneficiary and stakeholders. Stakeholders are those who have a vested interest in the outcomes of the organization—a genuine and legitimate interest—while not being those who are the actual focus of the mission. And the distinction must be maintained if we are going to have mission clarity because the mission is first and foremost about the customer, the *primary* beneficiary.

Thus, surely, for a university, the customer is the student. There are a whole host of stakeholders who have a legitimate interest in the outcomes, but when all is said and done, a university is about student learning and formation. A hospital is oriented toward a particular set of patients. A

---

[1]Peter F. Drucker, *Managing the Non-Profit Organization: Principles and Practices* (New York: HarperBusiness, 1990), 55-56.
[2]Ibid.

homeless foundation obviously focuses its attention on those on the streets of its city who need shelter when night comes.

When I was the president of small mission agency, our customers were theological colleges in the global south. The organization was created to respond to their institutional needs.

In some cases, the customer might actually pay for a service: tuition at the university, perhaps. But in other organizations those who are the immediate beneficiaries of the mission are not necessarily those who actually fund the agency. Thus for example, the homeless do not provide the funding for the homeless foundation.

Once an organization achieves true clarity about the primary beneficiary, we must ask this: Who are the key stakeholders in this organization? Every institution has them; they are vital to the missional identity of the institution. For a university, this includes the parents and families of students. But it is also the public schools of the region for the education program at the university, and it includes the businesses where business graduates might ultimately be employed. It is also accrediting agencies and the guilds of the professors— their disciplinary guilds. For academic institutions with religious affiliations, it is the church or religious bodies that endorse them—send them students, provide funding, or, in the case of seminaries, place their students. And for virtually all nonprofits, it is the financial contributors, those whose free will contributions actually make the institution financially viable.

An agency cannot fulfill its mission without attention to the stakeholders. Typically, they will find representation on the board of trustees. They have a stake, it is rightly noted, in the mission; they care about it, they are invested it in. Indeed, in a good pattern of governance, it is the board— representing those stakeholders—that actually in the end approves the mission and then holds the institution to its mission.

Stakeholders have a vested interest; they need to be heard; their voice matters and is indeed crucial to the organization and its governance. Yet organizations must clearly articulate *who* the mission of their organization is in terms of focus and critical institutional outcomes. The bottom line for a university is the student. Sure, we care about parents and spouses and accrediting agencies and, in some cases, church affiliations. But when all is said and done, we are here for these students who have been admitted to these programs. And the high point in the year is when the students cross the stage and receive their diplomas. They are what the mission is ultimately about. Assessment and outcomes and missional effectiveness are ultimately about student learning and formation.

For the hospital, insurance companies are a stakeholder; they are not the customer. And the customer ultimately shapes the defining focus of the mission. We do not dismiss the stakeholder, but we do not confuse the stakeholder with the customer. The fundamental vison of the hospital is the health and well-being of the patient.

For the Calgary Homeless Foundation, the customers—those who are the focus and intent of the organization—are the homeless. There are civic and business and church and other stakeholders. But the bottom line is always the homeless: Are *their* fundamental needs met? They are the focus, the reason for being, the critical outcome for which this organization exists. Other agencies—stakeholders—have a very legitimate voice and need to be heard. But we do not confuse the stakeholder with the customer. When all is said and done, we know who we are serving—that is, as the *beneficiary*, the primary beneficiary of our mission.

Most congregations have a number of external stakeholders; the most notable, of course, is the denominational body with which the church is affiliated. As often as not, this is the stakeholder that credentials those who serve in ordained ministry with the congregation. But the actual congregation, those who are present for worship and the focus of the congregation's ministry—they are the ultimate reason the church exists.[3]

So if you are interviewing for a faculty position at a university, ask yourself if this institution is committed to students and will support your vision as a faculty member to teach and to engage students. But also, ask the second and essential question: Who are the key stakeholders for this

---

[3]I realize that some might protest and insist that the primary beneficiary of a church is the community or the world, and that the church exists not for itself but for the world. The distinction may seem rather subtle but is nevertheless important. A congregation has integrity in its own right—as a liturgical, teaching-learning (catechetical), and missional community. And yes, the congregation is called and empowered to engage the world, witnessing to the kingdom in word and deed. But what I am suggesting is that this can only happen if the congregation is a vital and healthy and community of faith. External or missional engagement is one element or feature of what it means to be the church, and that mission is actually most effective when, ironically, the church is not reduced to being merely about mission.

institution? And what are the implications for how the mission of this university or this college is fulfilled?

Institutionally savvy faculty members are alert to the diverse stakeholders of the university, including those who have representation on the board of trustees. We serve the customer—the student—but in accountability to these diverse stakeholders. We take account of both, knowing who is the primary beneficiary and who is a stakeholder.

Institutionally savvy church members are aware of the denominational affiliation of the church and its implications for how this church fulfills its mission.

Institutionally astute relief and development workers are alert to the government bodies—both their own, that perhaps provide matching grants; and the government agencies on the ground, with which they must partner and work if they are to serve those who are, by virtue of their mission, the beneficiaries of the key action items of the organization.

But in the end, our vision, mission, and resolve is to serve our customers, yet we do so with intentional accountability to our stakeholders. I will be making the case that when it comes to governance, the board of the organization is very precisely the voice of the diverse stakeholders, all of which are external. The stakeholders have a voice; in a very distinct sense, the organization functions in direct accountability to the stakeholders. But it is crucial not to confuse the two, otherwise, the customer—the primary beneficiary—is merely a pawn for the sake of one or more stakeholders.

DISTINGUISH YOURSELF WITHIN THE INDUSTRY

Within your industry, taking account of your primary beneficiaries—not in a generic sense, but those who are very specifically the beneficiaries of your particular organization—you can now bring in a key qualifier or two to specify your specific focus. You can now look laterally to others who are perhaps in the same industry and consider what makes you unique within the industry. What is your particular niche? What makes you different? What particular segment of the potential beneficiaries are those for whom you have a particular responsibility or call?

As I have already stressed, this is not about being special or better than the other. This is actually an exercise in humility. It is about recognizing the particular ways in which your history, your sphere of influence, your stakeholders, and then, of course, your particular customers, define the way that you see and embrace your particular mission.

Universities in the same city will have a different mission. Each of them may be in the same industry, responsible to the same accrediting agencies, offering potentially a similar range of degree programs with overlapping student constituencies. But they will reflect a different history and ethos and identity and this will be reflected in an awareness of a distinct niche out of which each of them fulfills their distinctive mission.

Two churches across the street from one another could surely see themselves not as competitors for attendees on a Sunday morning but rather as having a complementary and mutually reinforcing vision for the community in which they have been placed. Their mission is not generic but particular—to their history, their calling, and their specific responsibility or vocation in that community. They do not need to be better than the other church; they can each affirm one another and then get on with being who each is called to be.

Consider from your institutional history, location, and resource base what you are positioned to do and, ideally, do very well. By what can you sustain what Jim Collins, in his book *Good to Great*, speaks of as the power of simplicity: the organization has focus and clarity of purpose.[4] We look laterally and as a church see that there are dozens of churches in this segment of our city. As a university, we can see that there are several other universities in our city. A relief and development agency can of course graciously and happily confirm that they are not the only group that responds to critical human need. We can recognize—using the language of calling or vocation—that in light of how God is surely calling others, we do not need to be all things to all people. We can accept our limits and consider our unique location and then embrace that good thing that is our particular calling. And then we can do it and do it well.

We can surely ask what we are positioned, among our peer institutions, to do particularly well. But the crucial piece is that we sustain a healthy and dynamic institutional humility. We are not comparing ourselves to the other similar agency. You can make your mission statement compelling

---

[4]Jim Collins, *Good to Great: Why Some Companies Make the Leap . . . and Others Don't* (New York: HarperCollins, 2001).

without suggesting that you are the only agency that is doing this good work and doing it well. You can sustain a healthy institutional humility while also speaking of your mission in a manner that invites delight and encouragement. With an appropriate humility, you can still identify what makes you different without suggesting that other similar agencies are not quite as good as you are when it comes to your core values.

I can be the president of a Christian university and still affirm the vital place of the public or secular university in the world of higher education. I can be the pastor of a Baptist church and still affirm and celebrate those congregations of other traditions—Presbyterian, Anglican, or Catholic. But the point here is that we ask, what is it that we are uniquely positioned to be and do?

CONSIDER THE CURRENT CONTEXT

Mission is always contextual—for this time and for this situation. It is often heard that mission remains static and fixed and vision is dynamic and fluid. And yet surely we need to insist that mission *does* change. People who argue that we are "faithful" if we are faithful to the mission fail to appreciate that we are not faithful to the original vision or mission until and unless the mission is changing—for the rather simple and obvious reason that the situation is different. We change to stay the same. Or better put, we change so that we can be faithful stewards of our vocation—our institutional calling. Context is fluid and thus mission must be dynamic and responsive.

The mission is consistent, of course, with the original founding vision— in continuity with that vision—but now the organization is responding to a new set of circumstances, opportunities, and challenges that the original founders could not have anticipated and did not need to anticipate.

A quick reminder belongs here: the organization does not belong to the original founders, and they do not have veto power on how the mission will be framed for a new context and setting. Rather, now—in light of our past—we consider and respond to changes in our world. We recognize the current needs to which we can and must respond. There will be continuity with the past, but with alignment and re-calibration for the present opportunity. Or, as Hugh Heclo puts it, "institutional thinking eagerly seeks to understand what has been received in light of new circumstances that are always intruding."[5] Heclo stresses that we are of course attentive to precedent, but we respond to the present.[6]

To determine mission means getting a nuanced and sophisticated read on the context, the demographics: the social, political, economic, religious, and cultural variables that are going to inform how the mission of this institution is going to play out. It means putting on a sociologist hat.

Our past represents a legacy, and, of course, the ideal would be that we are animated by that legacy. But now we find new wineskins in which to house and through which to express and implement the original vision and legacy. There will be discontinuity. Nothing is gained by clinging to outdated expressions of the mission that are no longer truly consistent with the founding vision nor compelling.

What we are doing is looking to the dynamic interplay between our history and the contemporary circumstances and the shifting needs or requirements and expectations of our customer, our primary beneficiaries. In other words, we are looking for a sweet spot between our story—our history—and current opportunities. When we find it, it is to our strategic and competitive advantage. It is leverage-able. It animates and provides clarity; it is compelling to both those we serve, the primary beneficiaries and the diverse stakeholders. We ask, what are we uniquely positioned to do? What is there from our history, from the weight and input of our various stakeholders, and our particular geographic and cultural context, that shapes our identity and institutional purpose?

A church asks how the neighborhood has changed and what that means for how we do ministry now. We can resist the change or embrace it. I am a member of Tenth Church in Vancouver, British Columbia. For years, this congregation was the establishment church of the downtown demographic made up of primarily of third and fourth generation immigrants whose roots looked back to northern and western Europe. But in a generation the neighborhood changed. Those folks moved to the suburbs. And the congregation languished until pastor Ken Shigematsu—very Canadian but very definitely not of northern European descent—came

---

[5]Hugh Heclo, *On Thinking Institutionally* (Boulder, CO: Paradigm Publishers, 2008), 99-100.
[6]Ibid., 109.

into leadership and now oversees a congregation where someone like myself, with Smith as my surname, is very much a minority presence. It is a beautiful thing. More to the point, it is the *right* thing, given the demographics. What pastor Shigematsu asked, very simply, is this: What does it mean to be this church now—not looking back, nostalgically, and not trying to compare ourselves or duplicate what other churches are doing? Rather, what does it mean to be this church now, in this time and place?

And for universities and colleges, faculty need to have an almost constant or ongoing conversation regarding how their students are different from them as students and how they are different from their students from four or five years ago. What has and is changing in our social context? And what does it mean for how we do this kind of work—the work of higher education—now?

Institutional location is also shaped by social, cultural, and national sensibilities. I have been part of a Canadian-based organization that was an affiliate to a US counterpart. This is not a unique phenomenon; there are UK and US nonprofits that set up shop in another country—Australia, Singapore, New Zealand, Canada. The danger is assuming that the affiliate is just the US or UK organization but perhaps writ a little smaller and, ideally, expanding the reach of the parent organization. But whether it is Langham Partnership, Overseas Council, World Vision, Food for the Hungry, or whatever the agency, the crucial piece is this: when the agency has an office in a different country, for both legal reasons and for reasons of institutional integrity, while there will be continuity between the parent organization and its affiliate, the affiliate will have a clear sense of mission and identity in its own right.

National identity will undoubtedly impact how the affiliate functions on the global stage. Thus, for example, a US-based agency will function with American sensibilities, no doubt—rightly or wrongly is not the point. The point is that the Canadian or Australian affiliate will function differently and appropriately so. A Canadian agency in Cuba will look and feel different than its US counterpart in Cuba. Both are needed; both reflect institutional integrity. Thus when affiliates are formed, the founding agency would be wise to identify itself as no more than a sister agency to its affiliates and recognize that they have a broader and more global reach by appreciating and affirming the diversity of sister agencies that reflect the sensibilities of different hosting nations.

MAKE IT WORK AND MAKE IT SING

Finally, the mission and purpose should be able to perform two functions for the organization. It should be practical. And it should inspire.

By *practical* we mean that it is eminently doable. The mission can and does inform strategic initiatives, direction, and institutional objectives. The mission is operational: you know what you are doing and what you are not doing. It is a compass that brings clarity not only in terms of when the agency says yes, but also when to say no to an opportunity, an invitation—whether an external or internal source of institutional pressure. The leadership can say, "That is not our mission." The mission provides this clarity and focus.

But being practical also means that the mission makes economic sense. The way the mission is fulfilled in the contemporary context or setting needs to be economically viable. We need to be able to answer the question of how we will *fund* this enterprise. Nothing is gained by an idealism or a utopian vision of mission that is not financially sustainable. Thus we will often have a dynamic tension between mission and money that informs our work.

All of chapter seven will be devoted to the economics of institutions. But for now, it is prudent to stress that the mission needs to be framed in a way that gains buy-in. Are there people who will buy into this service (such as those who pay tuition for an academic degree)? Are there donors who will invest in the mission? Can we secure government or foundation funding to make this operational? Or putting it differently, when we speak of mission, we have to also consider the pragmatics. Can we deliver on this mission? Does it have the potential to actually happen?

It is interesting to observe major denominations in North America rethinking how they do international ministry. The simple fact is that older funding models are no longer viable. Mission needs to be thought through from the ground up, with an eye toward the economics: What will international ministry look like now—with major changes in the works—and how will it be funded? Mission has to actually work—economically and otherwise.

These comments on the pragmatics cannot be the last word. Rather, I need to conclude this segment by speaking of the need for inspiration. The mission needs to sing—it needs to be not just clear, not just congruent with your history and traditions but also something that can capture the contemporary imagination. It needs to matter and be framed in such a way that it not only informs the work of the agency but also animates the work of those who are part of or influenced by this institution.

By this I do not mean that the mission statement itself is melodramatic and stated in a particularly exciting way. Rather, when you speak about your mission everyone knows you are talking about something that actually matters and matters a great deal.

Your mission may be about digging wells in African villages. You are clear about your mission, but then, everyone who speaks about it knows that water and wells are profoundly important for these villages. Without overstating, you are able to communicate how crucial these wells are to families and communities.

If your mission is that of an art gallery in the heart of the city that profiles the work of local artists, then the chatter about your art gallery is all about your enthusiasm for local artists and also for the significance of the arts in the life of the city.

The mission calls the organization to something bigger than the individual players, something worth investing time and energy and talent and resources in, something that calls forth deep aspirations. People want to be part of it. And in being a part of it, they know the joy of engaging in something worth doing. Without apology, we can use language of the heart: what it is that drives us, moves us, captures our imaginations. It gets us out of bed in the morning. It inspires us to persevere when there is a tough economic downturn or a major setback. It invites commitment. It solicits buy-in and it motivates excellence precisely because it matters.

We can talk about the mission in a way that is compelling. We can speak of the reason for which we are here and the purpose for which we exist. We can tell our story. If we are a university, potential students—and perhaps their parents—need to know about our mission and why they might want to study here. Donors need messaging that invites and inspires them to give. Potential faculty need to recognize this university as an institution that merits the investment of their time, their talent, that perhaps is even worth uprooting their family and moving to another city to respond to an invitation to be part of the teaching corp.

If we are a church, those who gather need to know what it is that makes this church this church. And if we are a relief agency, we are able to communicate to our supporters why they can give to this organization and in making this financial contribution they are making a difference— they are making an investment.

These questions—our industry, our primary beneficiary, our niche, our context, and what it takes to make this work and to make this animating— make for an ongoing conversation. We are talking mission and talking mission all the time. It is the institutional guide and compass.

The Shelf Life of a Mission

A mission has a shelf life—likely between eight and ten years. So while this work of discerning mission is not continuous work, it is regular work for an institution, not irregular or somehow strange. Each president needs to do this at some point in her or his tenure and every board member should have the opportunity during a typical term or set of terms to be part of a discernment process—the work of clarifying mission, purpose, and identity. And while we need to get on with it, it is tremendously important that a university faculty step back, with the president and administration, perhaps every eight to ten years, and review the history, the sense of purpose, in light of what has changed and evolved over the last decade.

A university faculty member—perhaps with the same institution over thirty to forty years—might protest the idea that this kind of intellectual and emotional energy needs to be invested three or perhaps four times in a typical faculty career, with the thought that this would be a distraction from the essential work of teaching and research. And yet two things merit consideration. First, if the process is well moderated and if the faculty are given voice but with sufficient external input from key stakeholders, the investment of time and energy will not be that great. And second, few things will be more intellectually and emotionally satisfying as the process that brings a faculty member into focused conversation with colleagues about the big picture, the shared vision and commitment that all have to a common objective.

MISSION AND ASSESSMENT

When you define the mission, when you come to clarity about your institutional purpose, then you have a basis for accountability—internally to the board and to external agencies, accrediting bodies, and, of course, those who invest financially in the organization. It means that you are able to get to this question: Are we doing what we say we are doing? Is the mission actually happening?

Mission has to be specific enough that we can list a set of outcomes—the indicators that we are indeed doing what we claim we are doing. Outcomes will be of two kinds: we speak of the key activities that implement the mission and the indicators that these activities actually deliver on the mission. Therefore, two questions will probe these outcomes. First, are you doing what needs to be done to fulfill the mission—the key activities? And second, are you doing these things in a way that is actually effective?

Key activities. We recognize that certain crucial activities implement and thus execute the mission. We ask, what key activities are essential for fulfilling the mission, and are we doing them? And are we doing them in a way that fits our core values and commitments? Mission must be, as Peter Drucker stresses, "operational." We should be able to translate it into specifics.[7] And, I would add, those specifics need to make sense. That is, there is a deep underlying logic to these activities; it is evident to each key player that this activity is congruent and essential to the mission.

We should be able to identify that key activities are happening: that courses are being taught at the university, that shelters are available for the homeless, that the injured are able to find their way to a wonderfully efficient emergency room.

Thus a Christian university would likely deem chapel to be an essential activity, an indispensable part of the overall program. But then we might also add an athletic program, focused residential life, learning services for those who have learning challenges, and a library. We ask, in other words, what activities are essential to our mission—that is, our mission happens because these very specific activities happen? Are we doing what we need to be doing in order to fulfill our mission? What is essential?

---

[7]Drucker, *Managing the Non-Profit Organization*, 4-5.

A church might consider that to be a church ("church" is the industry) requires that we have preaching and teaching along with the celebration of the Lord's Supper. We might conclude that these are essential activities for a congregation (see Acts 2:42). And so we ask, are we doing this in a way that is consistent with our identity, our very specific mission?

But then beyond this, in light of mission, what else needs to be happening so that we are consistent with our particular responsibility—our niche within the industry? We cannot and do not need to do everything, but what are the key programmatic activities—be they a children's program, a youth ministry, or a structured approach to community involvement? In other words, the activities are not a range of miscellaneous activities. Rather, we do what we need to do to implement our mission.

And with this, you can also consider what activities are peripheral— perhaps good in themselves, but not essential to your mission. This will be a particularly pertinent question in times of financial stress. A university, for example, might consider cutting out certain activities as a means to make the institution leaner and more financially viable. But you can only make these cuts in expenses if you have a clear sense of which activities are essential to mission and which are peripheral—the second being, perhaps, good in themselves but potentially expendable.

Notice a crucial sequence: activities follow mission. Mission determines the activities. We define our mission and then we decide the key activities by which the mission will be fulfilled. It is remarkable how often these are reversed. A seminary starts new programs without clarity about their mission and then retroactively revises the mission to incorporate the new programs. In other words, mission means nothing if you can just alter the mission to fit your activities. The challenge of new programs might very well be a catalyst for rethinking the mission. Certainly. But still, you begin with mission, even if it is occasioned by the opportunities. And then, with clarity about the mission, you identify the key actions, the programs, and the means by which the mission will be accomplished.

Are the key activities effective? But then we also ask, are these activities actually producing the outcomes that we intend to see accomplished through the implementation of our mission? A key activity might be that we teach courses. But just because we teach courses, we make no assumption that the mission is happening. We are not satisfied that courses are (merely) being taught. We ask the crucial follow-up question: Are the students actually learning? And is their learning consistent with the mission?

As a congregation, we might have as a key mission commitment that our members are equipped to think theologically about their vocations in the world and that as a congregation we are empowering women and men to be God's people in and through their vocations as artists, business people, homemakers, and educators. This is all good; but are we doing it? And if so, how do we know that we are fulfilling this dimension of our mission and identity?

A relief agency may have as a key activity that they are able to respond to a crisis in a timely manner. It should be straightforward to ask, assess, and conclude that this is actually happening. And in all of these cases, the boards of these institutions should know what are the KPIs, the key performance indicators. What are the ways in which as a board we can know that the mission of the institution is actually happening? An effective board is not satisfied with good intentions. They are only content when they have actual results—results that are consistent with the mission. (It is, of course, always necessary to recognize that we can only be held accountable through assessment for what we are actually responsible to do and over which we have direct influence.)

If the mission is happening, we ask what we can do to strengthen even further our capacity to fulfill our mission. Effective institutions are always coming back to the mission as their compass, so that financial decisions, personnel decisions, facility decisions are all oriented around the commitment to mission. That is always the baseline.

And if the mission is not happening? Then we ask the hard but necessary question: Why not? What are the obstacles to our institutional capacity to fulfill mission? Is it a structure of governance, an institutional culture, a lack of financial discipline, a facility limitation, or some other factor that is undermining the ability of this institution to be all that it is called to be? Do we have the leadership in place that can deliver on the mission? What is missing and keeping us from accomplishing what we say we are here to do?

CONCLUSION

It is difficult to overstate the priority of mission clarity: in the end, everything depends on this—knowing what it is that this organization is being called to do. Governance is about having in place the structures that assure that the mission happens. The annual budget is about mission. We recruit and make personnel appointments about the mission. The organizational culture is about animating mission. The facilities are about the built space that fosters mission. And, in the end, all strategic alliances and partnerships are about fostering missional capacity. It is all about mission. Mission provides the compass, the purpose, and the orientation. Those in institutional leadership will, without doubt, talk about many things, but they will talk about mission more than anything.

An Individual and Group Exercise

Here's an exercise that could be done on your own or as part of a team:

- Identify your industry: What kind of business you are in—and what difference does it make?

- Identify your key beneficiaries (customers) and stakeholders (other key constituencies).

- Identify how you are different within your industry. What is your particular niche? What makes you different?

- Identify the current context, the key social, political, economic, religious, and cultural variables that are going to affect how the mission of your institution is going to play out.

- Identify the key practical aspect of your mission.

- Identify why your mission matters and how it captures the imagination of the key stakeholders.

GOVERNANCE THAT WORKS, PART 1

Making the Right Things Happen

Effective organizations are effective precisely because they have in place the governance structures and systems that allow them to deliver on the mission. They have a clear sense of their institutional identity and purpose. But more, they also have in place the practices for knowing what needs to be done and the mechanisms for doing what needs to be done. Effective organizations make good decisions and implement those decisions.

They do not merely talk about what needs to be done; they have the institutional capacity to act. Things get done; what needs to happen happens. If the mission does not happen as often as not, it is a simple matter: governance is not working. The greatest impediment to the fulfillment of an institutional mission is the lack of adequate governance systems. When it is not working, we might be inclined to point to the lack of suitable leadership. But actually, when leadership is lacking, it is typically because of poor and ineffective governance.

And so we need to consider the meaning and character of governance, by which we mean the oversight and administration of the institution so that certain things can happen. When we speak of good governance that leads to organizational effectiveness, we mean that three things happen:

- An organization accesses wisdom, the knowledge and understanding of what needs to happen, through consultation.

- An organization makes good decisions, the fruit of good conversation and consultation, but specifically, conversation that comes to closure, to an actual decision.

- An organization implements it decisions with accountability.

All this is to one end, the mission.

Though it is listed third, following consultation and decision making, it is helpful to begin with the question of implementation: the capacity to act, to actually do what needs to be done. And for this, we have to speak about the place of power in the life of institutions.

EXERCISING POWER THROUGH SHARED GOVERNANCE

To speak of governance is to affirm what needs to be stated clearly and pointedly: effective institutions have intentional and transparent governance structures for the exercise of power. Without power, nothing happens; the mission is not fulfilled. Power is nothing other than leverage—the capacity of people, individually or collectively, to do what they are called to do. Power marshals intellectual, moral, and material resources to a common end.

Thus we can rightly be alert to the false idealism of those who insist on flat hierarchies that in effect undercut the capacity of organizations to get things done. Out of a fear of the concentration of power—or, rather, an actual fear of power—we end up with ineffective organizations where nothing gets done. The mission does not happen. When it is not clear who is responsible for what and where no one really has the power to do what needs to be done, the organization is ineffective and the mission will not be fulfilled.

Grant Munroe was a participant in the Occupy Wall Street protest movement. In a review of a book on civic protest—Micah White's *The End of Protest*—he speaks of his experience and observes and despairs that, as he puts it, "the nightmarish inefficiency of horizontal power sharing and cliquish nature of those contesting power within various groups was intolerable." And he thus notes that nothing got done and that consequently, "with nothing being done, my friends and I left." He goes on to deflate the naive idealism and notes that "open-floor direct democracy proved a horribly exploitable weakness." He speaks of this naiveté as a kind of "fundamentalist egalitarianism" and concludes that this refusal to accept the need for an actual structure, a hierarchy, will not deliver results. It will not win elections, run a legislative assembly, develop policy, and then act in light of those policies in a manner that brings lasting change.[1] It is, in effect, a useless effort. Perhaps worse than useless. In effect, power is not leveraged; whatever power was or could have been present was dissipated. It accomplished nothing. Michael Jinkins and Deborah Bradshaw Jinkins put it well when they make the observation that "impotence is not a virtue . . . power can and must be used for good."[2]

And yet power is tricky; it has to be regulated. Without discipline, accountability, and transparency, the exercise of power will be either unruly or ineffective or it will be abused. Power needs to be regulated for two reasons. First, of course, we need to be sure that the exercise of power does actually reflect the fruit of good conversation, good consultation, and thus that the actions taken actually do reflect the leveraging of wisdom. And second, power is so easily abused and used or misused for personal ends.

And thus while the exercise of power is essential for organizational effectiveness, there needs to be real and genuine accountability for all players within an organization for how power actually operates. A basic working principle could be stated as such: the leveraging and moderation of power is a two-fold essential element of good governance. The genius of institutions that work is that they get this blend right. They *steward* power and they *regulate* power in a way that fits their mission, their institutional strengths and potential, and they do so in a manner that is congruent with their values and organizational culture.[3] The stewardship

---

[1]Grant Munroe, "Review of Micah White, *The End of Protest*," *The Globe and Mail*, March 26, 2016, R9.

[2]Michael Jinkins and Deborah Bradshaw Jinkins, *The Character of Leadership: Public Virtue in Nonprofit Organizations* (San Francisco: Jossey-Bass, 1998), 32, 34. They are speaking of leadership and they set this observation up by stating, "If a leader wants his cause to succeed he must find the power to consolidate gains and buttress support."

[3]When it comes to "organizational culture," be alert to a pseudo culture—or better a pathological culture—that is averse to power. Either nothing will get done or there will be power but it will not be either a moderated or an accountable use of power. Be aware of institutions that naively think that we are just family, doing things by consensus, which can so easily be a cover for the lack of effective systems for the leveraging and moderation of power.

and regulation of power might look very different in different settings—contrasting a hospital with a university, a public library from the art gallery across the street, or the system of governance of the US Congress and how that compares with how a congregation or a Christian denomination is governed. And yet the fundamental principles will be remarkably similar. In each case we are looking for how to leverage and moderate power effectively.

We ask what the mission is and how we can, given our mission and our social and cultural ethos and location, work with a system of good governance that affirms the essential and thus legitimate exercise of power. But then also, in like manner, what would be the appropriate mechanism in this context and setting for us to moderate and regulate power in this organization or governance system? We explore this not as a way to weaken the capacity for power to be exercised or diminish its impact, but precisely as a way to hold it accountable while also stewarding and empowering those who have the responsibility to make sure that the mission is fulfilled. Thus the regulation and moderation of power means accountability, not dis-empowerment but the stewardship of power. For all of us in whatever organization we serve, we need to be accountable to somebody, some agency. The more power you have, the greater the need for a transparent structure of intentional accountability. But the point remains: the moderation of power does not mean impotence; it means accountability and transparency. We do not lose the capacity to do what needs to be done so that the mission happens.

Governance is always about the fulfillment of the mission, making sure that the objectives of the institution are accomplished. And more, the system of governance—whether in a church or a nonprofit—should be transparent: Where and how are decisions made? Who is responsible to implement a decision, and to whom are they accountable?

Knowing this is all part of institutional intelligence. Within the organization of which we are a part, we know where decisions are made, we know how we can contribute to the decision-making process, and we know who, in the end, has the capacity to act on those decisions. And there are no two ways about it: this means that we *defer* to the process. Believing in institutions means that we respect the critical elements that are essential to good decision making and thus to the capacity of the organization to fulfill its mission.

And one of the most obvious ways in which this happens is through what has been aptly called *shared* governance. Shared power does not mean diffused power. It does not mean that power is diminished. Ironically, the reverse is true. Shared power results in more power. The organization is more powerful, more effective, and more capable of fulfilling its mission as those within the organization recognize and affirm the legitimate exercise of power and appreciate the diverse ways it is expressed within the institution.

To put it more baldly, power is not a zero-sum game. I once heard a faculty speak of their institution as having a particular feature that they viewed to be a strength: they were marked by strong faculty, a weak president, and a relatively benign board. And they thus encouraged the search committee for a new president to seek someone out who would not lead but rather provide a kind of figurehead oversight to the institution where, they insisted, the faculty essentially "run things."

Could that kind of thinking be counterproductive and, ironically, disempowering of the faculty? Might the faculty actually be served best—and the mission of the institution that they all care about actually get implemented—if the president was empowered to be the president and the board was functioning fully as a powerful and effective board?

Could it be that universities need powerful faculty, powerful presidents, *and* powerful boards, all three? Could it be that nothing is lost and everything gained when each entity understands and embraces its role and effectiveness in the exercise of power and willingly responds to the moderating influences and wisdom of other necessary and legitimate entities within the organization?

Could it be that pastors welcome the opportunity to work with a strong and effective church council, recognizing that the strength of the governing board of the church does not diminish their power but actually is a means by which they are more powerful—more, potentially at least, effective in their work as pastors? And, conversely, boards and church councils must understand that part of their role is to empower the senior pastor or pastoral staff.

And yet shared governance only works if all entities—whether it be an individual role or a committee or board within the institution—clearly know what kind of power they have and how that power is to be exercised. Without this understanding, the only potential outcome is conflict, misunderstanding, and organizational ineffectiveness.

STRUCTURES THAT WORK

The reflection on governance and shared governance has led to a set of best practices that are essential for good governance within nonprofit agencies and institutions, evident, in part, in the recognition of three distinct areas or foci for the exercise of power: executive leadership, trusteeship, and mission practitioners.

Not all organizations or institutions will have three. But most will. And most crucially, it is essential that structure and decision-making systems are clear, integrated, and aligned: we know where decisions are made. And we know where and how decisions are made and to whom decision makers are accountable for the action taken.

We must speak of the role of the executive—the president and the senior administrators. And we need to consider the place of the board. Indeed, the vast majority of the literature on institutional governance will speak to the role of the board, the role of the president, and the way in which these two entities work together.[4] The exception to this is the university—the academic world—where, of course, significant attention is given to the role of the faculty in governance. But I wonder if we could make a case, as I will make it below, that the academy is on to something that is relevant to most institutions: those who actually embody and do the mission—what I will identify here as the mission practitioners— necessarily need to have a vital role in the governance of the institution.

Thus I will consider all three. Potentially they could be considered in any order, but I will begin with the role of the executive. First, though, a

---

[4]No one has influenced this conversation—the working relationship between boards and executives—as much as John Carver. See especially two publications: John Carver, *Boards That Make a Difference*, 2nd ed. (San Francisco: Jossey-Bass, 1997); and John Carver and Miriam Mayhew Carver, *Reinventing Your Board*, rev. ed. (San Francisco: Jossey-Bass, 2006). Much of what follows in these chapters on governance when it comes to board and executive effectiveness leans into and assumes the Carver wisdom on what he calls "policy governance."

crucial point must be made. One of the most significant contributions of John Carver to good governance thinking and best practice is a basic working principle that clarity is crucial: What is the role of the board and where does their responsibility begin and end, and what is the role of the executive? And then also, what is the role of the mission practitioners? It all needs to be clear who and what agency is responsible for what in the practice of good governance.

Executive leadership. First, there needs to be an executive; someone needs to lead, and it cannot be done by committee. Someone needs to give voice to the vision and direction of the institution along with attention to the means by which this is going to be fulfilled. Someone needs to be the president, the executive director, the principal, the senior pastor or lead pastor, the CEO, however it is designated—someone who has the immediate (immediate, not ultimate, since ultimate responsibility is located elsewhere) responsibility for the fulfillment of the mission. Someone needs to be empowered to pull this together and set the tone and direction of the institution.

When I hear of a church that has decided to establish a co-pastorate, or of an academic institution that appointed a husband and wife as co-presidents, I assume this reflects something in the history of the process of the appointment but I cannot help but think that it will not work. Might there be situations in which it would work? Perhaps there are, but at most in an unusual organization and, at best, for a relatively short period of time. Someone needs to lead. There needs to be clarity on who has executive responsibility and thus authority for the organization. And organizations must know who, in the end, reports to the governing board and who the board will hold responsible for the fulfilment of the mission.

Even if the president of a university works very closely with the senior academic officer, so much so that the perception within and outside of the institution is that they are deeply in sync in their vision and direction of the institution, the fact will still remain that one of them is the president—de facto or otherwise. And the person who has final responsibility to the board, to the key constituents, is the person who should be so designated as president. This is the person who, when all is said and debated, has to make the tough calls.

The executive may well include a senior cohort of vice presidents or senior associates. In larger organizations there will be an executive team. But here it also needs to be stressed that they serve at the pleasure of the president; they are an extension of the office of the executive director of the organization. The executive leadership of the organization could be small—one person—or larger, a president's cabinet with a cohort of VPs overseeing diverse areas of responsibility. But in the end, the executives, with and under the president and accountable to the president, function as one voice. They are one executive cohort who, through the president, report to the board and, through and with the president, oversee the institution.

When an executive is not appointed or if it is not clear who is leading the organization, then in all likelihood, someone is leading. But they are not leading from a position where they can be held accountable. It may be an influential board member or, in a college, an influential faculty member who, in effect, runs the place. And yet it is not done transparently, openly, and in a manner in which the individual or individuals can be held responsible.

Having clarity about who is the executive does two things: it empowers someone to lead, and it allows for clear terms of reference for accountability.

Effective executive leaders act: they do what needs to be done to lead the organization. True "servant leaders" provide executive leadership; they act. They are servants and this is evident in their leadership, in the well-considered actions that they take on behalf of the institution. And they are empowered by the rest of the organization—especially the trustees, of which I will speak next—to do what needs to be done for the health of the organization.

This applies to every institution with no exception. Leadership is critical to organizational health and effectiveness. Yes, there are leaders throughout the institution at different levels of functioning. But in the end there needs to be clarity about whom the board is holding accountable to make the critical leadership decisions. And the board supports the president to do what the president needs to do.

This is so also for a local congregation. William H. Willimon makes the sobering observation that congregations need pastors who can transcend their proclivity for empathy and actually lead. He notes that organizations only go somewhere when there is leadership. And more, congregations need leaders that name reality—the work of truth telling— and then in response to that reality, they do what needs to be done for the sake of the mission of the congregation, with the support of the board or church council. But, as Willimon notes, congregations "crave the placidity of the status quo and reward those who keep them comfortable."[5] And then he writes, "Caregiving, the default mode of most pastors, is always less costly than leading. But the problem with caregiving is that no group survives or thrives without continually refitting and repositioning itself—and certainly not an institution that's accountable to God."[6]

Congregations that are healthy, growing, thriving, and missionally engaged are congregations where there is clear and capable leadership that is allowed to lead.

Universities, hospitals, art galleries, publishing houses, social agencies, and governments are only effective when there is effectiveness in the role of senior, executive leadership. As Willimon notes, this is a "costly" role in the institution. This is so because leaders unsettle the status quo—naming reality (truth telling) and acting in ways that will not satisfy all. No leader is effective if all she cares about is that everyone likes her. But, when it is done well, both the institution and the leader know the joy of being part of an institution that actually works and fulfills its mission.

Trusteeship. Effective organizations also have an entity that holds the institution in trust. By law, most jurisdictions require as much: a committee, a collective, typically identified as the "board"—the governing board, the board of trustees, the church council. This is the body that appoints the executive and grants to the executive *immediate* responsibility for the organization's effectiveness. But the board has the *ultimate* responsibility for the fulfillment of the mission of the organization. They hold the mission and the institution's assets in trust.

---

[5]William H. Willimon, "Truth Telling in the Parish: Why Leaders Are a Pain," *The Christian Century* 133, no. 4 (February 17, 2016): 20.
[6]Ibid.

Much is made, and rightly, of the role of the executive in managing the operation—in assuring that the approved policies are honored and put into effect, that the lights are on, the bills are paid, the funds spent, all to the very simple end: the fulfillment of the mission. In contrast, the board has the responsibility of "trusteeship." First, to be clear, trustees ensure that the mission is happening; they are the trustees of the mission. Second, boards appoint a president or executive director to deliver on that mission. And third, trustees assure that the institution has the fiscal capacity and resilience to sustain the mission for the foreseeable future.

The board provides the essential link between the external entities that in effect own the organization and the management that then in turn makes the mission happen. Here is the fundamental working principle: both trusteeship and executive leadership are needed and something is lost when they are either diluted or confused. The board, representing key stakeholders, holds the organization in trust and provides the essential body of accountability for the executive. Peter Drucker stresses this point when he writes, "To be effective, a nonprofit needs a strong board, but a board that does the board work," which is, for Drucker, to be "the guardian of the mission."[7]

Ideally, the board is small enough to be effective—ideally no larger than fifteen (see chapter five for more on the question of group size and effectiveness). But it also needs to be large enough to adequately represent the external stakeholders of the organization. And that is the genius of the board: it represents *external* constituencies that have a legitimate say or voice in the mission of the organization.[8]

In effective institutions there is a vital and dynamic counterpoint between management and trusteeship. Organizations need both. Thus boards should

[7]Peter F. Drucker, *Managing the Non-Profit Organization: Principles and Practices* (New York: HarperBusiness, 1990), 157.
[8]I know that in many jurisdictions, presidents are actually voting members of the board. But this could easily be viewed as a confusion of function or role. The senior executive does not report to herself. And more, she needs a board that is truly "other"—a separate and distinct entity with a very different role or responsibility in the organization. A president may actually be more powerful and freer to provide executive leadership by not presuming to also be a member of the board. They are two separate functions. And, as noted, the board represents *external* constituents, thus not only not the president, but also not the employees—staff, faculty, or other internal stakeholders who participate in shared governance through other mechanisms.

not manage, for in so doing they inevitably step back from the crucial work of trusteeship. Effective boards keep to their knitting; they are trustees. And they appoint and then empower the executive to manage—to do what can only truly and finally be done effectively from the executive. This point is crucial: it is the responsibility of the board to appoint the senior executive, the president, the senior pastor—however this role is designated in this organization. They may well consult—and they should consult—but in the end, the board make the call.[9]

The board is the final line or court of appeal. But also, effective boards do have actual and real and effective authority over the mission and the institutional assets. Yes, there may be external constituencies that have a presence at the board by virtue of their affiliation with the institution— perhaps a denominational representative on a denominational seminary board. And yet it should be very clear that the board, as the final authority, does very genuinely have the capacity to act, as a board, without undue interference from any external agency or entity.

In this regard, the next point is crucial: the strength and power of the board lies in its *collective* voice. Board members function as one, and they foster their capacity—representing diverse constituencies perhaps—to speak with one voice, whether that be to the executive or to the diverse stake- holders. Board members may well differ through the process of deliberation on a matter, but in the end, the board speaks as one. And typically it does so through the office of the board chair.

The board appoints the senior executive, and that president or senior pastor reports to the board. This book includes a whole appendix on the relationship between the board and the president, a relationship that is absolutely crucial to the effective functioning of the organization. Yet here I will note that if the executive is not effective, it falls to the board to ask—collectively—whether the board is not providing sufficient support to and empowerment for the person in that office. And if it is, and if the presidency is still not working, only one body can act: the board. It behooves the board to act for the sake of the institution. When a president is inef- fective, the board must act. This is why, in part, it is problematic for the

---

[9]More in this regard in appendix A, on the relationship between the president and the board.

president to be a member of the board. This is why it is imperative that the board has clear criteria by which it judges the effectiveness of the president and in the end make a determination about whether the president or senior executive is effective.

What all of this implies but which perhaps needs to be stated clearly is this: an effective organization without fail has leadership that is empowered to lead but also leadership that is accountable and, more specifically, accountable to a governing board. This accountability needs to be real—clear, transparent, and meaningful. To be blunt, if the accountability has no teeth to it, no mechanisms for holding someone accountable—either no board or its equivalent—there is no real accountability. Pastors can only be accountable to the whole congregation in a very diffused and perhaps sincere way, but the congregation as a whole has no real way of holding the pastor accountable. Only a board or church council can actually do what needs to be done. Without a functioning board that has the power to hold the executive leader accountable, organizational effectiveness will be short term at best.

Effective institutions have both empowered leaders and transparent and workable mechanisms for holding those leaders accountable. When senior leadership is ineffective, it falls to the board to act, but this is only meaningful if they actually have the power to do what needs to be done to move the organization toward effectiveness.

The mission practitioners, the entity that embodies and implements the mission. Many institutions and organizations have another entity that represents a vital and essential voice and contribution to institutional governance. Typically, this is the group that embodies the mission and delivers on the mission.

For the university, good governance requires and presumes that faculty are not merely employees, but also—collectively, and I will stress this point, that they function collectively—have an essential voice that needs to shape the fulfillment of the mission.

It bears repeating that in a university the faculty are indispensable to effective governance. Their voice is crucial and needs to be heard; they need to shape the design of the curriculum and the policies by which academic excellence is sustained and expressed in this particular institution.

In a hospital, the medical staff needs to have a vital role in governance; in a publishing house, the editors; for a relief and development agency or a mission agency, those who are in the field, actually doing the mission of the organization. For an orchestra, it is the musicians.

Ask this question: In this industry, where you work, what is the appropriate role in governance or exercise of authority of those who actually do the mission? Do those in the field of the development or community development agency have a significant voice in the policies and procedures that guide their work? Do those who actually do the mission of the organization have a voice in whatever is most central and crucial to their capacity to deliver on the mission? In a university, the critical dynamic is among board, executive leadership, and faculty. In a church, it might outline the relationship among the pastoral staff, the church board, and the congregation.[10]

To summarize, effective organizations will be marked by these entities:

- an executive—president and executive cohort who are empowered to lead, functioning as one under the leadership of the president; or, in a church, the leadership of the senior or lead pastor

- a board that functions as one voice—members who have developed a shared identity and shared sense of the mission and shared trust and mutual respect that frees them to, collectively, be the trustees of the mission and of the institution as a whole and specifically to appoint the executive and hold the executive accountable

- another entity, be it the faculty of a college, or the medical staff of a clinic, whichever entity embodies the mission—individuals who function collectively and speak as one voice, in governing themselves and communicating with the president and through the president to the board

---

[10]Note: this might be delineated in quite different ways depending on the polity or theological convictions of a particular denomination. But the bylaws will still provide clarity on the relationship among the three entities.

BYLAWS AND INSTITUTIONAL ETHOS

Every organization or institution will have or should have bylaws. These documents delineate the way that power will work in this organization: Who has accountability for what and to whom? And effective organizations find the sweet spot where dynamic patterns of accountability do not limit the exercise of power but moderate it, keep it transparent, so that indeed good leadership can happen and so that the mission is fulfilled. Typically, the bylaws spell out the dynamic between the three entities indicated above.

And the main point is that while all three are needed, it is essential that their spheres of responsibility be clearly demarcated and integrated. Bylaws and policies lay out a functioning governance structure with clarity about the role of the president—both the responsibilities and the limits of the authority of the CEO—along with the authority and limits of the board as well as that of the faculty or the editorial board or the medical staff in a hospital. Make it clear! Good intentions and goodwill are not enough.

The reverse is also true: you can have great structures in place, but without goodwill they will not be effective. We need both: good structures, good terms of reference, and clarity about roles and responsibilities as well as people of goodwill who believe in and will respect the structure—faculty will work toward functioning as a collective and let the president be the president. The board will be the board and know its role and know what it means, through the bylaws, to empower the president to do what the president needs to do. And then, of course, the president will depend on, honor, and value the voice of the faculty and the board and encourage the faculty and the board to speak with one voice. And when they do, the president listens, heeds, and values this collective wisdom and authority. All three entities are essential to the fulfillment of the mission of the university.

When it comes to governance, if it works it is, as often as not, the lead executive who believes both in the stewardship of power and the regulation of power. It is the president or senior pastor who refuses to act without the support of the board and who defers to and fosters the capacity of the board to speak with one voice—refusing to "lobby" a segment of the board or to seek support from one part of the board over against the other.

We need presidents and lead executives who will act judiciously and courageously, doing what often only the president can do. We need leaders who are committed to the health of the institution and its missional effectiveness, even if they have to make less than popular decisions, even if there is a vocal and intimidating minority who lobby for their own concerns. We need presidents who hear and respect the voices of their constituents but in the end do what needs to be done for the well-being of the institution for which they are responsible. They do it in a way that is accountable to that very constituency and accountable to the trustees, of course. But they do what needs to be done.

We need pastors who affirm and work with the power of their governing boards. And they recognize and affirm the place of legitimate power of the congregation as a whole. We need pastors who value the voice and authority of the church council or board, and they value and insist on the voice and legitimate role of the congregation as a whole in the governing process. They value the wisdom of their congregational members while, of course, insisting that it is exercised collectively and that their final accountability is not the congregation as a whole but to the church board.

But then the reverse is also true: we need university faculty who recognize that the university will not thrive until and unless the senior executive is empowered to do what can only be done by the executive; and we need boards who, rather than trying to be the executive, support the need for an executive and empower the executive so that the mission of the organization is implemented. Nimble institutions and institutions that have the capacity to challenge the status quo in a time of financial stress, or in a time when difficult decisions need to be made, or when a senior executive must be empowered to do what needs to be done. Key decision-making authority needs to be located, unambiguously, in the hands of the president and the senior administrators of the organization.[11] Yes, of course, there

---

[11]Note the insistence on this point for universities and colleges in William G. Bowen and Eugene M. Tobin, *Locus of Authority: The Evolution of Faculty Roles in the Governance of Higher Education* (Princeton, NJ: Princeton University Press, 2015), 207. Bowen and Tobin use the word *unambiguously*, stressing that there is no doubt who has the authority to make the necessary decisions for the organization and thus who can and will be held accountable to make those needed

are limits. The board necessarily establishes the policies and the limits of
the president's responsibility and authority.[12] But the president can still act.

The genius of great institutions is captured in a particular dynamic, the
capacity to get things done in response to a changing and fluid environment:
to clarify the mission, to hire the best people, to find the resources to make
it possible to fulfill the mission, and to establish strategic associations with
other agencies. And they are able to do this when the three entities are
clear about their roles but also where the senior executive leadership can
actually lead. Yes, there is a legitimate concern about unaccountable pastors
or presidents or executive leaders. But with clear policies, leaders need to
have the capacity to lead and actually be accountable to lead.

As an aside I would note that a danger within a nonprofit is the disease
aptly called "vetocracy"—a term coined by Francis Fukuyama in *Political
Order and Political Decay*. His argument is that the United States does not
work because it has degenerated into a vetocracy, where the system of
checks and balances has become politicized and the outcome is that leadership is continually stifled.

In nonprofits, including churches, there is always a danger with a desire
for shared governance that a minority will effectively be allowed to rule
through veto, whether it be passive aggressive filibusters, emotional blackmail,
stonewalling, or—there is no other word for it—bullying. On faculty of a
college, I have seen a minority get their way through sheer dogged determination and an enabling, quiet, and acquiescent majority who wanted
to avoid the discomfort of conflict. Similarly, in churches, often people
comprising a loud and insistent minority—perhaps a founding member
of the congregation or someone providing significant funding for the
facility—are allowed to have a disproportionate influence because of their
insistence on something that matters to them. The result is that legitimate
leadership cannot be exercised for the healthy functioning of the organization:

---

decisions. I would add that nothing is gained by the sentimental talk of "we do everything by
consensus around here." Yes, we affirm the need for consultation, and yes, we affirm the need
for transparency. But when all is said it also needs to be unambiguously clear that the senior
leadership can and must and will lead; they will do what needs to be done for the sake of the
health of the organization.

[12]Thus the insistence of John Carver on what he has aptly called "policy governance"; see Carver,
Boards That Make a Difference, and Carver and Carver, *Reinventing Your Board*.

the board or the faculty cannot speak as one. In these situations, the role of the board chair or faculty chair is crucial: to recognize what is happening and insist on the capacity of the group to speak with one voice. Presidents and senior pastors need to learn how to act, but they can only do so if they have the unqualified support of their boards, the entity to which they are accountable.[13]

Does this mean that we completely ignore the voice and legitimate vote of the third entity: the people in the church, the people in the streets (for the government), the faculty of the university or the medical staff of the hospital? Of course not. If we ignore their voice, they can—literally or figuratively—go on strike. When a faculty vote "no confidence" in the university president, it is likely just a matter of time before the board has to act. When a congregation loses confidence in the church's pastoral leadership, they vote with their feet and with their checkbooks. Rather, my point is that effective leadership grants voice to the collective but—and this is crucial—has learned how to act, accountable to the trustees, taking account of the voice of the minority but not stymied or vetoed by that voice. They hear and affirm the insight and input from aptly called loyal opposition, but then in the end, they do what they have been placed in office to do.

Effective governance, then, moderates the voice and influence of those who might wield undue influence within the governance system—influence that is out of proportion to what serves the best interests of the organization. Unhealthy systems succumb; healthy systems—not just well-designed models, but systems that actually work—accept the presence and influence of a minority voice, but they manage to hold any undue influence in check.

Finally, in conclusion, remember that within the organization, you have institutional intelligence if you have clarity about a key question: To whom do I report? Or, to whom am I accountable for the work for which I am responsible? We are only effective within the institution when we know how to act and function and lead in a manner that is both transparent and accountable. A president reports to the board; functionally, as often

---

[13]The same dynamic can happen for much larger entities: a denomination is stymied in its workings by a small minority, a persistent sub-section that co-opts the capacity of the denominational to grow and flourish. Or, I think of government, where again, a strident minority can easily abuse the system—perhaps through filibustering—and keep the will of the majority from happening.

as not, that means the president reports to the chair of the board. But the president's boss is not the board chair. The chair only speaks on behalf of the board and provides counsel that as best as possible reflects the will and perspective of the board. But the main point is that the president reports to the board. There is a structure that provides accountability.

Board members are typically accountable—functionally, at least—to the board chair. If a board member is problematic in dealings and ineffective on the board, then it necessarily falls to the board chair to address the issue.

A faculty member typically reports to her department head or perhaps to the dean. And this is real accountability.

In the field, a team member for a development agency typically reports to a team leader.

Know where you fit within the system, and contribute to the system in a way that fosters the capacity of the system to work effectively. All of this leads, then, to the question of power and how it is exercised.

USING POWER RESPONSIBLY

Having established that power is a good thing—essential for the vitality of the organization and the implementation of the mission—we then need good and clear structures of accountability and reporting, along with clarity regarding who is responsible for which decisions and who is accountable to whom for these decisions. We need to know how power works in an organization and how that power can be exercised both effectively and responsibly.

Take for example the executive director, president, or pastor of a church. Whoever fills this role can only be effective if he has clarity about two things: first, for what am I responsible and second, in what ways and forms do I have the power available to me to fulfill that for which I am responsible? The two are linked: power and responsibility.

In speaking of power, then, it is helpful to recognize that there are different kinds of power. As a president, as an employee, as a congregational member, as a faculty member of a university, as a donor, as a student in the college, or as a client of the agency that is providing you with a valued service. Everyone has power, but there are different kinds of power. And those with institutional intelligence recognize what kinds of power they have and have learned how to exercise it responsibly. That is, they know how an institution works; they know where decisions are made and how they are made—who makes a decision and who has the right to either be consulted on that decision or actually veto that decision. This dynamic of power and responsibility is always institution specific. Presidents of universities recognize that not all universities empower their presidents in a similar way; pastors of churches come up against different dynamics when it comes to the relationship between themselves and the church board, and both pastor and church variably experience the relationship between the pastor and the elders and the congregation as a whole.

Ask yourself two questions within your organization: What kind of power do I have? And how can I exercise it responsibly?

I once heard of a couple who were upset that the elders of the church made a particular decision about the way that their church would observe the Lord's Supper. And they decided that as an act of protest they would walk out of the church every time the Lord's Supper was celebrated. Well, okay, I thought, they do have power. But is that a responsible way to exercise that power, through boycott? Sometimes boycott—of a product or service, as a client—is a legitimate form of protest and power. But in a church, it is hardly a constructive way to foster goodwill and good collective decision making. They have power, but they exercised it in a way that is not helpful to good governance and effective decision making.

So the first question is, what kind of power do you have? As a rule, it is helpful to think in terms of three kinds of power, each of which, to be effective, must be exercised responsibly.

First, there is *executive* power, the power to choose, to act, to decide: to sign the contract, to make the call on the action item that is on the table. For those in executive positions it is vitally important that they know where their power begins and ends. When can they consult but then act on their best judgement? And where and in what contexts do they only have the power to recommend, perhaps to the board of trustees? And where and in what contexts do they have the power to convene, to moderate a conversation that can perhaps in due time lead to action?

If you are a president, know what decisions are yours and yours alone—no one else can make them or make them for you. You know what power is given to you and what power is not given to you, and you exercise power in a way that is consistent with the role and the responsibility that goes with that role. Nothing is gained by a feigned insistence that everyone can be involved in a decision that in the end only the president can make and must make. Of course you consult, but in the end there are decisions that the president has to make for the well-being of the whole. So you make the call. You are accountable for that decision, which means that transparency through the process is essential. But in the end, institutions only thrive if there is someone who is prepared to act, as president, and do what the organization needs the president to do. This is executive power.

Second, it is helpful to speak of *legislative* power, the power that comes through the development of a common voice, whether this be for a board, a committee, or a body that is adopting actions, policies, regulations, and, potentially, direction.

In this case, the power is held collectively; decisions are reached through a process of deliberation and debate and discussion that leads to a vote and an agreement on a policy or an action item that reflects the will of the body. Legislative power by its very nature means that one learns to cultivate the power of the collective—to be part of a deliberative body that will make a shared decision. In this case, it means you know how to contribute to the process—under the authority of a moderator—toward a shared outcome. And it also means that you will own and respect the shared outcome: if the majority voted for an action and you voted against it, you use the meeting to express your views and make the case for what was not accepted by the whole, but in the end, you "accept," you live with, you affirm, you defer to both the process and the outcome. This is the only way that we can function with grace and integrity within an institution.

Third, it is also important that we acknowledge what might be best called *political* power—the power of association, of influence, of having the credibility where others follow you or at least acknowledge your voice and your will by virtue of the weight of influence you have with them. Executive power without political power is crude and ultimately ineffective. Legislative power is intimately linked to the credibility that one develops with one's fellow legislators—you gain credibility and voice, and thus influence, by virtue of the political and social capital one gets by the investment of time and association. As an aside I would note that as a rule those with political power are good listeners: they know how to be attentive to the felt needs of one or more constituencies.

So know what kind of power you have. Then ask how you can exercise this power effectively. What does it mean to be a responsible member of this organization with the large perspective in view? What is the mission of the organization? And as such, how can I—with the power that I have, whatever the form—use that power and influence to foster the capacity of the organization to fulfill its mission for the well-being of our customers, our clients, and our fiscal health, giving due attention to the crucial elements of a vital institutional culture?

And this means respecting the power of others. For example, soccer players only truly believe in and honor the game if they respect the authority of the referee and the assistant referee. A player may differ with the referee and be completely convinced that the wrong call was made. But it is crucial to the game that in the end the player respects and defers to the referee's decision. That is the only way that the game works.

It is a fundamental element of institutional life and thus institutional intelligence that we will not always agree with outcomes. We will get outvoted. But we respect the system rather than, when we are outvoted, decry or sabotage the process. We defer to constituted authority, and we free those authorized to implement a decision to actually do their jobs.

Thus a faculty member only truly uses her power when she acknowledges the legitimate role of the president, the essential authority of the board, and, of course, the rightful voice and vote of her faculty colleagues. And she only truly exercises her power when she does so in a way that is congenial and intentional with her colleagues—seeking, through political and legislative power, to foster a common faculty voice. We only exercise our power effectively when we recognize that others have legitimate power— our colleagues, the chair of our committee, the president, the board, and various other constituencies. We exercise the power that is given to us as part of a greater whole and out of commitment to the greater whole.

Appendix A, "Boards and Presidents," will provide further discussion for those for whom this topic is of immediate interest and relevance.

GOVERNANCE THAT WORKS, PART 2

Finding Wisdom, Making Decisions

Having already addressed the question of power, we can now consider how effective institutions not only get things done, but how they get the *right* things done. They not only have structures in place for the implementation, they also have structures, institutional habits, and practices by which they access the knowledge, wisdom, and insight needed to deliver on their mission.

Two things must be stressed. First, organizations must have the capacity to get the wisdom, the knowledge, needed to fulfill the mission. And second, they need the capacity for actually coming to closure on the decision that needs to be made.

We begin with the first, and the assumption here is that no one person in this organization has all the wisdom, insight, and knowledge needed to know how to assure that the mission happens. And so we listen and learn. We encourage good conversation. We look for insight and wisdom toward good policy and best practice. Effective institutions are learning organizations.[1] Organizations that get this know that consultation is crucial to the capacity of the institution to accomplish its mission. And so they consult widely.

---

[1]All of us who speak this way about organizations are indebted to the seminal work of Peter Senge, and particularly his publications, including: Peter Senge, *The Fifth Discipline: The Art and Practice of the Learning Organization* (New York: Doubleday, 1991).

It is helpful to think of this institutional habit—insisting on good conversation and good learning—as happening along three avenues:

- First, the administrative structure itself encourages and fosters consultation that leads to wisdom for effective decision making.

- Second, the institution encourages lateral consultation within the organization, between departments and divisions, conversation that might not follow official structural lines.

- Third, they go outside, speaking and learning from peer institutions—from divergent agencies, even—to learn from, adapt, and appropriate insights into their own context.

In what follows, each of these is considered separately. But what all three speak to is the passionate pursuit of insight into how an organization can effectively fulfill its mission.

WORKING WITHIN THE SYSTEM— THE GOVERNANCE STRUCTURE

When it comes to getting the wisdom, we begin by affirming that the structure—the administrative or organizational system itself—can be set up precisely to foster learning. The structure itself needs to be a conduit for good conversation toward getting an accurate read on what needs to be done.

The board meets to make decisions, of course. But good decisions require the prelude, good conversation. This is conversation marked by the give and take of good listening, mutual attentiveness, focused observations, and the capacity to say what needs to be said. Trustees come to the table eager to learn with their fellow board members and attentive to the ways in which together they will find the wisdom they need. We must always assume that no one person has the wisdom we need to proceed, to do what needs to be done. So we listen and learn and grow in our capacity to see the situation and the character of the challenges and the potential outcomes. And the key on the board is that the board itself represents diverse constituencies, perhaps from the business sector, or education and the arts, or perhaps from the social service sector. And they are learning together and from each other.

A pastoral staff or the president's cabinet of a university are colleagues learning together through the process of weighing issues and deliberating on those issues toward a good understanding that will lead, they trust, to good decisions.

The faculty of a college or university function as a collective, and there is no avoiding that to do so requires that they meet, as a faculty or in faculty committees, to deliberate on the options and opportunities that they are facing. They debate a range of issues from curricular revisions to academic policies to hiring recommendations. And they do it in meetings—search committees, program or departmental meetings, or full faculty meetings.

Meetings happen. We meet to talk with an issue at hand, an agenda with a list of issues that need to be discussed. And meeting together—either face to face or on the phone or through video conferencing—is *essential*, all to this end: to find the wisdom that we need to face the challenge or issues facing the organization. In saying this I am challenging the conventional wisdom that goes all the way back to management guru Peter Drucker's call for fewer meetings—treating them as an almost necessary evil, the fewer the better.[2] He suggests that we need to talk less and act more, that we need less conversation and more action.

We certainly need action. And no one needs ineffective meetings. I appreciate the call to action implied in what our Latino friends call *la paralisis de analisis*—that is, the lack of action because we are paralyzed by continual analysis. And yet we must insist that meetings are essential to the capacity of the organization to leverage the wisdom it needs to fulfil its mission. Implementation without conversation, consultation, and careful analysis is doomed to failure. And productive and informed analysis comes through meetings.

Of course we must come to closure and make a decision and implement that decision, but we must not get there prematurely. We first meet to listen and speak and learn. Wisdom is found through conversation. The decision to be implemented must reflect the best counsel of those involved in the conversation. But the basic assumption remains: we are looking for

---

[2]Peter Drucker, *The Effective Executive* (New York: Harper and Row, 1966), 44.

the wisdom of not one person but the group—wisdom that comes from the iterative quality of good conversation. Effective organizations generate wisdom, insight, and creativity by leveraging this good conversation. And the only hope for good meetings is if we realize that we need one another. And so we enter into the process, into the meeting, into the conversation with a fundamental generosity toward the other, attentive to the other, recognizing that wisdom is found in the very process of give and take.

Women and men of institutional intelligence know how to participate in this process. They know what it means to go to meetings where the focus is an agenda that has a potential list of items—issues or matters of common concern—that the group needs to make a decision about. They know that they have one voice in the process, and perhaps one vote in the decision that is to be made. They understand what it means to be a contributor to a decision-making process. And, of course, they know that they might lose a vote or speak in the minority. That is fine and is part of being a participant in an organization: you will not always get your way. But you invest in the process, you attend the meetings, you contribute to the agenda, and in the end, you respect due process.

Thus there are some things to remember. First, the role of the moderator of the committee—typically spoken of as the "chair"—is crucial. Simply put, the role of the moderator is to foster good conversation that moves the committee toward a decision in a timely manner. Every institution needs a number of skilled moderators: for the board, for the senior leadership team (typically the president), and more, for each committee meeting. The faculty search committee only functions well if we are clear about who is chairing: perhaps a dean or a departmental head. For a church board? Again, it is the chair who is essential to the effective functioning of the board and thus of the whole church. It is truly hard to overstate the significance of this role in fostering good conversation.

The chair is responsible to ensure that good conversation happens, to bring closure to the conversation, and to confirm that action will be taken and by whom; that is, chairs signal what decision has been made and who has the responsibility to take it from there.

The chair ensures that the group attends to diverse perspectives in allowing both sides of a potential issue to get air time so that the approved outcome is the best one for this institution at this time, as I will also stress in the upcoming chapter on recruiting and appointing the right people.

The genius of the role, the responsibility, of the chair is that as board chair or the chair of a faculty committee, your personal views are secondary—not incidental, but secondary—to the outcome you are seeking, the wisdom of the group. You are there to foster the very best conversation toward the best outcome. As chair, you are not there to directly or indirectly run things or get your agenda accomplished. You are there to foster the capacity of the group, the committee, to come to a shared understanding of the best way forward.

And yet, as noted, the role of the chair is also to foster closure. At some point, the chair makes the determination that it is time to call for the motion, in formal deliberations, or to simply say that the "sense of the chair is . . ." and put it simply: "Am I right to read the sense of the group that this should be our decision going forward?"

The chair calls for the action of the committee or board; the chair acknowledges the minority voice and allows it space in the meeting but also "moderates" that voice so that the minority voice does not co-opt the will of the majority.

Then also, good committee work recognizes that we know what agenda items properly speaking come to this entity—this board, this committee, this meeting? And when the decision is made, we know to whom is it referred and who has the responsibility to act on the actions taken by this committee. Meetings that do not lead to implementation are a waste of time.

Those who contribute effectively in a committee do so with a keen awareness of the parameters of this group, this committee, this deliberative body; they know when and where they have the power to actually decide; they know what agenda items are their purview. But then they also know where and when they refer or recommend their decisions to another body. And they work with not against the system.

Thus a US senator knows what properly speaking belongs on the Senate agenda and what is under the authority of the president. And the senator also knows when and where the president has the right of veto and respects and affirms this constitutional right. A faculty member of a university can contribute wholeheartedly to an issue under debate but also know that in the end, the matter at hand is being referred for final action to either the president or the board of trustees.

Finally, remember also this: diversity of views, opinions, and perspectives is essential to good conversation. An effective moderator will encourage the committee or the board to see an issue or question from diverse angles. Alternate views, perspectives, and opinions are encouraged. We do not need compliance. Now let me quickly add that organizations also do not need those who are in a habit of disagreeing as a matter of principle, a kind of proud-to-be-contrarian disposition. And yet we do need the diversity of perspective that can strengthen our capacity to find wisdom and make good decisions.

And this means that unanimity is not necessarily a sign of wisdom and a good decision. We need the minority perspective. And we need individuals who are willing to be in the minority but do so with all due respect for the process and the outcome: when all is said and done, you will defer to the will of the majority, or if the decision to be made is to recommend to the board, for example, you will accept the decision by the body that has the right to make the final decision.[3]

WORKING ALONGSIDE THE GOVERNANCE SYSTEM

A good and effective governance structure is about leveraging power so that what needs to get done gets done. Further, and ideally, that very structure should foster the capacity for good conversation to inform the decisions that need to be made. And yet the very structure, what we often think of as the hierarchy, can be both very good—essential for implementation, for action—and it can also be a problem if it somehow stands in the way of good conversation, good thinking, creative possibilities, and needed insight into both challenges and opportunities.

The structure makes implementation possible. But wisdom—understanding, good insight, creativity, and knowledge—does not always follow

---

[3]This means that perhaps we should resist the impulse to assume that if our decision is unanimous it is more likely to be the right decision. Boards and committees typically value the opportunity to say that "the decision was unanimous" as though this means that without any dissent the decision is a better one. Perhaps this is so, but this might only mean that no one had the courage to provide a minority perspective.

along the lines of administrative structures and direct reports. Some of
the best insights into how bank customers can be best served comes from
the tellers, and thus their voice needs to be heard and their wisdom incorporated into good decision making on how to manage how customers are
served. Wisdom, in other words, does not always travel along the same
lines as formal decision making and the implementation of those decisions.
And this means that strong and vital organizations have mechanisms by
which conversation can happen between divisions, or between areas or
zones of responsibility. They foster a capacity for not only "line" thinking
and conversation—along approved lines of authority and accountability—
but also lateral thinking and conversation. Sometimes the wisdom and
insight an organization needs comes through cross-pollination when the
administrative structure and system is either intentionally bypassed or, pro
tem—for the moment—flattened.

The potential danger with an administrative structure is that two people
whose conversation or shared wisdom would help address a problem are
not talking to one another, not because they have a problem with each
other but because their paths do not cross in the administrative structure.
They are never in the same meetings. They are not at table together
wresting with an issue that faces the organization.

An administrative structure is absolutely essential for the actual implementation of the decisions made from conversations that happen laterally
within the organization. Therefore, if we flatten the structure, if we open
up the conversation outside of the formal structures, it is only pro tem for
the purpose of getting wisdom and insight on a particular issue the
organization faces.

But we need this. We need to create the contacts, the connection—both
allowing them and encouraging them to happen, and creating the occasions to make sure that they happen. And, in like manner, we need to
have a system in place by which the wisdom of the network is incorporated
into the administrative structure and integrated into the strategic initiatives.

Thus the president might call an ad hoc meeting of five or six people,
including both internal and external individuals, to address an issue at
hand. Or two colleagues might meet over coffee—not covertly, but with
the full endorsement of their colleagues and their direct reports—to discuss

an issue that crosses spheres of responsibility and for which they have a perspective that might help the organization on a particular issue. A church board might ask four lay members of the congregation to meet to discuss a critical issue that is facing the church, asking them to bring their shared wisdom and expertise back to the board by way of a recommended course of action.

A selected group of university board members might create an open forum with students to get a read on the experience of being a student at this institution. A college president might sit down for coffee with the recruitment team to learn about their experience in the field with potential students. A mayor might create a town hall meeting to hear directly, not just through the formal governance arrangement of the city, from constituents in a particular part of the city or perhaps actually ride the subway and talk to the people who take it every day.

Sometimes, in other words, we bypass the structure. Early in my tenure as a university president, I asked this question: How should this institution, given its social and religious location, heritage, and commitment, respond to those who do not self-identify as heterosexual? It was a complex, controversial matter. I created a commission of eight persons from across the institution, who brought their own perspective but also needed to hear from others, together to help us all know how best to be who we were called to be, institutionally. Coming out of this commission, I brought a report to the president's cabinet (the vice presidents) and then to the board.

This way of thinking, acting, and entering into conversation needs to be part of the regular part of the fabric of institutional life. We have our systems and we need our systems. Wisdom should emerge from our systems, and we need our systems for implementation of our decisions. But we also need these other mechanisms that come alongside the formal administrative structure and foster good conversation that leads to the wisdom, knowledge, and insight that is essential for our mission.

GROUP DYNAMICS

For good conversation—both within the system of governance and alongside the system of governance—it is important to remember a simple working principle: the composition and size of the group can make all the difference. We need to consider two questions.

First, who needs to be at this meeting? Who needs to be part of this discussion, so that we have the wisdom we need to make the right decision? If we are determining policy, then who will actually be implementing this policy and living with this policy? Who needs to be at the table?

In some cases, we ask who has the right—by virtue of their office, their responsibility within the organization—to be consulted and part of the conversation? And we can ask, who needs to be at the table because, by virtue of expertise or experience, they bring an essential perspective to the table?

And second, we consider whether the group is right-sized for the issue that is being discussed. Boards are most effective when they are smaller. Larger than eleven and they are less effective, and if there are more than fifteen, they become unwieldy—not truly an effective decision-making body.

For working teams, four or at most five is a good number. The agenda items can be addressed efficiently or tabled if for some reason the group does not have the information in hand to make a decision. But either way the work gets done. Thus the presidents' cabinets that are most effective are likely made up of at least four and no more than five individuals, including the president.

And for a discussion on a complex matter, where every voice in the room matters and where you want to hear from every person in the room, then you want to have eight and no more than eight. There is a chemistry—the power of eight—to get the right balance or blend of the two things you need: diversity of perspective but also a small enough number so that each person is "at the table" and engaged in the conversation.

The science of group dynamics—typically a focus of research and insight from those who have expertise in social psychology—has given substantial attention to how groups work and how they work effectively. Group size matters. Large groups might have their place, but the larger the group, the more difficult it is to establish a collective cohesion, a shared and common voice, the coming to one mind. As soon as you have more than ten or eleven, there will be some who choose not to speak or contribute. But you need a group large enough to have diversity of perspective so that you are indeed getting the wisdom you need for the issue at hand. And it is these studies that keep bringing us back the power of eight—or, at least, less than ten: the right size for the input you need, but also small enough that each member of the committee or the board or the group can actively participate and be heard.

And what should be done when coming to an understanding on a matter and a resolution on a way forward involves a larger group, perhaps sixty, one hundred, or several hundred? Then, refer the matter to a group of eight with an effective moderator, and have moderators bring back a recommendation to the whole group. Smaller, in other words, is more effective.

LEARNING FROM OTHERS, INCLUDING SISTER AGENCIES

Finally, briefly, we also need to affirm the tremendous value that comes not only from internal learning but from others within our industry and, of course, from other agencies who have perhaps a very different mission.

University presidents are often on the phone with one another, and after the requisite comments on how well their own sports teams have done, they are asking questions of each other, learning from one another, and meeting each other at gatherings of their peers.

This can and must happen throughout the institution. Seminary deans and faculties find ways to bring congregational and denominational leadership into a conversation that leads to greater understanding of the challenges of theological formation. Pastors meet to discuss the challenges of congregational leadership. Relief and development agencies are in conversation with their peers but also with government offices and, of course, those entities that are in the field.

The main point is this: effective organizations are learning organizations. Their structures or systems of governance, designed for implementation of the mission, actually encourage good conversation, new learning, and growth in wisdom—both through the actual structures of governance and alongside those structures. They are looking for answers; they know that insight could be found in multiple sources. They encourage good conversation and are open to surprises and wisdom and solutions from wherever they might come.

WORKING WITH ROBERT'S RULES OF ORDER

If you sit on a committee—faculty committee or church board or just about any other formal meeting—you need to have at least an elemental working knowledge of "Robert's Rules of Order." They constitute a basic tool for working with organizations in the twenty-first century. Some entities, such as the British and Canadian parliaments, function by a different set of rules and guides to effective deliberation. But most non-profits both assume and actually work on the assumption that Robert's Rules provide the guidelines by which the organization will function in its various committees.

As a board member on a nonprofit, have a basic understanding of Robert's Rules. As a faculty member, you will be on faculty committees, senates, search committees, curriculum revision committees and other bodies that function, either explicitly or implicitly, by these rules.

Some might resist the idea that we are governed by rules and prefer a more shared-discernment approach or a more consensual approach to decision making, thinking that somehow these rules run counter to effective discernment and that making decisions by consensus is more communal and, in some religious circles, more spiritual. But such a perspective simply does not appreciate the very vital role Robert's Rules can have in fostering the capacity of the organization to do good work. It is a false polarity to assume that good processes, such as Robert's Rules, should be discarded for a more consensual approach to decision making.

This is so because the rules preserve and protect certain fundamental values of the process of good conversation and good decision making—with smaller groups but particularly with a larger group, and especially so with a large convention.

First, the rules are designed to allow for effective decision making that acknowledges the will of the majority—assuming, of course, that the will of the majority is valued by the organization. But, and this is crucial, the rules also give space and voice to the minority without allowing the minority to either co-opt the will of the majority or impede the organization from making the decisions it needs to make.

Second, the rules are only effective if there is a chair in place who knows the rules and applies them competently and recognizes that as chair, one is not partisan to the process but rather eager to foster the necessary conversation while also bringing the deliberation to closure when it is time to come to decision. The art of moderation includes recognizing when to call the question.[4]

Third, the rules require minutes. The minutes are not a diary, not a record of everything said, but the account of the actual matters on which the committee has acted. The minutes are recorded and kept on record as evidence that the organization is addressing the issues at hand and agreeing—deciding—on policies and actions by which the mission will be fulfilled.

Fourth, the rules encourage conversation but also decision making, and the genius of the rules is the capacity for someone to put a motion on the table, signaling that the group might be ready to come to a decision. They encourage us to come to closure. Yes, the group can decide to table something, convinced perhaps that they do not have all the information they need to choose well. But in due time, the motion comes off the table and is before the body, and a motion on the table signals a decision about to be made. And the rules keep the committee or the deliberative body on task—signaled, for example, in the chair's insistence that this is the motion that is on the table and that we will not move on until it is amended, acted on, or tabled.

And fifth, the rules are typically most effective when formal meetings that lead to closure through the use of the rules are complemented by other gatherings for conversation, deliberation, and shared reflection. Many organizations that follow the rules also have town hall meetings that become a means by which the group can have a conversation about a pressing matter that might inform the deliberative process. To come to a decision, it is wise and best that we be consistent and allow the rules to govern the process by which we bring a conversation to closure—meaning that a decision is actually made.

---

[4]On this point, it is always important to keep in mind whether this is a legislative body that can actually make a decision, or if it will refer a decision to another entity. Or is this a merely advisory committee—advising the president, the president's cabinet, for example, where the president has the actual say? Both are important: advisory and legislative. It is just essential to know the difference and to know what decisions properly speaking actually come to this body or committee.

When all is said and done, it is vital to remember that the rules are not an end in themselves, but a means to an end: fostering the capacity of the organization to leverage wisdom and, in turn, to leverage power so that the mission of the organization can be accomplished.

GOOD CONVERSATIONS

What needs to be stressed—again and again—is that all of this is only possible if good conversation is a basic mark of an institution's life, including but not limited to what has been addressed here, the dynamics of good decision making.

An appreciation of the place of good conversation could come up in chapter six, "The Right People," and the need for conversations that foster the capacity of the organization to hire well, develop their staff, review performance, and move toward a transition (when it is time to name the reality that something is not working and someone needs to be let go).

The question of good conversation could also come up in chapter seven on institutional culture. Vibrant cultures are marked by conversation that names reality with courage and does so in a way that is hopeful and encouraging.

In other words, good conversation is a thread or theme that will emerge at several points in a consideration of the elements of an effective organization. I raise it here, under governance, to get it on the table and raise awareness that indeed conversation—good conversation—is essential to our capacity to function effectively in an institution. In this regard many of us are indebted to Susan Scott's insightful book *Fierce Conversations: Achieving Success at Work and in Life, One Conversation at a Time.*[5] She speaks of conversations as "the work of a leader and the workhorses of an organization" and, as she puts it, that personal and institutional "success occurs one conversation at a time."[6]

My point in this chapter is that governance and administration is not merely about doing what needs to be done—that is, leveraging power effectively so that the organization achieves its purpose and fulfills its

---

[5]Susan Scott, *Fierce Conversations: Achieving Success at Work and in Life, One Conversation at a Time* (New York: Berkley Books, 2002).
[6]Ibid., xix.

mission. Rather, the genius of a great institution is that the *right* actions are taken and therefore that the organization has the capacity—through its governance structures, alongside of those structures as staff and leadership are encouraged to be talking to one another—for meetings that work. Such meetings are marked by good conversation, effective conversation that fosters the capacity to name reality, addresses potential outcomes and come to a shared wisdom that then, in turn, informs decisions and guides the strategic moves of the organization.

As Scott points out, good conversation is essential to learning and thus to effective decision making.[7] Conversations happen throughout the organization every day: in meetings, in the hallways, in one-on-one formal reviews and conversations, and in the ad hoc or serendipitous occasions that simply come up in the course of the day. This is an essential dimension of what it means to be an effective organization; the good work of an institution happens, as Scott puts is, one conversation at a time. We listen twice as much as we speak. We ask good questions. We know that wisdom is found together, through the very process of good conversation. We know it takes time and so we *make* time for conversation. And we learn to do it well.

CONCLUSION

So in conclusion, to summarize, the sequence is important. Effective institutions are marked by a threefold capacity to move from conversation to decision to action.

They foster good conversation toward insight, wisdom, and creative solutions.

They foster the capacity for closure—making the necessary decisions for organizational effectiveness.

They have the system in place—the mechanisms—to move from having made the decision to actual implementation.

All three are pivotal. Conversation without decision making will only lead to frustration. Decisions made that are not implemented will lead to cynicism. Actions taken without adequate consultation and a good decision-making process will lead to resentment at best and actual rebellion at

---

[7]Ibid., 107-18.

worst. And thus effective organizations do all three: conversation that leads to decisions that, in turn, leads to actual implementation.

An Individual and Group Exercise

Putting It into Practice: Getting Things Done

Individually or as a group, consider how governance works in your organization.

- Who is responsible for what in your organization? (Very specifically, where are decisions made? And who has the authority to implement those decisions?)

- What are the forms of power available to each to accomplish their responsibilities?

- Where is good conversation needed—within the system or structure of governance and laterally—and how could good conversation be encouraged?

- Who do you personally need to be in conversation with—so that you can do your job more effectively?

- Is there a bottleneck to effective decision making in the organization? If so, what is keeping the organization from doing what needs to be done to fulfill the mission?

THE RIGHT PEOPLE

Recruiting, Developing, Empowering

Institutions are only as effective as the quality of people they hire—more particularly, the character, capacity, and commitment of the people they appoint to responsibilities where they are uniquely positioned to contribute to the fulfillment of the mission.

An institution is an ecology of talent and commitment. People come together around a shared vision, the common belief in the mission. The governance structure leverages their capacity, empowering them to act together toward this common end so that the organization is truly a synergy of talent, the talent of those appointed or hired to serve together in this particular agency.

So yes, institutions need a compelling mission and an effective system of governance. But in the end it is *people* who deliver on the mission. An effective governance structure is not an end in itself, but a means—a tool—by which these people, with their capacity and talent and shared commitment, can achieve something together that they would not be able to achieve alone. In the end, it comes down to people: good people, talented women and men, who with good cheer, grow together, learn together, and deliver on the mission.

Typically, an organization has three major assets: the capital assets—the buildings, facilities, IT network; the financial assets—including investments and the various revenue streams; and the people. And the third, the people, are the institution's greatest asset.[1]

Thus we can affirm the so-very-appropriate line from Jim Collins when it comes to institutional thinking: get the right people on the bus (and the wrong people off the bus). He goes on to stress that people come first and mission comes second. He words it this way: first who, then what.[2] But, frankly, while his first comment—the right people—makes so much sense, the second comment—that people come first and mission comes second— is perplexing. Many readers, myself included, disagree. Is it not the case that an effective organization hires people who have the vision for and the capacity for the mission? And what brings them to the table is the desire to invest their time and talent in an institution that will deliver on that mission? In other words, mission comes first. This bus is going some- where. Now we need to be sure to get the right people on the bus to help and assure that we get where we need to go. And we will not get there until and unless we get the right people on the bus.

When it comes to people, effective organizations attend to three essential and critical practices:

- hiring and appointing well, including internal transitions or appointments

- developing, empowering, and encouraging effectively

- transitioning (from the verb "to transition") in a manner that honors people and reflects the core values of the institution

HIRING AND APPOINTING

Effective organizations attract women and men of talent who want to be part of something bigger than themselves and contribute to the mission alongside others of talent and capacity, people of creativity, innovation, and intelligence. Effective institutional leaders and managers recognize talent—are not intimidated by it, but welcome it—and they make judicious appointments when it comes to their hiring decisions. As a leader or

---

[1]Admittedly, there is perhaps a fourth asset, the reputation of the organization: its name and the credibility and association that current and potential constituents have with the brand. This too is an asset that needs to be nurtured and protected.

[2]Jim Collins, *Good to Great: Why Some Companies Make the Leap . . . and Others Don't* (New York: HarperCollins, 2001), 41.

manager in the institution, you are only as good as the people you hire. Your impact and effectiveness as a leader or manager will only go as far as the people you appoint to work with you and with others toward the common goal of the mission.

If you are a department head in a university or a team leader assigned to put together a cohort who will deliver on the mission—even if the final appointment or the confirmation of the appointment is made by another entity or board in the institution, and you are only the chair of the process by which a person is considered for a position—you are still only as effective, as a leader, as the people you recruit and see through till an appointment.

Whom do you hire? What do you look for? What kind of people are effective within an organization? And, more specifically, what kind of people will be effective in *this* organization? I say "this" organization because the particular institution will always be an essential referent: we do not hire for generic institutions, but for *this* institution. And yet some qualities and capacities are remarkably universal to all institutions.

First, as noted already, hire people who believe in the mission: they get it; it matters to them. They recognize its importance and they want to be part of it. People need jobs; they need employment and a salary. Of course. And yet what the organization requires is not merely individuals who need a job but men and women who through that job will contribute to the mission.

This applies to all positions in the institution, but some roles are clearly more pivotal. The board needs to be clear about the mission and their own belief in the mission. We recruit board members because they are going to be trustees of the mission. And their first loyalty and commitment is to the mission of the institution of which they are a trustee. Faculty in a university will likely have a loyalty to their guilds, rightly and understandably so. They have been formed within the guild—as historians, scientists, theologians, Bible scholars, and natural and social scientists. And there is a healthy and appropriate accountability within their guilds. But when they move into their classrooms, they teach to the mission of this university or college because they believe in the mission. They chose to accept an appointment to this university not merely because they needed a teaching assignment, but because they believe in the mission and know how to teach to that mission.

And then within the whole of the management system—each of those who are department heads or team leaders—they "get" the mission and it matters to them.

Second, hire smart, talented people. There it is, stated boldly and frankly: smart and, yes, talented. The corporate world always thinks about how to attract women and men of talent. But the nonprofit world has a history of hiring people of modest ability who are sincere and well-intentioned and available and willing to serve. The nonprofit world has a history of hiring family—promoting the sons and daughters of the founder, appointing friends who will promise loyalty (as often as not, an undue loyalty)—to the CEO. And yet the mission of the institution is too important and if the mission matters, then we need people who are intelligent, well trained, experienced and thus capable of making a substantive contribution to the effectiveness of the organization.

Some people will respond by saying that this sounds elitist, that there are many ordinary people who can make an extraordinary contribution, and therefore we should take full advantage of sincere people even if they are of modest ability. The word *elitist* almost sounds pejorative, negative. But in many respects it captures precisely the kind of commitment we need in our organizations. When it comes to your hiring policy and practice, be elitist—unapologetically so. Let's make the case that our institutions deserve the best: women and men who bring education, training, expertise, and intelligence to the table. But quickly, let me add that we need people of talent and ability—yes—but without two complementary qualities, their talent and ability is a detriment rather than an asset. First, they need to be learners—always learning, reading, growing, developing—so that their capacity, their talent and ability, actually matures. Beware of those who rest on their abilities rather than finding ways of improving on what they already do well. And second, hire people who are smart but who are also eager to work with others—to learn from and with others. On the one hand they are not intimidated by the intelligence of others, but more, they also know how to benefit from the learning and experience of others. They listen and learn with and from others. We do not need smart people who have either stopped learning or are dismissive of the wisdom of their colleagues.

Furthermore, while we certainly try to get the right people on the bus, we must also be concerned with getting them on at the right time. We need to hire people who fit the institution where it is at the moment. If you are in a time of growth and change, hire people that can adapt, are versatile, and are comfortable working within the unknown. A person may be a great cultural fit, smart, highly skilled, but cannot work in uncertainty. These people are much better for a time in the institution when it is implementing, consolidating, and fine-tuning.

Third, character matters. However illusive this quality may seem, women and men of virtue are a huge factor in the capacity of an organization to achieve its mission. Character matters. Institutions expand individual impact; a person's character is magnified as soon as they become part of an institution. From the receptionist who responds to a guest, to the faculty of the university, to the board chair, the institution will magnify their character flaws and their strengths. If you hire a person who lacks maturity of character, you have to face the implications for the whole organization. But the reverse is also true: to see the potential of a person—a person of depth and grace, of quiet strength and sterling character—appoint them knowing that their grace and depth of character will be enhanced and have a broader impact on the institution.

When board members or others within the organization fail to be transparent in their dealings with one another, subtly or less than subtly working behind the scenes to undermine the work of a colleague, the net result is always insidious, not only for the two people involved, but for the organization as a whole. All too easily these become patterns of behavior that get etched in the bones of the organization.

The opposite is also true: generous people have a positive impact well beyond their own spheres of responsibility. I think of the staff in an IT department at a university. Interestingly, their offices were at the center of the building and their reception counter opened up into a major hallway. It was fun to watch them work. They ate problems for lunch, as folks say. Their reception counter was a gathering point and their can-do attitude and good cheer—a credit to their team leader—had a positive impact not merely on the individuals who came to them with an IT problem, but directly and indirectly on the whole institution.

Fourth, hire people who work effectively in both line and lateral working relationships. By "line" functions we mean that a person understands and affirms and lives graciously with the governance structure of the institution. Institutional intelligence means that we not only know how to work within an accountability structure, but that we are not bothered by this—indeed, we actually learn to thrive within it. They do not feel diminished by needing to make a formal report to a boss. Hire people who welcome evaluation, who know how to be accountable within structures of constituted authority, and who in their accountability are eager to foster continuous learning, improvement, growth, and development. They view the accountability structure as essential not only to the organization but also the quality of our lives and our work. They are not resisting or continually frustrated with constituted authority.

But also, effective organizations hire women and men who, along with line accountability, know how to work *laterally*. They honor the structures of governance but also know how to work with another when neither of them is the boss—rather, as colleagues (neither of whom reports to the other) they can learn together, tackle a problem together, and come up with a solution and a way forward that represents the overall best outcome for the organization. They know how to keep their direct reports informed; they are not working surreptitiously behind anyone's back. But specifically, they know how to identify what needs to be done and how things that need to get done do not necessarily need to go through various approval processes. Thus with the encouragement of the board chair, two board members go for coffee to develop a draft policy statement. The biology professor and the campus manager sit down and work out how best to renovate a laboratory that needs upgrading. The finance officer meets with a senior staff person to reflect on the budget and come up with a way forward that will be good for that department. Neither of them reports to each other, but they are working together—as colleagues, laterally within the organization—toward a common goal: the best possible outcome for the organization.

People who work well within an organization—line relationships or lateral connections—know how to listen well, how to consider the perspective of another when coming up with a solution; they are looking for wisdom and insight wherever it can be found. Collaboration comes easily, almost instinctively.

Fifth, hire people who are diligent and thorough and who actually enjoy hard work. But—and this is important—they are not driven by work, a disease that inevitably and ironically creates a drag on others. Find a way, as you interview and assess a potential candidate, to know if they are detailed without being compulsive, thorough without being obsessed with more detail than is helpful or necessary. But mainly, find a way to determine if this person is someone who finds work to be something they do not avoid but actually enjoy. And this means that they don't "wing it" but have mastered their craft and exercise their responsibilities with a day in and day out commitment to excellence: doing, quite simply, their very best. It is a matter of personal honor to them to reject mediocrity and banality and deliver quality.

And yet we do not need just busyness and hard work. There is a growing appreciation in organizations for women and men who know how to do what needs being done—people who deliver, who can implement an idea or concept, and who have the tactical capacity to get the outcomes that are needed so that the mission happens.

Many people have wonderful ideas: they are dreamers and schemers. And we need their vision and their ideas, and we are perhaps inspired by the possibilities. But implementation is crucial and thus significant are those who know how to take an idea and put it into action in a way that is sustainable and which, of course, enables the fulfillment of institutional mission. They know how to implement—one step at a time—taking an idea and bringing that idea to reality. They are not busybodies; they work hard, but they have learned to do the right things—to prioritize, to leverage their time for those actions and outcomes that best help the organization fulfill the mission. Watch for a kind of lazy busyness—people who give the impression that they are working hard but actually do not know how to move toward key institutional outcomes. And watch for people who talk about what happened, perhaps in a previous job, but actually do not have a history of implementing good ideas. When you hire, you appoint people who have a history of delivering outcomes.

Sixth, hire people who will lower the anxiety level in the institution. In the upcoming chapter on institutional culture, the question of fear, anxiety, and worry will be profiled as simply crucial to the strength and effectiveness of the institution. Thus to highlight and stress this point here: effective institutions hire and appoint women and men who know how to respond rather than merely react, individuals who—whether in the hallways, or in committee or board meetings—moderate the tenor of the room. Reactors raise the anxiety level; responders lower the levels of anxiety and worry and in so doing foster an environment that is greater able to respond with courage and creativity to the problems the institution is facing.

And seventh, and finally, hire people that you enjoy having around—people who are, quite simply, fun to work with. They are civil, kind, generous, and winsome. They have a sense of humor. They move through our shared workspaces having come to work that day knowing that working in this place is a gift. And they go about their work with a mature peripheral vision—attentive to the personal and professional well-being of their colleagues. They are able to drop by another person's office and in a timely way be a fellow pilgrim on the journey. And they know balance; they drop in for a few minutes, but we both know that there is a job to be done. And yet neither of us is so consumed with our job we don't have an opportunity ask about the new baby, delight in the photo of a grandchild, catch up on how our favorite baseball team did on the weekend, and share the joys of the weather (or not!).

All of this matters. All of it. And yes, there are people like those just described. This list of seven qualities or characteristics is not unreasonable. There are people who are competent and a delight to work with; they can work diligently and persistently but also share a coffee, a few minutes of respite from the intensity of a committee meeting. We can trust them, depend on them and go home at the end of the day knowing that our colleagues are gifts—women and men with whom it is a privilege to work.

Thus be patient when it comes to hiring. If necessary, it is always better to wait so that you get the right person rather than to merely try to fill a position sooner than later. When I served as the vice president and dean of a small Christian college in central Canada, I managed to persuade the president and the other vice presidents that we needed to build a link—a walkway—between two of the buildings. It was not a major distance between these two buildings, but in our frigid winter climate I thought it only fair that the faculty offices in one building would be linked through a warm-air walkway to the main building.

This was approved. In time the vice president for campus operations came by with a visual schematic and asked me, since it had been my original idea, to sign off on the plan. Would this, he asked, do it? On paper it looked perfect and I endorsed it.

A few weeks later, with the construction of this link well underway, I dropped by to see how things were progressing. At first, I thought it would indeed be perfect. But as I stood in the opening at one end of the link, I realized that the passage way between the two buildings was much too narrow. Two faculty members would hardly be able to pass coming and going without adjusting their bodies, mid-course, to allow for their colleague to pass. I could already hear the jokes of how our football-player-sized faculty members would have to get advance clearance before heading to class!

When I expressed this concern to our VP for campus operations, he said that it was too late to make changes—or, at least, that making those changes would be very expensive. And, of course, he reminded me that I had signed off on the plans. *True*, I thought, *but those blueprints did not give me a capacity to appreciate what it would actually look like and feel like when the link was built*. And his reply was to say that he could only see starting over with the approval of the president's cabinet.

I felt I had no choice but to come, with a full-fledged mea culpa—no blame to anyone other than myself—and appeal to my colleagues asking that they approve a restart. I acknowledged that I had made a very expensive mistake. But I also stressed that I saw no alternative but to tear down what had been constructed and start over.

I have this very vivid memory of the response of the president, Dr. Bob Rose. He noted that while it was a mistake, it was not that expensive an error. We all protested, noting the dollar figure that had been quoted to us for the project to be restarted from the ground up. And his response, so perfect really, was that this was not an expensive mistake. While it was costly, no doubt, he stressed the following: the most expensive mistakes we make, by far, are hiring and personnel decisions that, in retrospect, we realize were not the right appointments.

And his words come back to me often. They are a reminder: do not rush; wait and get it right. And if you make a hiring mistake, then fix it sooner than later. With all due respect—and honor—to the person you hired, recognize that it was not the right appointment and arrange for a timely transition. But, of course, waiting and getting it right the first time is the ideal.

DEVELOP, EMPOWER, AND ENCOURAGE

Effective organizations care for their people. They work at making the organization a great place to work. They can assure anyone who works here: you will be a better person if you work with us and for us. We are committed to making this a place where your development and growth matters. We will support your growth in your area of expertise, we will provide opportunities for both further training where needed, and we will insist on the need for appropriate levels of rest and renewal. We value you as a member of our working community, and we want you to go home each day grateful that you work with us.

This kind of support will be evident in a number of aspects to institutional life. First, it is helpful to view staff and personnel support through the lens of "the first one hundred days." There is nothing magical about the opening one hundred days, of course, but it is a helpful benchmark for a new appointee. Establish some clear goals for those first three months on the job: an orientation to the administrative system and organizational culture, provision of the essential tools of the job—the basic elements that help that person be successful over the long haul. There is only one shot at a good start.

Second, it is vital to have regular performance reviews. An annual performance review is essential, but only as a benchmark. That annual review—the "how is it going" conversation—should have no surprises in that along the way, there have been regular times of reflection on how things are going, on what is going well, and on what needs attention.

Surprises indicate a lack of good communication in the normal course of the working relationship. Further, nothing—absolutely nothing—is gained by an annual performance that raises an issue that is six months old and should have been discussed at that time. Again, reveal no surprises in an annual performance review; it is merely a benchmark conversation that reaffirms what has been happening in the regular reviews along the way.

A performance review is only possible and only fair if expectations are clear, with a well-articulated position profile and fulsome conversation of institutional needs and priorities, so that both parties, both the employee and the person to whom he or she reports, have a shared understanding: how and in what ways is this positon contributing to the effectiveness of the organization?

When it comes to performance reviews, remember that an ineffective employee could be as much a result of the system—perhaps lack of support from a supervisor—as of the capacities of the individual involved. And so everyone needs to be reviewed within and as part of the system, not in a vacuum or in isolation from the dynamics that shape their work and thus their effectiveness.

Further, the focus of a review is the future. Sure, we benchmark the work of the employee and note with appreciation that which has been accomplished. But the primary agenda is the future: What can we do, together, to foster high performance moving forward?

As a rule, refuse to respond to anonymous critique or evaluation. Anonymous critique undermines trust, and in smaller organizations, it only raises questions about who has a problem with what. When we ask what this critique means, it makes all the difference to know the source. Thus I question the current fad of the 360-degree evaluation that presumes anonymity. Rather, why not have focused conversation with key and trusted observers, who can evaluate performance within the broader system in which they are doing their work? And, to put it bluntly, if you cannot stand by your critique of a person and share that critique in person, then perhaps it's just best to keep it to yourself.

Third, adequate staff support includes opportunities for training and development. For each person in the organization, consider this question: What resources and support—either in training or in other forms of equipping—are needed to encourage and maximize the possibility of this person's success? And one of the key forms of professional renewal is connections with one's peers. As a president of a small university, I find it tremendously valuable to be in regular conversation with other presidents. Each of our vice presidents is part of a cohort group of their peers. And the same can be said for many of the roles in the institution. I expect each of the key roles within the institution to be in conversation with their peers in sister institutions and with our accreditation association, which provides workshops and development seminars for new faculty, for development officers, for deans, and for finance officers. Some of these are webinars, where the entire learning experience happens online. And others bring colleagues together, across institutions, for shared learning from one another and together from an outside resource person.

Finally, a good workplace requires attention to several things:

- A just salary is provided. No one is trying to get rich working for a nonprofit, but a fair and equitable salary is a reasonable expectation, and thus we can speak of an appropriate remuneration with an edge of generosity (a cost of living increase; a salary that reflects the employee's responsibility in the organization and their experience; and a salary that is comparable to their peers in peer institutions). Nonprofits need to insist that there is an appropriate pay equity and ratio of executive-to-worker pay. Many times a supervisor does not have direct authority over the pay structure or system, but as a director or department head, you can advocate: you can point out inequities, you can be part of the conversation about what represents a fair wage within your industry and you, knowing the limits of the overall budget, can champion for the staff in your department.

- People have the tools to do the job effectively: good furniture, ergonomically designed working chairs, high Internet speed, and the software to do what you are expecting them to do. This is a basic cost of doing business.

- Accomplishments are celebrated. The institution affirms and rewards those contributions that fit the institutional culture and vision—excellence, collaboration, creativity, and innovation (in problem solving).

- There is latitude and patience in addressing problems at home or personal health issues that temporarily limit our full engagement in the work we share. We work together, in other words, to make our workplace one that believes in family; we recognize that our employees are part of family systems and so we are flexible in responding to immediate and, as the institution is able, ongoing needs.

- There is opportunity for each employee to speak to and be heard on working conditions, on what is needed, from their vantage point, to maximize institutional effectiveness. Healthy institutions have mechanisms in place for employee communication and feedback.

TRANSITION WITH DIGNITY

There may be people who stay with the same nonprofit organization for the whole of their careers—forty to forty-five years, perhaps. But they will definitely be the exception. Most people will give the organization a more limited number of years, anything from four to perhaps even ten years. And what this means is that organizations—particularly institutions with more than twenty or twenty-five staff—will have to manage transitions: those who discontinue their service with the organization or have their service discontinued.

First, it is important to stress here that institutions are fluid, not static: they grow, develop, and adapt to changes in the environment. While it might be the case that everyone who is on staff now is needed now, as the institution grows and develops, people will move on or the organization will move on. We don't assume that once hired, we have a job for life. Rather, we have a role to play at this point in the history of this institution. For most employees, a time will come when the question arises, is it time for me to move on? Ideally, we are ready to respond to a new opportunity— a new option for exercising our gifts and potential in a way that is consistent with our vocations.

Recognize that there is a shelf life to virtually every role in the organization. Some have suggested that the US presidency, with a maximum of eight years, is genius. There is something to this observation: organizations are fluid and we need to know—get a good feel—for when we have made our contribution and need to look for a new opportunity with another organization. And the ideal, of course, is that we know this first and make the move, rather than expecting the organization to initiate the change. As often as not, if we do not move on from the organization itself, we take on a new role or responsibility, a new challenge, *within* the organization.

Second, without doubt, another reason for transition is the lack of effectiveness in the assigned role or responsibility. When someone under-performs, the best thing to do is accept the situation and say, "This is not working." Drucker states it well: "To allow non-performers to stay on means letting down both the organization and the cause."[3]

You simply cannot know everything you need to know about a potential hire when you make the initial appointment. No matter how good your interview process and your background checks and the quality of the resume, you only really know a person when you have worked with them for a while. There is no shame in recognizing that it is simply not working. So, you find a way to graciously acknowledge this and bring about the needed transition. When you make a poor hiring decision, do what needs to be done sooner rather than later for the sake of the organization and for the sake of the person who is not performing effectively.

Then, of course, make the transition out of the organization one that is marked by a commitment to, as best you can, honor those who, whether for a few months or over many years, have given something of themselves. They deserve thanks and appreciation. How you say your farewells and care for employees in the transition—whether through events where they are honored and thanked, or through severance packages that bridge them for the immediate time after their employment with you—make it a com-mitment as an organization that you (1) hire well, (2) develop well, and (3) transition well.

And if the transition is involuntary, both parties need to work at making this as easy as possible. Even if I am the one being "let go," I leave with dignity, however unjust I think the decision may have been to terminate my employment. However disappointed I may be with the decision, the fact is that it only makes sense that I keep on good terms with the employer.

---

[3]Peter F. Drucker, *Managing the Non-Profit Organization: Principles and Practices* (New York: HarperBusi-ness, 1990), 154.

And the same applies for the organization: treat this person, as they leave, in a way that would make it possible for you hire them again in the future.

GROWING WITH THE ORGANIZATION

In all of this, it is helpful to ask, what am I being called to contribute to this organization? What is needed from me, particularly when it comes to what is needed here and now, in this organization, that corresponds to my areas of strength and expertise? And so, as noted, we adapt and grow with the organization. And yet a time will come when we see that what I have to offer is no longer what this institution needs, quite apart from whether it is an area of strength or not. It just needs to be done. Bill Robinson, former president if Whitworth College in Spokane, Washington, makes the following helpful observations when it comes to the alignment of our strengths with the needs of the organizations of which we are a part.[4]

First, and perhaps most obvious, if something is not needed by the organization and it is not our strength, then it is an easy call: we don't do it.

Second, if it is not needed, even if it is an area of strength for us, it is not something that we need to contribute. Very simply—regardless of whether it is a strength of ours, it is not needed. You might be an excellent writer, but that does not mean that this organization is going to lean into your writing skills. Either you park that part of who you are or, if it is an indispensable part of your identity and vocation, you find other avenues by which this is expressed.

Third, if it is needed and it aligns with our strengths, then we function from our strengths and lead from our strengths.

But then, fourth, what about those areas that are needed, but are not our areas of particular strength or capacity? Robinson suggests that even though we lead from our strengths, we still ask: what does this organization need from me, at such a time as this—even if it is not my primary area of strength?

---

[4]Robinson made these observations at the New Presidents Institute of the Council of Christian Colleges and Universities, in Washington, DC, in January of 2015. While the main point he made was with respect to the office of the president, it actually applies to virtually every role in the institution. Institutional thinking requires that we ask: what is needed of me by this institution at this time and in this season of the institution's growth and development?

But then, as noted, a time will come when we recognize that we need to move on. And when that time comes, we need to be the first to know. Do not overstay; take the initiative and work with your direct supervisor to manage, together, a healthy transition.

Here is another image that I have found helpful. When it comes to your work, your responsibilities within an organization, think in terms of three concentric circles. This works for just about any job—any role—in an institution.

With three concentric circles before you, write into the inner circle those activities and responsibilities that you simply and absolutely must do. The inner circle is the nonnegotiable part of the job.

The second circle includes those things that were very much included in what was expected of you when you were hired. But they are second-order—important, but not as crucial and essential as the inner circle.

And the third circle, the outer circle, are those other things you thoroughly enjoy doing—the elements of your job that you find personally satisfying, perhaps, and make the job particularly rewarding.

There is no problem attending to the third and outer circle and making that contribution. No problem at all, as long as you pay the rent, as my colleague Mark Buchanan puts it. You have got to pay the rent. The landlord does not care if you are painting the house, planting a garden and caring for the place. You still have to pay the rent. And that is the inner circle. Make sure that happens; make sure that you do it well. If you do, the responsibilities and contributions in the second circle will flow from it. Or, if not, if you do not get to these items as well and as effectively, you at least know that the items in the inner circle are cared for.

The third circle will happen, but only as there is time and space. Most if not all organizations value the contributions of those who have a third circle—something that you value and that is valued by others, that you contribute to the organization. But attend to the inner circle. Talk to your boss, your immediate supervisor; know what is in that inner circle. And pay the rent.

HUMAN RESOURCE POLICIES AND BEST PRACTICES

Effective institutions establish and maintain a range of policies and best practices that reflect the best in HR wisdom—written policies that guide and direct each aspect of the working environment, assuring that the institution signals that it values fairness, justice, and transparency, including due process on each policy that affects the people that work in this organization. At minimum, organizations need to have written policies for these functions of the organization.

1. Onboarding, or recruitment and appointment guidelines and policies. This includes the arrangement by which new positions are approved, new hires interviewed, and appointments made and what is provided for a person in their first one hundred days, to facilitate and assure their success, including their full orientation to their position, to the organizational structure, culture, mission, and goals.

2. Performance evaluation and development, along with compensation. Effective institutions have policies in place—and they follow them—by which they review employee performance, offer opportunities for growth and development, and provide equitable and appropriate compensation and benefits.

3. Health and safety. A mature organization has in place policies that reflect legal compliance with their local jurisdictions on security in the workplace, harassment and discrimination, and ergonomics, all with a commitment to a healthy workplace. The environment where we work should be giving attention to anything that might be toxic: relationships, air, noise, and any other source of undue and unnecessary stress that is not integral to the work required.

With all of these policies and practices it needs to be stressed that one of the most valuable members of an institutional team is the director of human resources. Smaller organizations may use an outside firm to advise or a person who works part-time. But in a larger agency, this is the person who works with the senior management and attends to the most valuable asset that the organization has: its people. A good director for human resources will assure that good policies are in place, that the salary and benefits packages are appropriate, that hiring and development and transitions are managed most effectively, and that crises or personnel problems are addressed in a timely, professional, and personal manner.

Finally, I conclude this chapter with an observation and admonition. Say thank you and say it often. Remember that everyone, even those on salary, could be working elsewhere. The institution is not entitled to anyone's time and talent; you cannot buy their time or their talent. Most if not all of your colleagues could earn more elsewhere. So we say thank you. We say thank you for those to whom we report, and we say thank you to those who report to us. We pause in the hallway and thank someone for their contribution to this place—to our shared mission and to what it is that we do together. We say thank you to the board who all volunteer their time. We thank our financial supporters and those agencies with which we partner. It is an institutional habit and a fundamental part of our institutional culture.

An Individual and Group Exercise

Putting It into Practice: Personnel Policies and Practices

Here are some questions you could discuss with your supervisor next time you get together.

- Are you clear about your own sphere of responsibility and how it fits with and contributes to the mission of the organization?

- What could strengthen your capacity to fulfill your job profile list of responsibilities and duties?

- Are you functioning in this organization in a way that reflects your personal strengths and commitments?

- What further training or experiences do you think you could improve your work and performance?

- What tools or changes in your work environment would have a significant impact on your performance?

- What policies, if any, are needed in your organization—personnel policies that would strengthen institutional capacity?

A GENERATIVE INSTITUTIONAL CULTURE

Fostering Hopeful Realism

Effective institutions have and nurture a distinctive and generative organizational culture. Every institution has a culture; the difference is that effective institutions cultivate a culture that is consistent with their organizational ethos and mission. And while culture may be the less visible side of organizational life, this does not mean that it is not powerful. To the contrary, everything—literally everything in an organization—is dependent on an animating culture.

The great classic on this topic is Edgar H. Schein's *Organizational Culture and Leadership*, where Schein speaks of culture as "the accumulated shared learning of a given group, covering behavioral, emotional, and cognitive elements of group members' total psychological functioning," in other words, all the fruit of a history of shared experience.[1] The apt phrase "psychological functioning" speaks to how the culture includes the affective dimensions of an organization—what does it feel like to work here? I use the word *feel* intentionally, in that what we are considering is the emotional tenor of the institution and how the affective dynamic of the institution sustains core values and the capacity of the organization to fulfill its mission.

On one level, culture is about whether this is a place that fosters joy in and through our shared work. Do the people who work here want to

---

[1] Edgar H. Schein, *Organizational Culture and Leadership*, 2nd ed. (San Francisco: Jossey-Bass, 1992), 10.

work here and be invested in the purpose or mission of the organization? But in the end, it is not just about good feelings. Rather, when we speak about culture we point to two fundamental reference points.

First we ask, does our institutional culture fit our mission? Is it consistent with who we are and with our institutional identity? Is it congruent with and in alignment with our institutional purpose?

And second we ask, does our institutional culture foster our capacity for change—specifically the kind of change that is essential to our mission if we are going to respond well to the inevitable changes in our environment?

CULTURE AND MISSION

Culture is first and foremost about mission. It is not ultimately about whether this is a fun place to work, but about whether we are fulfilling our institutional mandate and purpose. And the ideal, of course, is that the culture would infuse and give coherence to the mission of the organization—including its administrative processes, its approach to financial management, and the way the community signals what matters, what is important. But the key here is that the culture fits: it belongs and is consistent with the mission and core values of the organization.

Ralph H. Kilmann states it well: "Culture provides meaning, direction, and mobilization—a social energy that moves the corporation into action."[2] That is, the culture both fits the mission but also animates the organization to fulfill that very mission—to engage the future so that the mission is fulfilled. But it is *this* mission, the mission of this particular organization. And thus it needs to be consistent with the purpose of this organization; intuitively, it needs to fit and make sense. Culture knits colleagues together—affectively—reflecting a common identity, a common way of being, and a common vision for what it is that brings them together, and the common cause in which they are investing their time and energy.

Some leaders seem bent on trying to make the organization—be it a church, school, or mission agency—a place that feels good. Churches will often view the job of pastors as making everyone glad to be there on Sunday, as though their job is to foster good feelings. And if we have nice

---

[2]Ralph H. Kilmann, *Beyond the Quick Fix* (Washington, DC: Beard Books, 2004), 92.

feelings then presumably we will come back next Sunday. And worship is designed around fostering good feelings and the coffee hour is all about making people feel happy. While we would of course all like to be part of an organization or church that feels good—a fun place to be—the ultimate criteria for a vital and dynamic institutional culture is mission. Effective organizations are a great place to work because they are going somewhere. We enjoy working together because we have come together on common cause, with people we enjoy working with. But we do not confuse the institution and the joy of working in the institution with the very different joy of hanging out with friends at the pub.

Thus when we assess institutional culture, we look to see if there is a coherence between culture and mission. And we ask: do the elements of the culture mutually reinforce the mission? We *do* want our organizations to be enjoyable places to work. Of course. We are not steamrolling people toward our mission. And yet mission is always the bottom line.

This means we are alert to the ways in which a culture might seemingly be at cross-purposes with the mission. We ask, given our mission—our identity and purpose—what organizational culture reflects what we are called to do. And thus a church will feel—and yes, that is the operative word, *feel*—very different from a university, and the classroom will have a different feel from a relief and development team meeting. Different kinds of institutions will have a different affective quality. This is appropriately so.

But further, two sister institutions with a similar institutional purpose will also feel different from each other. As you visit two universities, for example, you will sense a different affective quality to each, reflecting a distinct organizational culture and ethos.

The point is this: the culture needs to be consistent with the institutional identity and purpose.

HOPEFUL REALISM

If the first question we ask about institutional culture is about mission congruence (does the culture align with the mission?), the second and necessary question is, does our institutional culture foster and animate our capacity to fulfill the mission in a fluid environment? Does the culture infuse the institution with sensibilities that allow the collective—the institution as a whole—to be responsive, adaptive, and innovative, able to handle change, crisis, and new challenges? Is there a *resiliency* in the face of new problems, obstacles, challenges, and opportunities?

And this capacity, this aspect or dimension of culture, is evident in two respects: first, the capacity to name reality, and second, the twin capacity—namely, hopefulness. The two elements of hopeful realism are inseparable; you cannot have the one without the other.

First, there is the capacity to name reality. A vital institutional culture is marked by a freedom to be fully present to this time and place—not nostalgic for a previous "golden age" of the institution, not caught in wishful thinking about the circumstances that the organization faces, not consumed by feelings of victimization due to the decisions or actions that have, from the past, shaped the current institutional context and setting. But rather we foster a simple yet powerful capacity to be in this time and place, without blame or envy or fruitless wishing that the circumstances were otherwise.

So many academic institutions and churches and other nonprofits seem to live with a huge disconnect from their environment. Often they are marked by a wistful longing for a previous time or era—"the good old times." My wife and I were once listening to a BBC broadcast of the London Philharmonic Orchestra when at the conclusion of the concert they led the entire audience in a rendition of "Britannia Rules the Waves." It was all very moving, of course, except for this: we were both wondering whether someone might best call London, urgently, and draw to their attention that it has been well over a century since they ruled the waves. Here is the danger: such sentiments are useless—nothing more than nostalgia. Actually, the danger is that this is worse than useless, for nostalgia can often keep us from effectively engaging our time, our place, our circumstances—facing reality as it is rather than as we might wish it to be. The culture has become static, one might say, locked in time, perhaps in a kind of nostalgia for a previous era or leader, with little courage to face the fact that the times have changed. The United Kingdom is at its best when it names the reality and asks, what is Britain being call to be now and what role does it have now on the global stage?

Sure, enjoy the nostalgia. But don't confuse nostalgia with hopeful realism. Don't confuse nostalgia with effectively engaging the world. I think here of churches that do not embrace the new reality of a changing demographic, of university faculty who fail to appreciate the changing patterns and ways of learning of their students or the economics of higher education, or of a relief agency living off the fumes from previous crises or ways in which the agency was funded.

There is the college, for example, with dwindling enrollment in a context where there was no real possibility for growth. The school had the opportunity to merge with another college and become part of a dynamic smaller university. The board supported the move; the senior leadership led the merger talks. But the faculty were resistant and fought the merger at each step of the way, as much as anything out of a concern that they would lose their teaching appointments if such a merger were to happen. And they managed to get enough constituents to make a protest to the board to eventually scuttle the merger talks. The net result was that the college continued on its decline and missed out on an opportunity that would have assured its future. Ironically, the faculty lost their jobs anyway as an actual result of their unwillingness to face reality.

A vibrant culture has a capacity for truth telling. Reality is named—outed—with courage, insight, and clarity: no nostalgia, no wishful thinking, no illusions. And this means naming the changes in the demographics, the changes in the culture and economy, the changes that mean we cannot proceed with business as usual. We will speak about hope, but we have no patience with a false or naive optimism. Our hope is grounded in reality, not wishful thinking.

We name reality and then, second, and this needs to be stated quickly, we also affirm the possibilities and options and potential that we have in the midst of that reality.

Rather than self-pity or fretful frustration with the circumstances, vital and engaging organizations are marked by a deep hopefulness about the possibilities for the institution in the ever-changing context and setting. They do not despair.

Given that environments are fluid—changing demographics, a volatile economy, changes in personnel (a key leader in the organization resigns or retires)—the genius of a great culture is its fostering of a capacity for effectively responding to change. Institutional momentum is sustained through the midst of change and uncertainty. Better yet, the organization has the emotional and entrepreneurial capacity to respond with creativity and courage to the new context or setting in which it finds itself. Just as a business is able to respond to changes in the market, a nonprofit is able to face its unforeseen future with confidence—able to respond and sustain institutional momentum.

Thus a healthy institutional culture is a generative culture: innovation flourishes, new ideas are encouraged and, of course, change is expected and actually sought.

Note something crucial here: the two go together and are inseparable. Without hope, we cannot face the full scope of our situation, which may be quite bleak. But also, we will only have naive optimism if we do not name reality. We need hope, not despair, of course. But we also need to name reality and not live in a fantasy world of good feelings that is disconnected from our actual circumstances. We do not need an inspirational speaker who can get us all thinking positively; rather, we need good conversation that names our reality—however dark it may seem to be—but always while also speaking of the possibilities that lie before us. We do not polarize information—knowing and stating our reality—from inspiration, the fostering of hope that will inform our capacity to engage those circumstances.

Nothing is gained by a naive optimism. This is but another form of wishful thinking. Nothing is gained by hoping that things work out, for example, when a situation is not tenable. When a church or a school or a college is no longer sustainable, the wise option is to consider the options moving forward—to explore options for mergers or for leveraging the remaining assets to contribute to something that will be sustainable. Thus we commend a congregation that has dwindled in size but, realizing that they are not sustainable, choose to contribute their assets toward a congregation that can make a go of it in that neighborhood. Or the small college with declining enrollments uses its assets to strengthen another institution in the area and in so doing strengthen a sister institution and also sustain their own legacy.

In this regard, there are two forms of what we might call false loyalty, or a false sense of duty. The first, not uncommon, is when a church feels an obligation to those who years ago gave sacrificially to this building or to the original founder or founders of organization. People express dismay at the thought that the church would be sold or donated to another church and not continue the original vision. The answer, of course, is that the situation has changed, the demographics make the current ministry unsustainable, and wise leadership considers the best way to invest and leverage that legacy and those assets toward a viable future.

When an institution is no longer viable, wise leadership assesses the situation and considers the actual and real options that lie ahead. The faculty of a college encourage this rather than block it: they too know that naming reality is crucial, that wishful thinking is a waste of time. Founding members of congregations, rather than steadfastly blocking critical thinking about reality out of an undue loyalty to how things used to be, actively support the process by which reality is named and new possibilities of mission unfold.

Then also, a dynamic institutional culture is marked by a refusal to either blame or play the victim. We do not blame others for our woes: the economy, the mistakes of our predecessors, the failures of others. We describe the situation we are and we get on with it.

Thus, to summarize, we come back to the two basic questions. First, does our institutional culture align itself with and reflect our mission, identity, and purpose? Does it reinforce the mission—reflecting the kind of institution we are called to be and the core values that are consistent with that mission?

And second, does our institutional culture foster learning and growth and adaptability—fostering our capacity to respond to fulfill our mission in a changing environment? Does it name reality and both see and respond to the possibilities by which we can fulfill our mission in this fluid environment?

GETTING A READ ON AN INSTITUTIONAL CULTURE

A vibrant institutional culture does not just happen. If we want to foster a culture that is congruent with mission and animates innovation, we have to be intentional. And this is the role of leadership—getting a read on, monitoring, and then shaping the institutional culture. Thus Schein insists that "[the] ability to perceive the limitations of one's own culture and to develop the culture's adaptivity is the essence and ultimate challenge of leadership," or, Schein again, that the key to leadership is to get a read on and understand the culture in which you are embedded.[3] Or, again, as Jinkins and Jinkins put it, organizational effectiveness requires *knowing* the culture: get a read on this and play to its strengths, even accept some of its limitations (this is what they are), and graciously accept some of the quirks in the way that this institution does things.[4]

But we must insist that institutional culture is everyone's responsibility. We can all be attentive to what it means to work in this place, and we can all—regardless of our roles and responsibilities within the organization—be alert to and aware of the cultural dynamics essential for organizational effectiveness.

Faculty can be attentive to their institutional responsibilities that may seem less like "requirements of employment" but are no less vital to their professional responsibilities: the need to connect over coffee with a colleague, the need to be part of faculty and staff social gatherings, and the need to enter into the classroom with a disposition and demeanor that is anchored in a deep hopefulness for their institution and for their students. Faculty individually and collectively have a powerful role to play in fostering a dynamic institutional culture.

And those who head departments and programs within the institution all need to appreciate this as well. They are the tone setters; they are either a drain on the culture and its capacity to fulfill the mission or they are genuine encouragers, supporting the mission in their attentiveness to the ways in which they need to adapt and learn as they respond to a changing environment.

Within an institution—particularly larger organizations—there will be subcultures, of course: the board, the faculty of a university, even specific departments within the university, whether it be the culture of the communication department at one end of the building or the development

---

[3]Schein, *Organizational Culture and Leadership*, 1-2.
[4]Michael Jinkins and Deborah Bradshaw Jinkins, *The Character of Leadership: Public Virtue in Nonprofit Organizations* (San Francisco: Jossey-Bass, 1998), 88.

and fundraising team at the other end. The key is for all people, but particularly those who give leadership to departments, to recognize their own sphere of influence and seek to be a catalyst for positive change. The president, of course, is attending to the cultural dynamic of the whole organization. But then everyone has a role—everyone, but especially those who have oversight of particular zones of responsibility, and they can learn to get a read on and then positively influence the institutional culture within their sphere of responsibility.

The genius, of course, is to know what is negotiable—you can just let it be—and what is pathological. What is not ideal, but secondary—those aspects of the institutional culture that we can just let be, because while not ideal, they are relatively benign. And what has to be challenged and changed so that growth is possible?

The sign of leadership in each segment or level of the organization is recognizing what needs to be challenged because it is either pathological and inconsistent with either our mission or our capacity to grow and adapt. I say pathological, but that may be a bit melodramatic (though sometimes it certainly is pathological). And yet at the very least we ask what in our institutional culture is inhibiting us from fulfilling our mission or being adaptive, responsive, and innovative. What is making this a less than animating place to work?

Thus a key capacity for institutional leaders, whether presidents, program heads, departmental directors, or board members, is the practice of ethnography, a skill that we typically associate with the discipline of anthropology: recognizing and interpreting a culture—getting a read on it so that we can discern how and in which ways the institutional culture fosters mission.

And so we ask what about the culture—perhaps that you have inherited—is deeply consistent with the mission, vital to the distinctive institutional identity of the organization and, therefore, needs to be encouraged and reinforced. What is there in the very walls of the institution, one might say, that needs to be encouraged because it fuels mission?

Then also, what is there about the culture that is inconsistent with our mission or undercutting our capacity to fulfill that mission? Thus, Jinkins and Jinkins write,

The nonprofit organizations we lead are located on various points along a continuum that range from very healthy to very sick. Our approach to leadership must be sensitive to the organization's relative health and realistic about the prospects of change in this particular organization.[5]

On this, though, we also need to affirm that leaders—presidents, of course, but also board members, department heads, and directors—have to be able not merely to live with the culture but actually be animated by the culture. Jinkins and Jinkins insist on this point, stressing that in leadership we have to accept some of the key core values because one cannot lead unless and until one is viewed as "one of us." The authority of a leader to bring change is based on the confidence that one can be trusted, that one honors the history and identity of the organization. Again, Jinkins and Jinkins state, "the leader who cannot learn to represent (and re-present) the culture of the group will not remain leader."[6] This is all so critical because a leader of necessity must be a representative of the culture.

But I would add that this principle would apply to every person within the organization—whether it is a board member of a local church or a faculty member of a college. We read the culture and live with it, but more, we do not merely tolerate it but actually find that the culture is animating and fuels our work and our contribution to the mission. For leaders within the organization, at all levels, it means we do an audit; we get a read on the emotional tenor and psychological health of the organization—all ways to get at whether we have a healthy and dynamic institutional culture.

We begin with history; culture is always something we inherit. A new leader within an organization does not receive a blank slate. We attend to the history of the organization, to the shared experiences of those who work with the institution; all shape the institutional culture, including shared assumptions and shared experiences. New leadership within an organization must always take account of that history. A new CEO, for

[5]Ibid., 92.
[6]Ibid., 89.

example, can bring in new beliefs, values, and assumptions, as Schein notes, but there must always be a deep pragmatism; one has to live with and take account of what one has received, what has been inherited.[7] Or, as one college president put it to me, we need to ask what is in the walls, in the very DNA of this organization. New leadership does shape culture, but only in a way that takes account of the beliefs, values, assumptions that are in the air, in the halls, of this organization. Someone new to a position has little choice but to work with the actual proclivities and sensibilities that one has inherited—not fatalistically, but merely as part of recognizing that while institutional culture is malleable, it is so only to a degree as we nudge the organization toward greater psychological health or, very specifically, toward hopeful realism.

THE SIGNS OF HOPEFUL REALISM

On the one hand, the first question we ask is this: Does our culture fit our mission? Does it fill our institutional identity and purpose? But then, as noted, we need to ask if we have a culture that fosters our capacity to be responsive to a changing and fluid environment. And here is where it is helpful to ask five essential and critical questions looking for the signs of hopeful realism.

First, is the culture a *learning* culture? Is this an institution that is committed to finding knowledge, understanding, and insight wherever it might come from, so that the wisdom can inform good decision making? We are learning about the industry itself—together, asking questions, seeking input, reading books, discussing the mission and how we can do it better. We learn from clients, financial supporters, board members, and staff colleagues. We are in conversation with peer institutions—again, looking for insight into changes in our environment and how we can respond. We have a culture that is liberal, using *liberal* in the best sense of the word to signal that we are not fearful of ideas or change, but that instead we are open to possibilities, to new vistas, to ways in which we can adapt to a changing context or environment.

---

[7]Schein, *Organizational Culture and Leadership*, 202.

Second, what is the character and tone of what happens in meetings, in conversations formal and informal—both scheduled meetings and casual hallway conversations?

And while it is certainly not the only read on culture, humor is one of the ways in which we can test the character and resilience of an organizational culture. I am often a speaker for groups, events, agencies, and churches, and humor is an important part of what I am presenting and speaking to—not in the sense of "did you hear the joke about," but rather and always humor that is integral to the occasion and integral to the lecture or sermon. What I find helpful is that humor, fairly early in a public lecture or a sermon, can give me a read on who it is that I am speaking to in terms of their cultural ethos and orientation. I listen for the laughter and ask myself these questions:

- Is it awkward laughter, suggesting that they want to laugh but do not know if they have permission to lighten up, to relax and enjoy themselves?

- Is it polite laughter, suggesting they want to be kind to the speaker who obviously thinks what has been said is funny and as a courtesy to him—that is, me!—they laugh at my attempt at humor?

- Or is the laughter easy—comfortable, indicating that this group knows each other, are comfortable with each other, and are not willing to let the challenges they face unduly weigh them down emotionally?

Humor, and thus laughter, is not incidental to our shared lives and thus our shared work and our lives in institutions. It signals our mutual enjoyment of being together and working together. But also, when it is easy, when it comes naturally within the context of shared work, it signals that we believe in what we are doing but also that we are not taking ourselves too seriously. It is one way to get a feel for the quality of an organization's culture.

Third, is there conflict—or perhaps better put, healthy conflict, meaning generative conflict? The lack of conflict is typically not a good sign. Unhealthy organizations are marked, as often as not, by either the lack of conflict, meaning that, in effect, conflict is either not tolerated or it is sublimated, or they are conflicted, meaning that conflict is now institutionalized: the conflict has become entrenched and unaddressed; the conflict has perhaps become personal. The conflict is no longer a dynamic that encourages growth and wisdom but is something that actually undercuts the capacity for institutional growth even as it loses the capacity to respond to diverse perspectives.

Healthy organizations are marked by a diversity of opinion and diversity of perspective and often these diverse views will be held strongly, with deep conviction. Conflict is a sign that the mission matters and getting our decisions right also matters. And as soon as we have more than two people in the room—well, even if we have only two people—we will have a diversity of perspective. The only question is whether this diversity will be encouraged and allowed to inform a healthy process of fostering wisdom and good decision making. And this means that the conflict is generative.

One sign of an unhealthy working relationship is that you are hesitant to raise a matter of contention—a potentially difficult matter—because you fear the reaction of the other person. Healthy organizations do not fear conflict; they are open enough and honest enough with each other that they raise difficult matters and work them out, seeking common understanding around shared mission and core values. Healthy institutions manage conflict with generosity and courage, not fear; they recognize that conflict can lead to new learning.

And so we can ask: is this organization marked by either the avoidance of conflict or by entrenched and unresolved conflict? Do we have a culture that allows for diversity of opinion—where we do not expect or require compliance, where diversity does not polarize or threaten? Do we have a healthy enough community that conflict does not threaten the whole, the common vision and identity, and where conflict is resolved effectively and actually strengthens institutional mission?

Fourth, is the culture marked by a dynamic that is both professional and personal? *Professional* signals two things. First, it signals competency: the people in this organization are good at what they do. And what they are doing matters. Professionalism is about doing something that is worth doing, something that needs to be done and done well by those who have the competency to do it and do it well. And we signal this in our symbols, our rituals, and most of all, of course, in the way that things are done.

And we speak to this. We encourage excellence in our performance; we signal that this is an organization where people want to succeed and are given every opportunity to succeed. And more, we have a culture that encourages continuous improvement, learning and growth—learning to do better what we already do well, recognizing where new organizational strengths and capacities are needed and can be developed.

Personal indicates a fundamental affirmation that each of the people we work with is an individual, that those with whom we are engaged are persons before they are anything else—before they are students who pay tuition, or colleagues who have particular responsibilities, or attendees to our church who increase our church numbers, or donors to our cause. No one is ever just a number or just a direct report, a boss, or a financial contributor. They are persons. And we treat them accordingly as the base line of how we relate to one another.

And what I am suggesting is that we do not need to choose between being professional and personal as though if we are professional we are not personal or that by being personal we will somehow compromise our commitment to be competent, accomplished, and effective. Rather, we are secure enough in our competency that we can be first and foremost a fellow human being to the other who has crossed our paths. In being professional, we are not for a moment discounting our commitment to treat persons as persons.

How we dress in many respects captures this point precisely. Airline pilots dress the part; we have no doubt that they are qualified for the job, are credentialed for the role, and can be trusted to turn left as they board the plane while the rest of us turn right, so that as pilots they can deliver all of us safely to our destination. The uniform matters. No one thinks of it as pretentious. Rather, in every culture, actually, we signal that this person is a professional by the symbols of dress.

Informal or casual dress may *seem* more personal—and some within academic environments or churches we are inclined to think that casual dress signals that we care about people. We are just "folks"; and no one wants to show up inadvertently in a suit or a formal dress that might be read as "professional."

This is a false polarity. My physician is a consummate professional, and when I show up at his office he signals this with his dress. But he always treats me first and foremost as a person—not a problem to be solved, not his 11:15 a.m., but a person with a name. But while he is very personable, I need him to be professional. Why would this not apply to the liturgist on Sunday morning or the preacher to whom we look for competence—able and more than capable of expositing the Scriptures with authority and grace? Why would it not apply to the work of a professor in a classroom or faculty or departmental meeting?

And then, perhaps even more crucially, surely we should avoid using the word *family* as an attempt to signal that we care about people, that we are committed to being personal. The line "we are all family here" is often used in organizations as a way to stress the human and personal quality of our relationships as colleagues. But is this really helpful? Perhaps in the church, sure: to speak of the faith community as family has biblical precedent. Indeed, a case could be made that the church as family takes priority over the nuclear family for these indeed are our sisters and brothers. But nonprofit organizations are not family. They are institutions with a mission—with a job that needs doing, with lines of accountability, with consequences if we do not perform our responsibilities. And the senior leadership are not parents and surely should not try to have a parental role with their staff.

Yes, we can and need to be deeply personable—invested in each other's lives, as colleagues, caring for one another, finding friendship, and nurturing relationships that will be significant to us through times of difficulty, knowing that we have others in our lives, whom we know through our spaces and venues of work, who will share our joys and our sorrows. And we will drop by each other's office to see how the new baby is doing and how our colleague's son did in his first day in school. And we will attend funerals when there is loss. These relationships matter.

But, family? Not quite. This is not the most helpful metaphor to describe the very real community that constitutes the important social glue that is essential to our institutional culture. Some, of course, like the language of "team," often using it as an athletic metaphor. And this has possibilities, as long as we avoid the assumption that this presumes competition with our peer institutions.

Fifth and finally, does the culture foster the capacity to get things done? An organization can have great clarity on its mission, and it can put in place the appropriate governance structures and procedures for managing the affairs of the institution, and it can hire tremendous people—qualified and more than capable to do what needs to be done—and yet still not be effective.

All is for naught if the institutional culture does not free and empower the institution to make difficult decisions when these are called for—with courage doing what needs to be done. Culture can foster good conversations—effective deliberation—that lead to good decisions, which in turn empower action. Or the culture can hinder—subtly or less than subtly—the capacity of the organization to act with insight and courage.

A dynamic and healthy organizational culture is evident, in part, in a hopeful realism that is marked by the capacity to do what needs to be done, with a clarity about where decisions are made complemented by the capacity to implement those very decisions. Does the institutional culture foster good conversation that leads to good decision making, which in turn leads to action? Is there enough trust in the network of relationships—between staff, between staff and the board, and between middle management and the senior leadership—to free one another to do what needs to be done to fulfill the mission of the organization?

And we need a workplace culture that affirms that once we decide, we act. The decision is implemented. We have a culture that respects the due process and the authority of those who have to implement the decision. In other words, sometimes the inability of an organization to act and do what needs to be done indicates that the institution does not have good governance structures in place. But the point is that an organization could have a very well-designed approach to governance but still be inept because of a culture that consistently blocks the process toward critical actions that will lead the organization to implementing the mission effectively.

The Insidious Power of Fear

If an organizational culture undercuts institutional functioning, as often as not the root problem is one of fear. Fear always lurks around the edges of an organization. The danger, of course, is when fear gets into the DNA—when it is in effect institutionalized, embedded in the organization's way of being and seeing and thus acting. Fear can so easily be rationalized and become so much a part of the fabric that change and growth and good decision making are almost impossible. In those cases, there are two options: effective leadership that over the long haul, builds slowly and incrementally a climate of trust and institutional confidence; or a crisis that forces the institution to face reality and do what needs to be done—to intervene and do what needs to be done.

GRADUAL INCREMENTALISM

Culture does not change quickly; it is strengthened and encouraged through—the very best expression for this—*gradual incrementalism*: consistent behavior and consistent messaging over an extended period of time.

There is significant potential and impact in the benchmark events in the life of the organization—not so much crises, to which I will speak below—but, for example, the opportunities of a new senior pastor or a new CEO to make some definitive moves in the opening one hundred days with the organization: the first sermon for that new pastor, the first hire for the new CEO, or the first person fired. And on that score, what is noted is not only who was let go and why, but also how—the "how" of a dismissal will say a great deal about the way that the new leader will be shaping institutional culture.

The same goes for a team leader or for a faculty departmental head. Pay special attention to your first one hundred days in a role; it is a one-time opening to shape the culture of your segment of the organization. There may be one or two key things you can do to make a substantive impact.

But substantial and lasting cultural change comes slowly. This is so because culture runs deep in the patterns and rhythms of the life and work of an organization. There are ruts in the psyche of the organization—ways of doing things that reflect habitual patterns and behavior, ways of being and responding. Some of those are good patterns; they merit attention and reinforcement. Some are not so good—inconsistent with the mission, undercutting a hope-filled realism, and undermining the capacity of the organization or the department to do the right thing. And this is where new patterns are encouraged and then reinforced and then reinforced again and again and again until the new habit—consistent with mission, and reinforcing the learning culture—becomes second nature.

Yet even when it comes easily, consistent messaging and consistent behavior always need to be reinforced over an extended period of time. We might long for dramatic and immediate change, but deep change—change that is imbedded in the very social architecture of the organization—by its very nature comes slowly.

So, we attend to what *we* can do to foster a dynamic institutional culture. Ralph H. Kilmann puts it this way: we "control the culture by changing the stories, myths, symbols, and history itself," or "by managing the norms."[8] And he notes that negative norms need to be ignored, starved, or confronted. That is, we need to be both alert and intentional in our response. Then, norms that are consistent with the mission and with the capacity to be responsive and adaptive need to be encouraged and sustained through two things: consistent behavior and consistent messaging. And it is important to stress that it is both—consistent behavior and consistent messaging—and, of course, that ideally what we say is consistent with what we do; they reinforce each other.

As a leader within the organization, begin with mission. What needs to be affirmed, celebrated, and profiled because it is consistent with our mission and identity? What are the symbols and indicators of missional identity that need to be encouraged and referenced? And then consider what needs to be done to foster a culture of hopeful realism.

Schein speaks of "culture-embedding mechanisms" of two kinds.[9] First there is what he calls "reinforcing mechanisms" for fostering cultural identity and ethos. These include such things as these:

---

[8]Kilmann, *Beyond the Quick Fix*, 105.
[9]Schein, *Organizational Culture and Leadership*, 231.

- the organizational governance design and structure

- the mission statement and statement of core values

- the rites and rituals of the organization

- the physical space: building design, facades, furnishings, and public art

And second, Schein also speaks to what he calls "primary mechanisms," such as these:

- what leaders pay attention to

- what leadership chooses to allocate resources to

- how leadership respond to crises and critical incidents

- how people are recruited (and who), promoted, and fired

- what leadership says in strategic moments: reports to the board, public events, special ceremonies

This says it all, really, and it is a very helpful reference for the daily work for each of those who take their roles seriously when it comes to organizational effectiveness.

CRISES: WHAT THEY TELL US AND HOW OUR RESPONSE MATTERS

Crises will come. We can assume they will happen, whether a sudden resignation of a senior leader, a major budget crisis that leads the board to declare financial exigency, or an act of violence in the church parking lot or on the college campus. Or there may be a major blowup between two employees—where a conflict becomes public knowledge and creates sides, perhaps because a decision was made over which there is major disagreement.

A crisis of any kind is obviously something that everyone wants to avoid. But crises are also moments that call for the best in institutional leadership and test the organization's cultural resilience.

First, crises tell us something about the organization. Does it handle crisis well? Do people respond personally and professionally? Do employees— or church members—act as professionals, doing the right thing for the sake of the organization? Do they respond with a deep attentiveness to the personal dignity and worth of each person involved?

Second, a crisis is also always an opportunity not only to test the cultural resilience of the organization but also to strengthen institutional capacity. Thus Schein observes, "responses to crisis . . . provide opportunities for culture building and reveal aspects of the culture that have already been built."[10] But then also, a crisis is also an opportunity in which a leader, Schein notes, "creates new norms, values, and working procedures and reveals important underlying assumptions."[11] Each crisis is a new opportunity for learning.

Two more observations on crises must be noted. First, every crisis is an opportunity to test the level of hopeful realism in the culture—noting, in particular, the level of anxiety and fear within the culture. Healthy and dynamic cultures will experience fear, for sure, but it will not be a crippling fear but rather will call for the very best and appropriate response.

And second, we must also ask if there is ever a time and place to actually *create* a crisis. Might there be a time when an intervention is needed: the culture has become so entrenched, the decision-making processes have made leadership impossible, the undercurrents are pathological and run so pervasively through the ways of being and acting that no amount of "gradual incrementalism" will ever break the deep seated patterns of behavior that are crippling the organization? Schein suggests that this would not typically be an intentional strategy.[12] Rather, as a rule, radical reform is possible because an opportunity emerges—a financial crisis, perhaps, or a merger between two agencies—that brings about the opportunity for restructuring, re-envisioning, rebirth. While that makes sense, I wonder if there is not the time and place, that rare occasion, when the leadership recognizes that the organization is at a complete impasse, and that gradual and incremental reform is simply not possible, thus something radical needs to happen. I think here of the church in Vancouver that had become so dysfunctional that the leadership resigned in mass, called on the congregation to accept an interim arrangement where the pastor would take the church through a complete—from the ground up—restructuring of the ways in which the mission would be conceived,

---

[10]Ibid., 67.
[11]Ibid., 237.
[12]Ibid., 331.

governance would happen, decisions made, all with a view to, as they put it, "starting over." They had tried and tried and tried, but the culture was so ingrown and incapable of animating any kind of effective governance and missional growth that they felt they simply had no choice but to, quite simply, do radical surgery. This would, of course, be the exception, something done only in the case of an intractable institutional culture that no amount of gentle and consistent leadership would be able to renew. But it has to be an option for the board to authorize an intervention or actually manage such an intervention when the circumstances so warrant.

CULTURE AND RELIGIOUS SENSIBILITIES

All of my professional work has been done in religious institutions—churches, as a pastor, but mainly in executive leadership within academic institutions that would identify themselves as Christian. And I have wondered whether and how and in what ways that Christian identity and commitment should find expression in the institutional identity and thus its culture.

Within churches it is fully expected and appropriate, if not essential, that references to God—God's provision, God's presence, God's guidance—dominate public speak. But what about the board meeting or the meeting of the pastoral staff? What about those events or activities that reflect the more institutional character of the life and mission of the church? Should God-talk similarly dominate that aspect of the church? And what about a Christian university, or a theological seminary or a mission agency or service agency that has a religious affiliation? How explicit and overt should the language of God be? And what difference does it make?

Some would no doubt find this to be a rather strange question. Surely, if we are a Christian college, some would say, speaking of God should be common—not just common, but standard—because to be religious is to be talking about our religious identity as a way to infuse the whole of the organizational culture with this broad and ever-present awareness of our religious or Christian commitment.

Thus from this perspective, a Christian university class would begin with a prayer led by the professor, and the professor would regularly highlight the religious implications of what is emerging in the class—not just the religion or theology class, but the class in biology, sociology, or music would not only begin with prayer but also include a regular opportunity to bring God into the picture. Board meetings and committee meetings would begin with a prayer and perhaps end with a prayer.

But I wonder if another approach might be to suggest that if we want the whole of the place to be infused with a religious sensibility—a theological, ethical, and spiritual orientation—that perhaps subtlety might be more effective. Perhaps a more understood rather than expressed Christian ethos—implicit rather than explicit—would actually run deeper in the institutional culture. Perhaps we recognize that Christian or religious talk is not itself transformative and that a religious ethos that is subtle, perhaps implied in the way that the class is taught or the committee is moderated, ultimately alters and shapes our way of being. Teachers speak of this as the hidden curriculum.

Christian faculty in a public university understand this. In this context, it is necessarily the case that a professor's faith is not explicit. And thus it is often the case that a student becomes aware—slowly, over time, perhaps—that her history professor shares her Christian faith. It is caught—picked up—not by explicit prayers and references to Christ Jesus but by the asides and the way of being and the way that students are treated and the way that the material is handled in class. Now of course, some would say, "Is it not wonderful in a Christian university that we can be explicit about our faith and our religious commitments? Of course it is. I am only saying that there may be a place for a quieter witness. Subtlety might, in time, in the life of a student, for example, actually have a deeper and more lasting impact. What makes a religious institution religious is not our God-talk, but the way that our religious sensibilities find expression in the way we handle texts in the English department, cadavers in the biology lab, and the way we consider the horrors of war in a course in twentieth century history.

CONCLUSION

In conclusion, consider two brief points. First, art can play a very significant part in shaping culture—public art, both in the way that the visual arts grace the walls of the facility or the music that graces either public worship for a church or the chapel of a Christian university or college.

Does the art signal a deep awareness of the human predicament—that of the world at large and the world of those who live and work within this organization? Or is it escapist—seemingly disconnected from reality? And, of course, is it hopeful? Can we embrace the visual and musical arts that signal that all is well and will be well and that evil will not have the last word? Can we sustain throughout the building or the campus or the church facility the statement "this is an organization that does not fear reality but also knows that in the midst of whatever might be faced, there is the potential for good"?

And finally, and this point cannot be overstated, when it comes to organizational culture, the role of the team leader and department head is crucial. Likewise, for the institution as a whole, there is no avoiding the pivotal role that the president plays in setting the tone, keeping the culture on mission, affirming and recognizing and reinforcing those elements of the culture that are consistent with the mission and maintaining a resilient hope in the face of environmental changes, setbacks, and new opportunities. But leaders must display a hopefulness that reflects not a naiveté about reality—the circumstances in which the institution finds itself—but rather a confidence in the capacity and resilience of the institution to respond to those very circumstances. One of the most powerful ways that leadership shapes a hopeful culture is by avoiding—eschewing—a culture of blame. It is so easy to blame past leaders—one's predecessors—for the decisions they made or to blame external agencies, subtly suggesting that as a leader and as an organization we are victims of the misguided decisions of others. Or we blame the economy for our financial woes.

But if our orientation is one of hopeful realism, we name reality—without blame, without complaint—with an equanimity of spirit. And then we foster a good and vibrant conversation on how as an organization we can most effectively respond to the reality in which we have found ourselves. We embody the hopeful realism that is needed throughout the organization.

And while deeds need to match our words, few things shape culture as powerfully as rhetoric: the words we speak, the timeliness of our words, apt words spoken in season—"a timely word," to use the language of a contemporary translation of Proverbs 15:23 (NIV). But the "apt word in season" captures it best: to know what to say in the right time and place, words that shape our vision of reality and empower the organization to respond with courage. We all know this: pastors, coaches, team leaders, deans and department heads and, of course, presidents. We know that our words matter and that few things shape culture as powerfully as these words. As long, of course, as our deeds match our words.

FINANCIAL EQUILIBRIUM

Making Economic Sustainability a Priority

We cannot speak of institutions and, specifically, *effective* institutions without speaking about the economics—the funding and the financing and the money that is an inevitable part of our world, our work, and, of course, our institutions. Whether homes or families; churches or religious communities; schools or universities; hospitals; mission or community agencies; or the government. They all exist in an economic universe. Institutional intelligence requires an appreciation of the economic character of institutions and a recognition of one's own role, within the institution, of fostering financial equilibrium and sustainability.

There is no doubt that the finances of an institution are a primary concern of certain individuals: the president or CEO, the treasurer and finance officer, the person responsible for donor relations, and others. Effective presidents, for example, are very present to both the revenue and expense side of the budget; their long-term effectiveness is dependent on the fiscal health of the university. The same applies to pastors: effective church leaders are attentive to the financial health of their congregations. But everyone—whether the faculty of a college, the director of a department, or a board member—needs to appreciate some basics of the relationship between finances and mission and know how to support and work with those for whom this is their primary responsibility.

Anyone who thinks institutionally will be aware of and attentive to the financial health and vitality of the institution of which they are a part. They will understand the relationship between the budget and the mission, between the budget and the key sources of revenue for the institution, and they will take none of this for granted; they will all know that financial health is the fruit of intentional practice.

MISSION AND MONEY

Simply put, an effective institution operates with a balanced budget that delivers the mission. Institutions that work know how to secure the revenue for their mission, and further, they leverage financial resources for the mission.

There is nothing gained by sentimentality or idealism. The mission happens *and* the bills get paid. Mission happens because the economics are cared for; core values are expressed in the hard realities of budgets. "The love of money is a root of all kinds of evil," the Scriptures say (1 Timothy 6:10), but most certainly evil also runs rampant when we do not have a fundamental *respect* for money.

Effective nonprofit leaders run their organizations with shrewd business sense. And more, all the key players in the organization recognize and affirm that the financial health of the whole institution matters—not merely their own personal well-being or the financial resources that they hope would be allocated to their department or division.

But we always begin with mission; we assess an organization around questions of mission rather than money. The key issue is whether we are fulfilling our mission, not whether we are making money and are financially viable! Who cares if you are financially sitting tight if you are not fulfilling the mission? You are content and happy, perhaps, but irrelevant. I know of a college that makes a big deal of the fact that they have a balanced budget and have consistently balanced the budget for the last several years. But I almost want to say, "So what?" given that they are not able to draw or pay qualified faculty and that they have gone through several years of declining enrollment.

The goal is not a balanced budget, but a budget that delivers the mission. Board members and others are often impressed with a balanced budget as though that is a sign of institutional health. Boards should instead ask the hard question: What did it cost to balance this budget, and was the cost too great in that the mission is compromised? Does the balanced budget deliver on the mission? Financial equilibrium is a means to an end. Budget is a means, not an end. The end, of course, is the mission.

Something else must be stressed in speaking of mission and money. The fact that there is an economic dimension to effective organizations is not a problem, as though financial issues are a kind of necessary evil. Rather, it is helpful to remember that there is an economic element to the way in which we are created. See, for example, the witness to the wise woman described in Proverbs 31: her wisdom is evident, in part, because she attends to the economic well-being of her household and her community. The financial dimension of life is, actually, a gift: money is a means for fulfilling the mission. One could almost say it is the God-given means by which mission is fulfilled—the mission happens when we steward and thus leverage the financial resources of the institution, both its actual resources, the assets, and the potential resources, so that the mission of the institution is fulfilled.

As an aside, I would note that we would all wish to have huge amounts of money—to be well funded with substantial resources, so substantial that we do not even need to think about money and budgets and the fiscal year end. But there is an irony here: financial limits are actually a kind of gift in disguise. I am not suggesting that poverty is a gift; financially stressed institutions are only effective, if they are effective at all, in the short term. We need well-funded institutions that can thrive in fulfilling their mission. But financial limits are not an inherent problem or something we should immediately bemoan. Financial limits call us to make some decisions, forcing clarity about what matters most. We are required to make hard choices, as often as not personnel choices, forcing us to choose what is most important. Effective institutions do not do everything: they are lean and they are focused. Financial limits help make sure that mission happens in the most effective and focused way possible.

We can make a comparison in our personal lives, perhaps. We all wish we had more time so that we could do more things. But there is a grace in what is aptly called "the poverty of time." We only have so much time and we often buck against it—protest it and wish it otherwise. But could it be that this is actually a gift and that the limits of time, of our days and weeks and hours, means I have to make a choice? Limits force us to choose what is most important; we have to focus on what is most crucial to us. If I cannot do everything because of the limits of time, then I am forced to do what matters most. I learn to focus.

In like manner, the limits of our financial situation mean that we have to attend to what matters and give particular attention to what is most essential to our institutional mission. Personally we might really feel the pinch of having to say no to an opportunity because of the limits of time. But wise women and men know that this is the only way to live well. And, institutionally and organizationally, we learn to live within the limits of our means. This is not a curse but an opportunity to focus.

Financial limitations are never an excuse for tolerating an underfunded institution that does not steward its finances effectively so that the mission happens—not minimally, but as fully as possible. As an organization grows and matures, its financial situation should grow stronger. Presidents and chief financial officers should make it a rule of thumb: when you leave, after six or eight or more years, for however long you are in the role or responsibility, you will leave with the organization in a stronger financial position than when you arrived. And by stronger we mean that the organization is more effectively positioned to deliver on the mission with excellence.

That always remains the bottom line. We need to be mission focused and driven, but financially astute. This is a particular challenge when we live and work and oversee our institutions in a very volatile world and a fluid and thus uncertain economy.

THE INDICATORS OF AN INSTITUTION COMMITTED TO FINANCIAL EQUILIBRIUM

As a senior leader or board member of an institution, it is helpful to ask and confirm that certain things are in place for the institution of which you have responsibility as an administrator or trustee. If you are a faculty member of a college or a senior staff person, these are your concerns as well; if you have institutional savvy, you are letting others—the finance people—do their jobs. But you also know what it takes for an organization to have financial credibility, and you recognize the importance of financial equilibrium. An effective organization will have certain things in place—the marks, one might say, of an organization that recognizes the importance of the finances to the mission.

There is clarity about the financial position of the institution. Effective organizations are marked by clear and accessible financial statements that provide a read on the financial situation of the institution, including such questions as these:

- What is the annual budget, and does it accurately reflect the financial situation of the institution? Is the annual budget linked to the key functions and responsibilities of the organization? Does the budget express the costs of the key activities that further the mission?

- What are the financial assets and liabilities, and are the assets greater than the liabilities? This means, of course, that an institution knows what the assets are and that the liabilities are manageable. That is, managing the liabilities does not unduly limit the capacity of the organization to keep on budget and fulfill the institutional mission. And this presupposes a financial statement that provides a summary of the total assets, liabilities, and thus the net worth of the organization. Key constituents need to be assured that any debt the organization has can be managed without limiting the capacity of the institution to fulfill its mission.

- Is there sufficient cash flow to meet the institutions obligations? Cash flow is king; accountants will stress this again and again and . . . again. It is acceptable, of course, to have accounts that are restricted, but the key sign of financial health is liquidity—the capacity to fund operations. Thus vital institutions generate enough income each year to fund modest cash surpluses (an operating margin). And, of course, as a rule, effective organizations do not borrow to fund operations.

- What are the indicators of financial equilibrium for this kind of institution? For every "industry" there is some measure of institutional health—the key performance indicators for churches, schools, hospitals, or mission agencies—and it is essential to know what they are for your institution. (There is, for example, the Composite Financial Index for colleges and seminaries.)

- Is the financial position of your institution communicated in an accurate, accessible (meaning understandable) and timely fashion so that the data—the statement of financial position, the monthly and annual budget statements and updates—are able to inform good institutional decision making?

- Are the financial statements monitored by an external agency—or, putting it differently, are they audited, subject to an analysis that provides appropriate external accountability?

- Finally, does the organization have a system of internal controls in place and an adequately engaged board aware of these policies and assured that they are followed, so that the organization stays on mission and minimizes the possibility of fraud?

What all of this speaks to is the statement of financial position as a key indicator of the institution's financial health and vitality. The financial position—its health and resilience—is not known through a review of one financial statement. Rather, the key is to observe what is happening over several years. It is not a great crisis to have a single, one-time deficit budget—as long as (1) it is strategic or (2) it is clearly temporary—meaning you can demonstrate that this is a short-term or one-off situation. Financial stress happens, but it is another thing when it is chronic, meaning that the stress is happening over multiple years. When financial stress is the norm—year to year and year after year—then the only thing that boards discuss is not mission or vision but the financial troubles of the institution. And the only thing that presidents and senior leaders think about is the financial condition of the organization.

There is clarity regarding the institution's economic engine. Effective institutions know what sustains their economic engine and they strategize accordingly. Yes, we do need to speak about multiple streams of revenue. And we will. But first we ask, what is the economic engine, the centerpiece, the key revenue stream that assures that the mission of this organization will happen?[1] The economic engine should be consistent with the mission but the mission and the economic engine are not one and the

---

[1]The language of "economic engine" comes from Jim Collins, *Good to Great: Why Some Companies Make the Leap . . . and Others Don't* (New York: HarperCollins, 2001), 104-8.

same. It is not necessarily true that those who benefit directly from the mission fund the mission. An agency that secures shelter for the homeless will not be funded by the homeless. And yet the two, the mission and the economic engine, are linked logically and organically.

It is certainly possible to have an organization with a stream of revenue—perhaps from a for-profit business—which in turn funds the mission. Possible. But the ideal, without doubt, is that the identity, purpose, and mission are organically linked to the economic engine, so that what makes it possible for you to fund your mission is in continuity with the source of your financial health.

Thus, we are back to asking this question: What would it look like for this organization to have a sound economic engine? What key economic denominator can be linked to strategic and measured goals so we know if we are making progress and actually strengthening the financial capacity of the organization? And then it follows: organizationally you would focus your energy and strategy in a way that leverages your critical point of economic strength and capacity.

When I was the president of a nonprofit organization, the economic engine was clear: we were entirely dependent on free-will charitable contributions—financial donations—to the operations of the institution. We received significant designated or restricted contributions for particular projects. And we also received foundation grants—typically, again, for specific projects for which we had submitted a proposal. But what we also learned was that we could not survive, as an organization, let alone thrive, without a cohort of individuals who were giving regularly and generously to operational expenses.

Many supporters of the organization resisted giving to operations; they wanted to give to designated projects. That was fine, of course, but only to a point. The fact was that without undesignated giving to operations, we could not deliver on the very projects they were so keen to fund. Further, on every designated gift, we allocated a percentage of that gift—in our case 15 percent, which by industry standards was modest—toward administration. And sometimes donors would protest that this was an unfair "tax." The man who supported our efforts to build a theological library

in Haiti insisted that 100 percent of his funding would go to the library
and none, as he put it, to the "tax."

But this perspective is, I fear, naive: it reflects a failure to understand
precisely what it takes to deliver the very contribution he wants to make,
the theological library in Haiti. Without the infrastructure—the administrative oversight of the gift and the agency capacity to secure the finances,
work with the local administration in Haiti in the implementation of the
project, and then assess the effectiveness of the investment—the gift would
not be a wise investment.

In other words, informed nonprofit contributors actually *want* a percentage of all giving to go toward administration and many will actually
make operations a focus in their financial contributions to the nonprofit.
Jim Collins make this point brilliantly in his smaller book *Good to Great and
the Social Sectors*, where he emphasizes that

> social sector funding often favors . . . a specific program or restricted
> gift. . . . But building a great organization requires a . . . strong, self-
> sustaining organization that can prosper. . . . Restricted giving misses
> a fundamental point: to make the greatest impact on society requires
> first and foremost a great organization.[2]

Thus effective organizations recognize the priority of their primary
mechanisms for fostering economic sustainability by attending to the revenue
source and sources that make operations possible. For a smaller organization
like that referenced above, we had to ask two questions. For every designated gift, what portion of that gift—a percentage, perhaps 15 percent—
is needed for operations to make it possible to deliver the intended outcome
through the designated gifts?

But second, we went further. We asked, given the size of our staff and
our potential to connect with our donor base, and given our budget, can
we actually calculate how many donors with whom we can have an active
connection and how much they need to give, on average, so that we stay
in business and deliver on the mission? And in the end we focused our
attention precisely on this group: those who were able to give a basic

---

[2]Jim Collins, *Good to Great and the Social Sectors: A Monograph to Accompany Good to Great* (New York:
HarperCollins, 2005), 24-25.

amount, each year, to operations—an amount which, when averaged out, would help us meet our annual budget commitments. And we focused on recruiting board members who, in turn, would reflect this capacity for and conviction about giving to operations each year. That core group—those who would give that base amount, each year, to operations—were our economic engine.

I serve as the president of a small university. There is no doubt that in our case, as a private university with a minimal endowment, our economic engine is tuition revenue. Even though that only represents 40 percent or 45 percent of our annual revenue, it is so basic that we monitor enrollment projections very carefully. We are not endowed, and in contrast to other universities in our city that have substantial government grants that keep them in business, we depend on tuition. Our donors who give to operations are so very important, of course. Without them we are not in business. But they *supplement* the tuition revenue. Tuition is still our "engine."

And this means that we ask, if tuition revenue is so important, then we need students, and where do our students tend to come from? And what does that mean for how we profile the institution? In our case, the vast majority of our students come from evangelical congregations and this necessarily means that our relationship with church constituencies is pivotal to our financial equilibrium. And, of course, all of that ties in directly to our mission. Other agencies can and must do the same exercise, to ask, what is our engine, and how can we leverage that source of revenue and nurture the connections and relationships so that the organization can fulfill its mission?

There are multiple streams of revenue. Even with clarity about the financial engine, there is yet another key feature of vital organizations: they have *multiple* sources of revenue. They are not overly dependent on a single revenue stream that would, if that revenue stream were to falter for any reason, put the institution and thus the mission in jeopardy.

I think of the theological college in Colombia, South America, for which the annual operations budget was basically underwritten by a single North American–based foundation. When the foundation advised that drastic cuts were forthcoming, the college was in no position to respond. Both were at fault: the school should have been using those funds to foster

multiple streams of revenue; the foundation should have known better—
that is, rather than create and encourage dependency, they should have
insisted that their support fostered capacity building.

Or I think of the mission agency that has two major donors, whose
support represents, between the two of them, almost 80 percent of the
annual operations budget. Additionally, they serve as chair and vice-chair
of the board. Without being unkind I can simply say that the organization
is their hobby. It cannot be an effectively functioning board. It would take
extraordinary courage, with much awkwardness, for the president to differ
with these two individuals or, actually, for anyone on the board to outvote
them. It is, essentially, a two-man operation. They fund; they control. The
organization's leadership is necessarily beholden to them and if either of
them gets a bit disgruntled, the organization is no longer viable.

Or consider the church that, while small, is meeting its financial obligations but doing so because there is a single major donor who takes pride
in being the one whom the church depends on to stay in the black. In
both this and the previous example, there is an inherent vulnerability for
the organization: they are, there is no other word for it, *beholden* to their
funding source and overly dependent on that source.

Or consider the university that is overly dependent on tuition revenue
to meet the operational budget. While tuition revenue will, as a rule, be
a major source of revenue for the school, when it gets too high, tuition
rates outpace the capacity of students to pay for their education or, if they
do, they end up with significant debt. And if student numbers suddenly
drop—given the inevitable ebbs and flows in enrollment rates—the school
is put in a vulnerable position.

Or consider the nonprofits, including universities, colleges, and seminaries, that were heavily dependent on endowment returns and income
to fund operations, which then, with the events of the latter half of 2008
on the stock market, were left floundering, having relied too heavily on
one source of revenue. Thus, wise financial leadership strives to foster
revenue diversity.

When the Money Does Not Fit the Mission

While we must cultivate multiple revenue sources, it is important that we avoid approaches to funding that are inconsistent with the mission, that is, a revenue stream that while providing funding for the mission, in an unfortunate and ironic way undermines the missional integrity of the institution. One example might be when a major revenue stream for a university comes through academic programs that are only quasi-academic and not approved by the faculty; they provide a bit of a "cash cow" but not in a way that makes the institution feel an integrity between the funding source and the key institutional values. We need to avoid a disconnect that subtly or less than subtly undermines institutional integrity.

Or I think of the huge pressure for academic institutions to pay the bills by offering online courses, which are typically viewed as another source of revenue. This might be the right thing to do, but the leadership and the faculty need to ask: is this approach to education consistent with our understanding of core institutional values when it comes to the transactional distance between the professor and the student?

In other words, institutions can and must ask two questions. When is a funding source either directly linked to mission or perhaps only secondarily linked to mission? Both might be fine, as long the economic engine is linked to mission. And when is a funding source inconsistent with institutional vision, purpose, and core values?

Qualified, skilled, and capable women and men who manage the finances of the institution. Vital and effective organizations have in place qualified individuals who manage the finances of the organization in a manner that is marked by efficiency, accuracy, and transparency. These individuals are invaluable to the organization—essential to managing the economics, working with the board and the senior administration toward financial resiliency so that the mission of the organization happens.

They need to be qualified; spare no effort in finding and appointing individuals who are fully certified for their responsibilities.

Ideally the treasurer, chief financial officer, or the vice president for finance will be a senior member of the organization, serving on the president's cabinet in a larger organization or, in a small agency, with a direct report to the president and able to speak directly to the board on all matters that affect the financial health and well-being of the organization.

And in academic institutions, it is essential that faculty view senior-level finance officers as their colleagues and give them voice and participation in the academic planning process.

An effective chief financial officer or treasurer will have the following qualities and commitments.

First, they believe in the mission. They are not merely numbers people. The mission of the organization matters to them and they have a keen appreciation of the nuance in the relationship between the mission and the funding that makes the mission possible. Their goal is not a balanced budget but the mission. Having said that, they are unequivocal that the organization needs to live with a budget in which revenues more than match expenses.

Second, they provide clear and accurate financial information to the key decision makers of the organization. This means, for starters, that they are not inclined to paint a rosy picture when things are actually not so good—though my experience with accountants is such that I cannot imagine a financial officer giving an overly rosy picture! But the opposite is also the case: they are not melodramatic and they do not understate the institution's financial position if that position is actually quite good. They name reality, providing clear, accessible information.

Third, they work well with others—coming alongside the board and the president, of course, but more: they know how to help each department head and each of their key colleagues work through the financial implications of the decisions that are before the institution. They are colleagues and not adversaries; they attend to the finances out of a disposition of service to the institution and to those within the institution.

Fourth, of course, they do not presume to be the president. Be alert to an institution where the finance committee of the board or the treasurer or the CFO becomes the de facto CEO because they exercise or presume to exercise veto power on the decisions of the program leaders. Effective organizations are mission driven—and this perspective comes from and needs to come from the president. Within an academic institution, the faculty will have a primary voice in both the mission of the university or seminary but also in the academic planning process. So in the end, the CFO gives the president good information; and the president (with the board and in an academic institution, with the faculty) is well advised to make the CFO a primary advisor. And the CEO would rarely be inclined to make a decision with which the CFO disagrees. But in the end, the organization needs the president to lead and keep the institution on mission.

In every organization, there are certain pivotal working relationships. And when it comes to the chief financial officer, he or she has two relationships that are vital to the effectiveness of the institution: with the president and with the chief program officer. In an academic institution, then, few relationships are more crucial than these two, the senior finance officer with the president and the senior finance officer with senior academic officer.

Then also, an effective CFO provides the institution with a critical and essential contribution: managing the budgeting process and the budget itself.

And this leads to the next point.

The institution has a budget that works. It does not take long within an institution to realize that there are few decisions more loaded than the annual decisions around the budgeting process and the final decision on the budget that will inform the finances of an institution for the upcoming fiscal year.

When it comes to the budget, we begin where we need to begin. Who, in the end, has the final say, the final ownership on the final numbers in the budget? It needs to be the person or office that in the end has to deliver on the mission, the person who in the end is able to say that the mission happened. And that is the president. The budget, in the end, is the president's. Yes, the board need to endorse the budget, and ideally the senior leadership team has signed off on the budget. And yes, in an academic institution, the faculty will have a significant voice in the academic planning process and the establishing of academic priorities for the university or seminary. And the president is well advised to have a CFO who owns the budget sufficiently to be able to present that budget to the board. But, in the end, it is the president's budget.

Every budgeting process will involve some tough decisions. And for the most difficult decisions—including personnel cuts or the allocation of scarce resources—the CFO will turn to the president and, in effect, advise the president of the following: we need to make a decision at this point in the budget to balance the budget. The CFO can advise one way or the other on the potential benefits one way or the other—financial and otherwise. But in the end, the budget is the president's. The CEO needs to make the final call—accountable to the board, of course—but the person in this position simply must make the final decision. The president is responsible before the board to deliver on the mission. And the budget is a tool, a management tool, to accomplish the mission.

This does not mean that the budget would not go to the board for their endorsement. Indeed, in some jurisdictions, this is actually required. And, of course, this might be one of the means by which the board would confirm that it is aware of the financial circumstances of the organization. And they need to be. But their main concern is mission.

Thus the board can review the budget but then press and ask: the proposed budget is a balanced budget, but what did it cost to balance the budget? What tough decisions were made? And they might well question those decisions. And if they do, they do so in light of the mission and the capacity of the president, with the senior leadership team, to deliver on the mission. And the board has every right to challenge the administration on whether there are financial implications of expenses that are peripheral to the mission—or core elements of the mission—that are being sacrificed to get to a balanced budget. These are all fair questions. But in the end, the budget belongs to the president, who has the final responsibility to the board to deliver on the mission.

Having said that, one of the key contributions of a finance officer is to work with department and divisional heads within the organization, throughout the budget process, so that there is wide ownership of not only the process but the outcomes. Everyone in any institution knows the following: (1) that finances are limited and that therefore decisions—tough decisions—have to be made on the allocation of those resources, and (2) that the president will make the final call, in close collaboration with the chief financial officer and other senior leaders and, in the end, with the support of the board of trustees.

Finally, there are three crucial rules of thumb. First, approve no deficit budgets. It is critical that the institution lives not only within its means but also with some margin—actually budgeting for a modest surplus and thus building up cash reserves year to year. In the rare situation a deficit budget is called for, it needs to be demonstrated that the deficit is strategic—as a means of leveraging institutional growth, including revenue.

Second, when budgeting, be conservative on the revenue side; avoid creating immediate stress on the organization or on sectors of the organization because you have created a budget that overstates potential revenue. Rather, estimate expenses while also providing for latitude for the unexpected.

And third, look further down the road than just the next fiscal year. Consider the growth and development of the institution for the next three to five years and what that will mean for the budget cycles upcoming.

Most of all, of course, it is always about mission. The budget is designed for the upcoming fiscal year with the mission uppermost in mind.

AN INTENTIONAL SYSTEM AND PROGRAM FOR FUND DEVELOPMENT

It is very much the exception that nonprofits exist without a system of intentional connection to donors—to the charitable gifts, the free-will contributions of those whose financial resources are given to support the operations and capital needs of the organization, making it possible for the mission to be fulfilled.

In small nonprofits, the senior administrator—the president—is both chief executive officer and the chief development officer. In larger institutions there will typically be a vice president or director of development and donor relations as one of the key senior positions in the institution. But either way—with a senior development officer in place or not—the president is necessarily a key participant in fostering the connection with the network of individuals and agencies whose contributions and grants support the institution. And yet the larger the organization, the more critical it is to have someone who gives leadership to this side of the organization's development.

Fundraising as vital to mission and ministry. When I became the president of reSource Leadership International, an agency that supported theological schools in the global south, I knew I was facing a new challenge: I had served as the vice president and dean of three different theological schools where I had never had a direct role in fund development. But now, if I was going to give leadership to this organization, I would have to work in the area of fundraising—meeting with those with the financial means to identify with our mission and, through their giving, make it possible for us to make a difference globally. A few weeks after I had started in this new assignment, I met someone who said that he too had been a candidate for the job. He then added the observation that when he realized that fundraising would be a major part of the job, he withdrew himself from consideration for the job, adding, "I could not see spending so much of my time fleecing people of their money."

What an interesting view of the place of fundraising and fund development in the world of the nonprofit! The irony for me was that this gentleman was a faculty member at a theological college and, of course, his salary was being paid in large measure from funds that were secured through what he called "fleecing." Such a perspective is an indicator of remarkable institutional naiveté.

To the contrary, the mission of nonprofits flourishes as those in leadership within these agencies invite women and men with financial means to come in as partners in the mission. And inviting their participation in the mission requires attention to some fundamental working principles that necessarily guide this side of institutional life.

A theology of abundance rather than scarcity. Without presumption, we can be confident that the funding is there for this organization to thrive. If the mission matters and if we communicate that vision effectively, we can work from the vantage point that the support needed is there; it is available. No, it may not be low-hanging fruit. And no, we cannot assume that if we build it, they will fund it. Donors are not ATMs! We still need to do our due diligence to highlight the mission and cultivate the relationships that are needed for the financial health of the institution. There is no place for presumption. There is no place for assuming that funds will always be there if we just carry on and do not ask hard questions about sustainability. And yet we can, in humility, be confident of divine provision.

Donors are members. Those who contribute financially to the bottom line of the organization are partners who work with us and contribute to the organization through their financial gifts. And they deserve, then, good communication that is both informative and inspiring.

Mission animates fund development. The primary work of the president is not fund development; rather, the CEO's primary role is to articulate and affirm and provide essential leadership to the mission of the institution. Thus the president of an academic institution provides conceptual, intellectual, and educational leadership—defining and affirming the mission and the institutional core values. And it is the mission that drives fund development. In the end, donors to not give to the budget; they are investing in the mission. They believe in the mission. And thus fundraising is all about communicating the vision—telling the story, profiling the organization's identity and values, and inviting support for the mission.

Thus wise institutional leaders are prepared to graciously decline a gift—a contribution—that is not consistent with mission. The organization is mission driven, not donor driven.

Trust is the essential glue that connects a donor to the institution. There are no significant contributions without trust. Thus fundraising is about, in many respects, fostering trust, building a relationship of mutual trust and respect.

Finally, we can always work with the assumption that there is deep joy in giving. It is a privilege to invest in an organization that has a mission that matters and has capable and qualified people who are implementing the vision. It is a deep joy to meet a real need and contribute to something bigger than ourselves as full partners in the work of this institution.

Fundraising as science and art. Religious organizations rightly approach fundraising out of a deep recognition that the ultimate provider for the organization is God. And senior leaders know that they do their work in deep dependence on this providential care. And yet they are also diligent and intentional and attentive to best practices when it comes to the work of cultivating the network of supporters who are key partners in the economic health of the organization.

They set realistic goals, allowing the organization to grow at a solid but incremental pace. Nothing is gained by overstating the potential of the organization. Set challenging goals, of course, but keep them in reach.

They remember that giving arises out of a relationship. And it takes time and patience to develop the relationship so that giving is based on trust and reflects the partnership into which the donor is being invited. Be patient.

They know that the genius of every effective nonprofit is the network of donors who give unrestricted contributions to operations. They get it: the growth and development of the organization needs investment directly in helping the organization meet its budget. There is, of course, the investment that donors will make in special projects—capital projects or new programs. But the strength of the organization is found, when it comes to development, in the direct support for operations. And so the key to fund development is not the one-off fundraiser. It is relatively easy to raise funds for a one-off crisis event, perhaps. But the genius of the strength of good program is long-term relationships—people committed to the annual fund year in and year out.

When approaching a prospective contributor, wait until you have met with this potential donor at the very least two if not three times before asking them for financial support. Get to know them, and let them get to know you and your organization. But then, when you have established the relationship, do not be shy about the ask: give them the opportunity to make the investment.

Further, effective fund developers avoid the year-end appeal. There are no doubt times that the organization will be facing a year-end challenge and there are those supporters who appreciate knowing this and will help the organization end the year "in the black." But don't make a habit of the year-end appeal. This kind of fundraising is so easily nothing more than emotional manipulation.

Fund developers also know that fundraising is first and foremost an act of listening. Yes, we have a conversation about the organization—our mission and our vision and our current challenges, of course. But we also listen. We attend to the heart of the potential donor, to see what matters to them and what has captured their imagination. Donors want to feel connected with the mission of the organization. And so a fund developer will listen first and get a sense of what matters to this particular donor and why and how they might want to invest in this particular organization.

Finally, make it a rule of thumb that you reject manipulation and melodrama. Respect the integrity and intelligence of the potential donor and respect their decisions. Instead of a we-do-not-take-no-for-an-answer mentality, respect the decision of the donor who in the end is responding to the call of God in their giving. Trust them with that.

When I first moved into a senior role that included responsibility for fundraising, a wise counselor gave me the rule of the three "I"s: invitation, investment, and integrity. Fundraising is an *invitation* to participate in the mission of your organization. Giving is an *investment* with a tremendous rate of return; with the funding that you invest in this institution, you will make a tremendous impact on a generation. And donor communication has *integrity*—it is open, transparent, consistent, and accountable.

Finally, for those who serve in a senior leadership team or on a board, there are three questions you can ask of the organization as indicators that the organization is attentive to the due diligence that is needed to sustain a giving constituency. How many regular donors does that organization have giving annually to the general fund, and is this number growing? What is the average gift and what does the average gift need to be for the organization to have a significant stream of revenue from contributions? And what is the retention rate; is the organization effective in sustaining loyalty from its supporters? And, of course, is the board invested? As Peter Drucker observes, the first constituency in funding the organization is the board; the strength of the organization requires that board members both give and connect the organization with potential donors.[3]

CONCLUSION: MONEY AND DIVINE PROVISION

Many nonprofits are sustained by religious sensibilities—a keen sense that the mission or the organization reflects the purposes of God in the world and further, that the institution is actually, therefore, sustained by God. It matters to God, and God will provide the means by which the economics of the organization will be sustained. And often this is expressed in a need to pray and ask for God's provision.

This is all good—indeed, very good. It is wise for leaders to cultivate a keen awareness of the need to depend on providential grace. And yet

---

[3]Peter F. Drucker, *Managing the Non-Profit Organization: Principles and Practices* (New York: Harper-Business, 1990), 56-57. Or, as he puts it elsewhere, "If the board doesn't actively lead in fund development, it's very hard to get the funds the organization needs." Ibid., 157.

wise leaders know that radical dependence on God is and can be matched with a keen insight into the economics of how organizations work: how revenue is secured and how funds are managed and accounted for. It is all, in the end, a matter of good stewardship.

A PLACE TO BE

Creating Built Space

Space and the use of space matters. A classroom instructor knows he must not only read the classroom to which he has been assigned for his fall introductory course but also know why the room for his senior-level seminar needs to be a different space and why. A liturgical leader understands what it means to work within a particular space and know how to maximize that space for purposes of authentic Christian worship. A university board member understands the motion on the table regarding the renovation of a campus facility, why that renovation matters, and how it fits with the institutional mission and vision.

Institutional intelligence necessarily includes spatial awareness: understanding and appreciating how an institution is housed and functions within built space.

Effective institutional leaders know that a place—well designed and well used—can foster good work and encourage institutional vitality. Conversely, they know that if we fail to attend to the particulars of good space, our institutional spaces will subtly, or less than subtly, undermine our capacity to fulfill the organizational mission.

THE IMPORTANCE OF BUILT SPACE

Built space is not a matter of theological or architectural neutrality. Attention to built space rests on a theological premise that the human person is an embodied soul—or, perhaps better put, an animated body—and that as human persons our relations with ourselves, with others, and, of course, with the Creator, are shaped by the places in which we live, worship, and work. Place makes a difference, a profound difference, because we are not merely disembodied souls—not even "essentially" souls—but actual bodies that move through space and live in space and are shaped, substantially so, by the spaces we inhabit.

Finding our place—our location—is essential to our personal health and well-being. We do not land, we do not find ourselves, until and unless we find our place. We "aren't" until we are en-placed. We can only "be" when we are located. The same is true for organizations.

Indeed, I wonder if it could be said that salvation is always local and particular, because the salvation of God is always embodied, evidenced by the incarnation of Christ himself. And we, in turn, are always embodied and located in particular spaces and places.

We will all have transition times. As children, we followed our parents when a new job meant we had to leave one neighborhood and move to another. As adults, we will change jobs and have to accommodate a new workspace and new building in which we seek to do the good work to which we are called. We will leave high school and have to navigate a very different building—a university, perhaps—in a different city, perhaps even a different country. That is fine, but only to a point. Eventually, if we are going to find ourselves and be ourselves, we need to settle. We need to find our place. Transitory times can only be that: transitory. They can be fruitful times, potentially, for a number of reasons, but only if they are temporary.

Thus we need to speak about space or, more specifically, about *place*. John Inge makes an insightful distinction between space and place.[1] Place is built space. Place speaks of intentionality in the way in which we engage a particular space. And it is not a place until it is designed in such a way that works, that makes sense, that is congruent and fitting and functional. It becomes a place for you, a place to be.[2]

---

[1]John Inge, *A Christian Theology of Place: Explorations in Practical, Pastoral and Empirical Theology* (Burlington, VT: Ashgate, 2003), 1-2.

[2]The phrase "a place for you" is borrowed from Paul Tournier, *A Place for You: Psychology and Religion*, trans. Edwin Hudson (New York: Harper and Row, 1968), a book that for many of my generation first fostered our appreciation of the importance of place.

A PLACE TO BE

Institutions need places to be. More specifically, institutions need to be housed in generative spaces, locations that fuel and animate the work the organization is doing—specifically its mission. To this end, it is helpful to think in terms of place as providing and encouraging three aspects of institutional capacity: identity, purpose, and community.

Identity. A building should reflect and reinforce the identity of the institution. In the words of the classic on space and buildings, *A Pattern Language*, "A building is a visible, concrete manifestation of a social group or social institution."[3]

Identity speaks of meaning: What does it *mean* to be a university, or a church, or a hospital? What does it *mean* to be a government service or a business and, in particular, *this* kind of business? On identity, Inge puts it this way: "if identity . . . is at the root of the problem, then there can be no escape from a revitalized sense of place, since identity . . . is formed, nurtured and fostered by place."[4]

Thus this question naturally follows: Does a building need to "look" like what it is used for? Does a school need to look like a school? A country club like a country club? A church like a church? Is there such a thing as a generic building? Or does space matter in such a way that a building needs to reflect the institutional purpose and identity that it houses?

What does it mean to speak of a facility as "multipurpose"—as one often hears for churches that choose to hold church in warehouses or box-like structures? Does it matter to use a facility where the space is not in sync with the purpose for which it is being used—or, perhaps better put, where the space is not intentionally consistent with the identity of the institution?

Do the facilities that house a university need to look and feel like a place for critical thought, good conversation, teaching-learning, and research? Or can it look like an office building, or a church, or a mall? If not, why not?

---

[3]Christopher Alexander, Sara Ishikawa, and Murray Silverstein, *A Pattern Language: Towns, Buildings, Construction* (New York: Oxford University Press, 1977), 469.
[4]Inge, *Christian Theology of Place*, 130.

Does city hall need to reflect something of what happens inside it and how it relates to the city and to its environment? Do we signal civic virtues by our buildings?

When you approach a building, does it need to read in a particular way? If so, why?

To respond to these questions, so much depends on our understanding of the human person and whether indeed our embodiment actually matters. Using for example Christian worship, does it matter whether it takes place in a venue or space that explicitly and intentionally actually fosters worship? Does it need to be a liturgical space? A sacred space? If we are just rational beings and our greatest need is information, or if we are essentially emotional beings and our greatest need is to feel good, then perhaps multipurpose is fine. But if we are animated bodies—and if our being in bodies makes a difference, and, perhaps, makes a huge difference, even a defining difference—then surely the space needs to be congruent with what we are trying to be and do in that space.

A space needs to foster the kind of relating we hope to do in it: whether that be worship, thus encouraging our relationship with God; or learning and thus fostering our capacity to learn from a teacher and with others; or governance; or the whole range of human activities. In particular it needs to support and reinforce—house, in a generative way—those activities that are consistent with the institutional mission.

Furthermore, built space can be a determining factor in fostering and sustaining the core values and commitments of the institution. Conversely, the place—the built space—can not only not be in sync with organization's identity but actually be at cross-purposes with the institutional mission.

Purpose. Built space can also be thought of in light of institutional purpose: What is the mission of this particular agency? This is more specific than identity in that two universities may both look and feel like universities, and two churches may be rather different, but no one doubts that they are both churches. But the purpose question considers whether the mission of this institution is fostered by this particular facility or building. Is our purpose fulfilled in this space or as with identity, are we subtly fighting the space—running up against the limits not merely of the amount of space we need, the size of our place, but the way in which the place itself is not congruent not just with who we are called to be (identity) but with what we are called to do (purpose)? Thus, while all three look like churches—Presbyterian, Baptist, and Anglican—in practice, they look quite different in that each of these denominational traditions approaches worship quite differently. They have a distinct purpose.

Thus, for example, Tyndale University College in Toronto has a challenge: they purchased a convent and now need to repurpose the convent for a liberal arts university. That is challenge enough, but it will be interesting to see how the chapel in particular will serve the purpose of the university. The inherited chapel is a magnificent space and ideally suited for the worship forms and liturgies of a Roman Catholic monastic community. But how will this work for the worship forms of an evangelical Protestant institution of higher education?

And this leads us to one of the great working principles of built space, attributed to the American architect Frank Lloyd Wright: form follows function. The space needs to work—it needs to function and facilitate what it is that we are trying to do in this space. We protest ostentatious spaces or decoration, or any intention to impress—whether as a home, a school, or a church where form interferes with and does not support function. This is not to discount the value of beauty—not for a moment— or even spaces that foster a sense of reverence. But the working principle remains: form follows function.

It is one thing to have a beautiful buffet—exquisitely laid out, food that appeals to the eye and invites you to enjoy a good meal. But do the people who set up the buffets ever actually use them? Thus, I register a mild protest. Please put the utensils at the end of the buffet line, so (1) we do not have to attend to carrying utensils in one hand while also holding a plate that we seek to load up with the other; and (2) we do not have to go back to the beginning of the line to get a spoon because, in the end we did decide to have soup after all! Think function: how does this actually work?

Thus, for example, a room that is too large for a small intimate gathering does not foster purpose—the purposes for which we have gathered. The conventional wisdom, which makes sense actually, is that you want a room that is 80 percent full—less than that, and there are spaces that become psychological spaces, gaps, like a missing tooth that keeps drawing the attention of your tongue. But more than this limits options for seating, increasing awkwardness for those who are new or feeling uneasy in the space, who would prefer some social distance as they process what is happening in the room. This is why churches that are reaching more than 80 percent capacity Sunday after Sunday will not typically grow. Sure, you can get away with this on an Easter Sunday—pack it out—but not week-in and week-out.

But purposeful space is not just 80 percent of capacity, it is also a matter of the configuration. The organization asks, what works best, what is it that we are trying to do, and what is the best configuration to make it possible for that to happen?

I resist invitations to speak at banquets. The reason is simple: you are trying to accomplish two very different things with a similar layout. For a meal, the round tables are good—very good, but for a plenary presentation, even if you invite those with their backs to the podium to turn around, the result is still a room designed for one function that now only somewhat works for another. If you want a combination of public presentation with small group conversation, then you will need a different format and setting for each function to maximize both activities.

At home, you may want a living room that fosters good conversation. For that, you will need to reflect on seating configuration, the size of the room as a whole, but also the kind of seating, the distance of the setting of the seating options, the size and location of a coffee table, the access points and the ease with which any one person in the room can make eye contact with others.

You may know you are in a school or a university when approaching functional spaces for an educational identity. But then we ask, is this particular space configured and designed in such a way that the mission of this college or seminary or university is able to happen? This has to do with the amount of space, of course: does the university have the right number of classrooms and offices and fitness rooms to deliver on its mission—the practical question. The question of purpose always then considers the kind of spaces that exist and whether they reflect what this university is trying to do—at this time and in this location. If you have a science program, you will without doubt be asking about laboratory spaces.

Or for a church you will be asking, what is the right size of auditorium or sanctuary for a congregation—one that is congruent with the mission of this church? Architecture is always, in the end, about effective functioning—for the accomplishment of the mission of this particular organization.

Community. And this leads us then to the question of community. Spaces are always places of encounter in various working relationships and connections. Our built spaces are always about people in relationship. We encounter others—colleagues, clients, and others—in built spaces. Place shapes and informs these connections; indeed, it could almost be said that place is the final arbiter of a relationship. All human relations are linked with both time and space. Only the naive think they can form community and build relationships without attending to the quality and character of built space. The design or mis-design of a place will trump our best intentions for fostering human connections.

For churches, of course, the venue for worship needs to be conducive for worship, for communion with God. But then also, a church can ask: are we building community as the people of God, in communion with God, sure, but then also in communion with one another? Does this building encourage community in a way that reinforces our core commitments and values? At the very least two dimensions of community need to be attended to in the design of place: hospitality and good conversation—the two essential features of genuine community.

First we ask whether the facility fosters hospitality (assuming, of course, that this is a core institutional value).[5] Whether it is a church or a hospital or a school, each institution typically recognizes that the facility plays a vital part in encouraging ease of access for those who are new to the building and thus to the organization.

Can a facility be welcoming rather than intimidating? Can the entrance be both grand and friendly—signaling that what happens in this place is

---

[5]Christine Pohl, in her *Making Room: Recovering Hospitality as a Christian Tradition* (Grand Rapids: Eerdmans, 1999), makes the case that hospitality is a core Christian value. As such, hospitality is not merely a pragmatic value—that is, something the organization does because, for a university, for example, it might bring in more students; it is a core value because it is a deeply held *religious* value.

very important, but also that this institution is accessible, eager to receive those who are new to this place? Can the transition space into the facility encourage and foster a sense of welcome, hospitality, and even love?

Newcomers are trying to read the building and are eager to move into and through the building in a way that is relatively easy. Are they able to navigate the space in a way that is accessible, not threatening—a space that is easy to read, not overly crowded, not overly designed in a way that only makes sense to the initiated?

It is interesting to compare older and newer church buildings when it comes to the built space between the street and the sanctuary—the venue for gathered worship. Older facilities from the seventeenth and eighteenth centuries had literally no transition space: one moved directly from the street into the place of worship. Then architects in the nineteenth and the first half of the twentieth century provided for some transition space, but still, typically, nothing more than a small narthex. But in a post-Christian, more secular, and pluralistic society, liminal space is crucial. And this transition space needs to be inviting and non-threatening, allowing for a slow progression into the pace of worship, which may, at first at least, be a relatively unfamiliar space. Thus many newer churches are building expansive foyers with coffee shops and a design that signals hospitality with gathering spaces for small groups to meet for conversation prior to the formal event of worship.

Hospitality also means that a person feels safe. Hallways are inviting rather than ominous and intimidating. Transition spaces allow a people to get their bearings as they move into and through the building. They do not have to approach a private space, an inner office, without adequate intermediate space. Thus, for example, offices that are off a major corridor create challenges. Those who work in them likely often feel exposed and those who come to visit those offices are likely often feeling, intuitively, the lack of transition space. An outer office provides for that safety—for both the person who works in that space and for the visitor. The same is true in a home; we come in through a transition space—a foyer, or narthex—and recognize the importance and integrity of public spaces where guests are received and inner rooms where only a few are admitted.

The authors of *A Pattern Language* make that observation that "unless the spaces in a building are arranged in a sequence that corresponds to their degrees of privateness, the visits made by strangers, friends, guests, clients, family, will always be a little awkward."[6] They speak of an "intimacy gradient" (what a wonderful phrase) to help readers appreciate how both those who host and those who are guests make sense of and move through built space.

The question of hospitality then leads us to a further consideration of whether a facility encourages conversation, genuine and effective human encounter through animating and encouraging exchanges. Do those who need to be in conversation with each other find that they are in adequate proximity to each other so that they foster good work, together, for the sake of the mission of the organization?

Then also, while the design needs to work for the newcomer—respecting the need for accessibility, but then also the need for privacy for those who work in the facility—it also needs to function, in terms of connections, for those who actually work there. The distance between offices—work stations—matters. Effective buildings are good places to work in part because of the way that office and work stations are situated. The authors of *A Pattern Language* make the observation that if offices are too far apart and distant, people do not meet, formally or informally, as often as they should, especially if they are on different floors.[7] But then also, if they are too close together, the need for focused work is too easily interrupted. Staff need their space; they need to feel that they can work without having someone watch them or watch over them, or too easily interrupt them. Thus a most effective facility strikes a balance between privacy and connectivity.[8]

Gathering spaces for both formal and informal conversation are also an essential feature of a good working environment. Most organizations will need a venue where the entire working team—the college faculty and staff, perhaps, or the entire staff of a nonprofit organization—can meet for an agenda that necessarily brings the whole working cohort together.

---

[6]Alexander, Ishikawa, and Silverstein, *A Pattern Language*, 610.
[7]Ibid., 408.
[8]Ibid., 717.

But beyond this, good working environments include gathering spaces—generative spaces—for groups of two, three, eight, and fifteen. And the genius of a great space is that it is the right size for the group—not too big but also not crowded. Effective buildings are marked by multiple gathering spaces for good conversation, whether it is meetings with a formal agenda or ad hoc gatherings for connecting over a coffee.

What we seek and need is built space that fosters identity, purpose, and community. The same is true of our personal space—the work station or office to which we are assigned within the organization. The key is to design our workspace in a way that most fosters identity (our role in the institution), purpose (what it is that we need to accomplish in that space), and community (hospitality, good conversation, and safety). We can ask, do we want an imposing desk in a huge room, with the desk between us and our guest and then a large space between them and the door through which they entered? Or do we want an accessible space, not cluttered, but organized, with clarity, simplicity, and open lines—that is, a good place for good conversation, where a guest is safe? They can have their back to the wall, the space is not intentionally intimidating, and therefore, overall, this office, this work station, works for all involved.

INTERPRETING BUILT SPACE: PLACES THAT WORK

Women and men of institutional intelligence are marked by a capacity to read built space: recognize when a space works and when it does not work, and know why it does not work and what can or should be done—if at all possible—to make it more workable. As we navigate our way through buildings, facilities, and designed spaces, we need a conceptual framework for engaging a particular place—for thinking about, interpreting, and experiencing space, and, of course, for moving through and working in the built space in a way that is consistent with and encourages the institutional identity and mission.

We need a guide, perhaps for the prospective faculty member of a college who is coming to the campus for interviews with the hope, perhaps, of getting appointed as a tenure-track professor; or for the couple who have just moved to a city that is new to them—a new job—and now they are visiting a church that is for them potentially a new church home. Or

I think of my first time through the buildings of the institutions where I came on staff—as dean of Regent College in Vancouver, and then years later as president of Ambrose University, in Calgary, Alberta. In each case, I approached the building differently than might otherwise have been the case in a casual visit. This works similarly with an airport or a hospital. As you approach the building and enter in—for whatever reason—you are, consciously or unconsciously, interpreting space.

How do we approach a facility, enter into it, see what needs to be seen, and consider whether it works or, perhaps better, how it works?

Several elements should be considered; together, these elements make all the difference in whether a space is a generative place. If an architect were to coach a potential new faculty member or a couple visiting a church, here is what those in the field would offer them—the basic guide, the conceptual framework to seeing and responding well to a facility. Following architect Witold Rybczynski, we note and read the building by asking—consciously or unconsciously—some key questions that help us make sense of this building.[9]

Location and siting. We begin with siting: the location of the facility, within a city and in which part of the city—urban or rural or suburban—and then how the facility is sited on a particular piece of land.

What are the main views of the building and what does one see from diverse angles as one approaches the building? What are the immediate surroundings, both in terms of designed landscape and other buildings and facilities?

As I write this, Food for the Hungry Canada, based in Abbotsford, British Columbia, is coming to the end of their lease on their current office location. And as they think through their options moving forward, they are keen to move to a new and more open space—fewer hallways, more light, not necessarily more space, but a better configured space than where they are currently located. And it was interesting to hear of their options: Would they move their offices into an industrial zone—with a lower rent, no doubt, but with a facility surrounded by warehouses and minor industries? Or would they move their offices into a thriving community

---

[9]Witold Rybczynski, *How Architecture Works: A Humanist's Toolkit* (New York: Farrar, Straus and Giroux, 2013), 80.

of street level restaurants, coffee shops, and individually owned stores? The decision they make will invariably shape the tone and character of their work.

And this question is perhaps most crucial: How does the building face or engage the sun? For buildings in zones along the equator, the question is whether there is shade around the building and especially on the approaches to the facility. In northern countries, southern exposure is, as they say, "gold." It is northern exposure, of course, for those in the southern hemisphere. For those in northern zones, "South is the most important point on your compass" writes Rybczynski, who urges those who design buildings to position the longest side of a house or an office building "within thirty degrees of due south."[10]

The most critical question when it comes to siting is the orientation toward the sun. With that settled, the next issue is how one approaches the building. And in this regard, there are three things to consider.

First, as you leave your car and approach the building, or as you walk toward it from the train or bus station, note the orientation toward the sun. As Rybczynski observes, "it is always best to enter a building on its sunny side if possible, for that is where the façade will appear to best advantage, with sharply defined shadow lines and contrasts."[11]

Second, the main entrance should speak "welcome." This may seem more essential for a church building or a college than the US Capitol, which may try to be a little intimidating. But as a rule, buildings are designed for people. Even the US Capitol building speaks of a facility that houses government by the people and for the people. A university is, as often as not, keen to communicate the value and importance of higher education, but still, surely we can and must insist that nothing is gained by intentional aloofness or alienation. And in this regard, a facility is most welcoming when it is clear that the main entrance is the main entrance. Signage helps, of course, and it should ease the approach for a person who is new to a facility. But ideally, with no signs, it should read, "Enter through here."

---

[10]Ibid., 100.
[11]Ibid., 12.

And finally, Rybczynski suggests that things like mail delivery, storage, garbage bins, "such messy impedimenta are ideally located away from the entrance . . . screened from public view—at the back of the building."[12]

There is a certain irony in the facility that is the main building of the university where I currently work. The parking lot is on the back side of the building, and this unfortunately means that the majority of those to visit the campus and come to the main building pass by all the garbage bins en route to the most obvious access from the parking lot into the building! Some architect was not thinking about how the space actually works. The beautifully designed main entrance is actually rarely used for the simple reason that the parking lot is out back. The same often happens with church facilities: the parking location leads worshipers to come through a side or back door rather than the door that best reflects the welcome and purpose of the church building and the transition into the worship space.

The plan of the facility. Second, we take note of the layout, what is often spoken of as the *floor plan*. Part of reading a building is asking how the various functions happen in the building, how a person moves through the building, and what is the emotional quotient that comes from the layout itself.

If you are coming to a church for the very first time or if you are coming for your first meeting as a prospective faculty member of a college, be observant. You can ask such questions as these: Does the floor plan have symmetry? What are the axes—the major exterior and internal routes through the building? Symmetry is emotionally satisfying; with axiality, symmetry fosters a sense of logic, order, and well-being. Or as Rybczynski puts it, quoting Graham S. Wyatt, "Axiality and symmetry are formative principles that everyday people understand as they experience them in three dimensions and for a lot of people they imply formality, maybe even a degree of gravitas."[13] Symmetry and axiality give the facility meaning, so that it has a logic that resonates; it makes sense. And those who are

---

[12]Ibid., 95.
[13]Ibid., 121-22.

relatively new to a building can find their way around with ease. They are able, consciously or unconsciously, to read the building.

Again, as noted under the reflections on the siting of the facility, the points of entry—and particularly the main entrance—are quite important. The authors of *A Pattern Language* observe that after siting, the most important feature of a building is the main entrance, noting that

> when a person arrives in a complex of offices or services or workshops, or in a group of related houses, there is a good chance he will experience confusion unless the whole collection is laid out before him, so that he can see the entrance of the place where he is going.[14]

And then, from the entrance we move through the building, and what I am suggesting is that there should be a rationally satisfying approach or sequence of spaces that make sense and allow us to move through the space with a reasonable degree of confidence. Actually, it would be interesting to ask an astute newcomer to find the office she wants to visit with no signage to help her along the way, to see if she can simply read the facility. In other words, the layout should make sense, and signage could be an almost non-essential confirmation of what our instincts are already telling us about how this building works.

Structure, skin, and details. If a building is satisfying, if it gratifies and is a place to be—a place where people want to work, or worship; for a school, to study; and, for a home, a place that people want to live—siting is very important. And layout matters; it should make sense. But then we move to the critical third feature of a generative space. When you approach a building and when you move through the building, those who are observant of buildings will note three things beyond siting and layout that merit closer observation: structure, skin, and details. Again, each of these gives meaning to the building and thus to the institution.

By *structure* we mean the bones of the building. What holds up the roof, and how it is constructed? Some argue that how a building is constructed should be clearly visible. No artifice. No hiding the beams and bones of the building—brick, steel girders, stick construction for a typical home

[14]Alexander, Ishikawa, and Silverstein, *A Pattern Language*, 500.

structure—that in any structure, they should be clearly evident; a person can clearly see what makes this building stand up. But while it is sometimes fitting and attractive to reveal the structure, many spaces work best when there is an internal cladding. Drywall is very common and it has the huge advantage of being cheap, relatively light, easy to mount, and wonderful to paint. The main point here is simply this: What kind of building do we have? Is it a steel structure? Stick? Wooden beams? And how are the various components of the structure joined?

Skin makes the first impression. It is the cladding. It protects the building from the elements. But it is not merely functional: it is the face of the building—glass buildings, brick buildings, siding. What kind of building do you have or want? Glass may be rather dramatic and may seem to be all about light; but it also exposes, quite literally, everything. Do you want to work in a fish bowl? Surely the ideal is a combination of materials for the sake of interest and, of course, function. A glass exterior to a main entry makes the entry more inviting—one can see just beyond where you are entering in, which makes it more accessible to a newcomer to this space. But beyond this, glass should be used discriminately.

Then we come to the *details*—such things as the windows, frames, doors, baseboards, fixtures, and door and window handles. Each detail matters. Details should be beautiful—visually satisfying. And they should be functional. Hopefully any institution of which we are a part has rejected the kind of pseudo-details that were popular in the 1970s, such as suburban house construction that seemed infatuated with fake shutters that were neither beautiful nor functional, in that they were just pieces of shutter-looking plastic affixed to the wall next to the windows.

As Rybczynski observes, details set the tone and express architectural ideas and thus give meaning to the building and provide what he calls a "coherent visual logic."[15] But more, they should be consistent with the identity and purpose of the building—features that speak domesticity for homes, with civic and perhaps historic allusions for public buildings. A church, for example, might well have a cross, signaling, potentially even very subtly, the religious identity and purposes of a place of worship. The

---

[15]Rybczynski, *How Architecture Works*, 179; see also his comments on building details on pages 202-3, where he stresses the need for coherence and consistency.

details do not need to be in-your-face. They can be understated. Those who are observant will note and pick up on these smaller but no less significant features of the building. The details of a university campus or of a hospital or a retreat center would each be consistent with the intent for which the building was erected. The details reinforce the reason for being of the building; they signal and actually affirm what happens in the space.

Finally, on details, there are two more observations. First, we cannot avoid that staircases are a particularly important detail. They are obviously transition spaces, but they are also inevitably prominent and potentially serve as both a means of moving from one floor to the other but also functioning as a kind of sculpture, often at the very heart of the building. Something is lost, for example, when faculty slip in the back door and up the back steps into their offices and miss the feel, the sense of place, that comes with entering the building and taking the central steps so that even as they are in their offices and off to their own classrooms, they have a feel for the whole.

And then, second, we need to make an appeal for authenticity. The details of a building need to reflect institutional core values and commitments. And so, one would think, a church would avoid the use of faux flowers or stone, or anything that is not actually what it appears to be. Surely, for a university where critical reflection on ideas and truth matters, we would want the details of our construction to speak of integrity and authenticity, transparency and quality. We would avoid the merely novel and curious or anything that defies logic, as well as anything shoddy, unkempt, or out of proportion to the building as a whole.

Practicality. While all that has been stated thus far about siting, plans, structures, and details might imply that all of this actually functions, it also needs to be stated explicitly: the building needs to work. It needs to function in a way that allows the building to be used for the purpose for which it is built or is being used.

A university needs an appropriate number of offices, classrooms, athletic facilities, meeting spaces, common areas, storage spaces, washrooms, and parking spaces. We can simply ask, what is needed here? No idealism. If we have a second floor, we need a stair case and an elevator. If we build a chapel, we need to attend to sight lines, sound, and accessibility.

And when it comes to practicality, safety matters. And it needs not just to be safe; it needs to feel safe. Railings on the balcony need to not only be secure but also give the person on the balcony an ease to be there without fear that the structure will not support them. This is particularly the case for stairways. In few areas of the building will people feel the safety of the building more keenly than in the stairwell. Are the stairways well lit, with appropriate hand rails, with the edge of the step easily visible, with each step the same height, and with an ease of transition from the last step to the lower or the upper floor?

Safety also speaks of accessibility—for those who have mobility challenges, for children, for the elderly, and for those who are visually impaired.

Finally, consider the simple things: Do the doors open and close and stay slightly ajar when you want a door left ajar? Does the plumbing work? Are the light switches well located, so that as you enter a dark room, you know where to reach to find a light switch? All of these are but a subtle way of reflecting on the institution as a whole. But it happens, as often as not, subconsciously. We read the facility as a window into the institution as a whole.

Sustainability. Then also, attending to the facility demands that we also ask about sustainability. If, as a potential faculty member or as a church-goer, questions of sustainability matter to you, then you will approach the building and move through the building asking of this building not only if it works but if, further, it reflects a commitment to environmental integrity.

Sustainability suggests relative ease—it is always "relative" ease—of maintenance. The facility needs to be maintained, and the design should take account of the need for cleaning, upgrading, and the replacement of those elements that have worn out. More on this later in this chapter.

Most of all, sustainability speaks of whether the building is designed in a way that fosters environmental integrity. Anytime we are talking built space, we need to consider the environmental implications of the process and outcome—both what it means to build something in a way that honors the ground, the water sources, the air quality and, of course, the long-term implications for sustainability not only of this particular building but for the planet as a whole.

One helpful approach to thinking of sustainability is that provided through the Leadership in Energy and Environmental Design (LEED) rating system.

LEED is an approach created by the US Green Building Council in 1998 that provides a way of thinking systemically and comprehensively about built space: how we can build in a way that minimizes our environmental footprint, is efficient both in the process and the outcome in terms of the consumption of nonrenewable energy sources, and effectively manages water runoff from snow and rain. All this is, of course, typically within the context of the urban location of the facility. (An isolated location that requires major commuting—when employees, for example, to do not have access to public transportation—gets a lower LEED rating.)

Some key elements of the rating system include these:

- Energy conservation—a key factor: quality of insulation, windows that minimize heat loss, roofing materials that are "green" in orientation, and minimal use of nonrenewable resources

- Water management: both the use of recycled water and how rain and snow and storm waters are used, including proximity to rivers subject to spring runoff; and minimal use of turf for gardens and lawns (that is, lower ratings when 60 percent or more of your property requires watering)

- Density: proximity to other buildings, accessibility to power lines, water and sewage lines, and size of footprint

- Quality of materials used: recycled, not imported from a different continent with high shipping costs, but also materials that in themselves are not just quality materials but materials that reflect a commitment to environmental integrity

The LEED rating is of primary significance in the development of—the design and siting—of a new building. But it can also be a helpful reference with an older building as the facility is renovated and upgraded to take account of building and design and facility use that reflects a commitment to the environment. While not the only factor in what it is that makes for an appropriate facility to house an institution, it is surely an essential consideration.

Beauty. Does beauty matter? Beauty actually is the sum total of what I have spoken to thus far—siting, structure, details, cladding, and a practicality and sustainability that has you feeling like this works—it is both beautiful and functional, reflecting the familiar line commonly attributed to William Morris, "Have nothing in your house that you do not know to be useful or believe to be beautiful."

In the design and use of our buildings, we seek durability, comfort, beauty, decorum, functionality, and economy. We seek buildings that reflect our intellectual and moral virtues—theological and personal convictions—reflecting mature moral and aesthetic perspectives.

Ideally, we are part of institutions that have a profound distaste for shoddy workmanship, for clutter, for kitsch.

Beauty is crucial to shaping institutional culture. Art can make such a huge difference that the real test of the importance of art is whether the art in our facilities fosters a hopeful realism. We can and must decry kitsch, nostalgia, prettiness, blandness, and sentimentality. We need art that acknowledges the deep fragmentation of our world, that captures human pathos and suffering and yet does so in a manner that fosters a capacity for hope even in the midst of the darkness.

Thus we reject nostalgia, whether this be a pseudo "main street" that harkens back to a small, 1950s American town, a Disneyesque escape from reality, or even a chapel design for a Christian university that bespeaks a kind of "old-time religion" that is not consistent with or engaged with current social and cultural challenges.

Remember that everything matters. Everything. Consider colors, textures, lighting, landscaping, sight lines, public art, architecture, and movement, both traffic (external) and people (internal). And the big three aspects that we can monitor all the time are surely these:

- The power of natural light: open spaces, and open blinds that bring in the light. I am struck by the bold statement from the authors of *A Pattern Language* when they write that "buildings which displace natural light as the major source of illumination are not fit places to spend the day."[16]

- The power of greenery: living plants and even indoor trees, but also the landscaping around the building(s) that is cared for

- The power of uncluttered space: respecting the need to avoid clutter with constant vigilance in both our shared spaces and our personal working office or work station. As stressed already, everything counts: nothing extraneous, nothing that distracts, nothing that does not foster the capacity of a space to be used for the purpose for which it is being used.

BUILDINGS THAT ARE CARED FOR:
LEARNING, MAINTAINING, ADAPTING

Buildings may initially strike us as relatively static and stable entities, but the more you live in, worship in, and work in a building, the more you realize that buildings are constantly being impacted, intentionally or unintentionally, by their environment, by the way that they are used and by the level of use. And thus buildings require constant attention to confirm and assure that they are indeed working effectively for the mission of the organization.

Buildings that learn. In her exquisite book *The Geometry of Love*, Margaret Visser considers a building, a church, not far from the ancient walls of Rome, Sant'Agnese fuori le Mura (St. Agnes Outside the Walls). It is a church that has been on that site for over 1360 years. Early on, the church was, obviously, outside the walls of the city of Rome, but now, with the growth of the suburbs over the last hundred years, it is very much in the city. What makes her book so interesting is not only that she considers the church in its present form and how it serves the parish community in which it is located, with its current liturgies and practices, but that she also reflects on how the church has evolved, adapted, grown, and now exists as a building that is very different from the original chapel that was built on that site to mark the grave of St. Agnes. As Visser puts it, "the church . . . has known many vicissitudes down the centuries. . . . It is a building that feels as if it has been on a very long journey out of the

---

[16]Alexander, Ishikawa, and Silverstein, *A Pattern Language*, 525.

past, has altered and suffered and gathered accretions, and now it is here with us, still bearing its cargo of memories and still carrying out the purpose for which it was built."[17]

Buildings learn; they are never really finished. There are new and unforeseen requirements, along with technological changes, changes of purpose, even changes in style or taste. Ideally, buildings are actually designed with growth and potential change in mind.

And here is where everyone in the institution needs to avoid any kind of propensity for nostalgia—for clinging to the form of the building that was perhaps ideal in a previous era. A downtown church might need to do a major renovation to accommodate more transition space between the street and the sanctuary. Another church might recognize the need for much more natural light and actually open up a wall that is more than a century old in order to accommodate this very commitment to make accessibility to natural light a stronger feature in the building.

And, of course, some buildings will go through a complete transformation. They may have been built for one purpose and are now repurposed for a new opportunity.

Perhaps we also need to acknowledge that a building may need to be abandoned. I think here of the Vancouver School of Theology that was for years housed in a magnificent building, fondly spoken of as "the castle." But with substantial changes in student enrollment patterns and the sheer cost of maintaining such a facility, the board and administration made a courageous move: they would sell the building and invest in a much smaller and more workable facility that would more than adequately meet their needs and better facilitate the fulfillment of their mission. They indulged in no nostalgia, no false loyalty to a building that just did not work. They did what they needed to do to get into a facility that served their mission.

Maintenance. As noted, maintenance is essential. As you move into and through a facility, ask yourself, is this facility well maintained? Are those who manage the facility attending to what is worn out, that which

---

[17]Margaret Visser, *The Geometry of Love: Space, Time, Mystery, and the Meaning of an Ordinary Church* (Toronto: HarperFlamingo Canada, 2001), 3-4. I am struck by the line Visser uses to describe the church, when she writes, "Sant'Agnese's is a building that is intentionally meaningful; it reveals itself most fully to people prepared to respond to its 'language.'" Ibid., 4. Her book is essentially a guide for learning how to read a church.

needs upgrading, areas that need to be repainted and that which needs to be replaced?

It is a sign of institutional health that renovations and maintenance are happening. All buildings wear out and require maintenance. Is this building cared for? Is the painting up to date? Are the ceiling panels stained? Are worn elements of the building replaced in a timely fashion? Is the carpet worn, stained, or odorous?

In other words, the mission of the organization requires constant attention to the facility in which it is housed.

INFORMATION TECHNOLOGY

The digital revolution has changed the way that we move through, live in, and experience built space. Everything that has been said so far about generative space—how we design our spaces, read those spaces, and live in them—now needs to include the reality of digital space.

A line frequently attributed to Franco Berardi makes this point: "The Internet is not a tool, it's an environment." And increasingly the Internet is changing the way that we conceive of space, in that the digitalization of our work changes our way that we engage the built space in which and from which our institutions operate and fulfill their missions.

The built space of an institution, in other words, includes—necessarily includes—institutional space on the world wide web (www). This means at the very least two things. It means that when we are in the physical and tangible space of walls and roof and staircases, we are connected—digitally—to innumerable other spaces. And then also, of course, we recognize that one of the most critical and vital spaces of an institution is its own presence on the web—its website.

And at the very least, the Internet connection and web presence of an institution needs to consider the following:

- connectivity: the capacity for a level of Internet connectedness that is consistent with what is needed for this institution to fulfill its mission, which might mean, for an institution with a wide level of national or global commitments, the capacity for video conferencing and other such high-demand Internet requirements

- hospitality: a website that is informative and easy to navigate
- community and conversation: an Internet capacity and web presence that fosters not just Internet connectivity but personal connections, so much so that those who are on the website feel—and that is the operative word, *feel*—that they are on campus and as present to the institution as if they had walked into the physical plan or facility of the church, school, or hospital

Effective institutions recognize the priority of an Internet presence and it is evident in their staffing; they empower those who have direct responsibility for the organization's digital connections. Their role is pivotal in fostering the capacity of the institution to be located online and thus to fulfill its mission. I observed above that the facility needs to do three things: it needs to foster hospitality, an intentional welcome, especially to a first time visitor; it needs to foster good conversation; and, of course, it needs to work. And a good information technology team knows how to do this—how to make your web presence hospitable and interactive, how to keep it working, and how to get it back to working when for whatever reasons it is down.

CONCLUSION

Over time, of course, we are not always making an overt read on the facilities in which we live, work, and worship. We are just there. But knowing how to read a building and a facility gives us a capacity to appreciate the building, know why it works well or, if it does not work so well, know why it does not and, hopefully, know what we can do to mitigate the limitations of the built space in which we are teaching, worshiping, or meeting with others.

STRATEGIC PARTNERSHIPS

The Synergy of Collaboration

One of my two sons has, with his wife, recently launched into the restaurant business. It was an educational experience to be near the operation during the weeks leading up to the grand opening and then see how they managed all the necessary connections that come with getting such a venture off the ground. I was impressed with many aspects of a business that I had only previously experienced from the table, where I had wondered what to choose off the menu. One thing in particular caught my attention: this little restaurant was not only a hive of activity on a busy evening when most if not all the tables were taken, but it was also a rather busy complex behind the scenes, with the remarkable number of businesses and agencies that were essential to the operation and the success of The Groove—Island Kitchen, as it is called.

You do not get the restaurant business if you do not get this, if you do not know two things. First, if this business is going to work, you need to know and work with the suppliers; the government agencies that give out business and liquor licenses; and business associations, such as the chamber of commerce. And second, you need to know how to work effectively with them. You will not maximize your potential if you try to be a stand-alone entity.

In like manner, every college, church, orchestra, and nonprofit agency is the hub—whether smaller or larger—of a network of agencies without which the mission of that organization will not happen. No agency, school, church, hospital, or art gallery can manage to fulfill its mission as an independent, autonomous, and self-sufficient entity. All institutions without exception are dependent entities, dependent on a whole range of businesses, agencies, and organizations. As often as not these are mutually dependent agencies. Therefore, effective organizations are intentionally linked on multiple levels to a whole host of other agencies, organizations, businesses, and church bodies and recognize and live with this as a key aspect of their missional capacity. They do not feel that they are self-sufficient, and they do not strive for self-sufficiency. Rather, they see these associations and alliances as an actual point of strength. Those with institutional intelligence get this and have learned to thrive in these diverse connections and partnerships. The central and basic point of this chapter is captured well in a line from the book *Forces for Good* where Leslie Crutch-field and Heather McLeod Grant write, "Great organizations work with and through other [organizations] to create more than they could ever achieve alone."[1]

Institutional effectiveness depends on such affiliations, on finding synergy particularly with agencies that have complementary strengths and missions. Institutional intelligence requires that those who give leadership at each level of the organization—including board members and faculty members of a college or university—appreciate that this web of associations and relationships and organizational connections are essential to the prospering of our institution and thus the fulfillment of our mission. But second, it also means that institutional intelligence includes knowing how to cultivate and work within these partnerships for the strengthening of their institutional capacity and fulfillment of their mission. And this is more than just learning how to work with others. As I will stress, this is a unique capacity: knowing how to work in bi-lateral connections and relationships, with agencies and organizations that have a different mission and different and distinct institutional culture. The end goal, of course, is to leverage the full potential of the organization to achieve its mission.

---

[1]Leslie Crutchfield and Heather McLeod Grant, *Forces for Good* (San Francisco: Jossey-Bass, 1998), 19.

FORMS OF AFFILIATION

It can be immensely helpful to put together a list of the agencies that are
or could be vital partners for your organization. Consider doing a taxonomy—putting down on paper a list of the agencies without which your
organization or church cannot fulfill its mission. This process does two
things. First, it profiles how critically important it is to have this network
of affiliations and partnerships—to help those within the organization see
and appreciate how deeply dependent this agency is on the good work of
other agencies. And second, the process will also highlight the gaps where
a partnership might be called for because it would strengthen your institutional capacity. An agency that works with the homeless, for example,
might recognize the need for partnerships with local businesses, with
government agencies, and with sister agencies in other cities. A business
faculty of a university might recognize their need to work more closely
with the local chamber of commerce. A publishing house will determine
that they are best off to contract out the final printing of their manuscripts
and that it behooves everyone in the organization to appreciate that this
partnership is rather critical to whether their publications see the light of
day. In the case of a denominational seminary, for example, it is simply
imperative that everyone on the faculty recognize, affirm, and even appreciate the vital connection of the seminary to the church with which it
is affiliated.

If no institution is self-sufficient, it is helpful to lay this out visually so
that it can be seen and felt and thus appreciated, so that this network of
affiliations and associations is adequately resourced in terms of financial
and time commitments, and so that these connections can be assessed—in
that they may not always be fruitful partnerships even though they are
consuming time and emotional energy. We need partnerships, but we also
need to be discerning and astute. Nothing is gained by a kind of sentimental idealism that leads to a huge investment of time in the name of
partnership when in actual fact neither agency gains from the connection
that is being nurtured.

Ask the mission question: What affiliations and partnerships are essential
for the fulfillment of our institutional mission? Which are in place? And

which need to be established or strengthened—meaning there might be gaps and thus a sign of a need for establishing a connection or partnership? Or which associations are missionally crucial and need to be strengthened and more effectively stewarded? And which, perhaps, are drawing more energy that is appropriate for purposes of our mission and institutional capacity?

As a side note, let me stress that there will often if not always be some institutional values that lead to an institutional partnership that might seem to have limited benefit—at least limited tangible benefit—but which as an organization you deem to be essential to your institutional identity and your core values. A congregation might invest substantially in ecumenical relations with other church bodies out of a deep commitment to the unity of the church. And they might not see, in that it might not be immediately evident, that there is a tangible benefit to the congregation. But they still do it; they work with others, in partnership for the sake of a common cause, because it represents a fundamental theological conviction. We do not judge every association by whether it feeds into our bottom line or as a church if it draws new members into our house. And yet, with a wide appreciation of what constitutes institutional mission, generally speaking each affiliation will bear a positive benefit for the institution as long as it is linked to mission and to our institutional core values.

So, do a taxonomy: What are the affiliations, strategic associations, allies, and partners that are essential to your institutional identity and to the fulfillment of your mission? It is helpful to think of affiliations and partnerships under the following categories.

Allies and coalitions. This is the category of affiliation that highlights the value of sister agencies wherein by working together, the linked agencies can leverage their shared institutional weight to achieve common cause or, of course, learn together how to fulfill their respective institutional missions more effectively.

University presidents invest considerable energy in meetings with fellow presidents—within particular jurisdictions—in making common cause with government officials. They meet with the leadership of sister institutions within their theological and denominational traditions where their meetings focus on common learning as they face similar challenges and opportunities.

And these kinds of connections are found throughout the university as the finance officer meets with colleagues from other universities or the athletic directors are off to a conference with other university varsity coaches to hone their skills, learning from each other and learning together. As a young pastor in my first congregational assignment, I came to recognize very early on that there was a significant network of mutual encouragement and support in the local ministerial association.

A denomination is, in many respects, a vehicle that fosters the capacity of an individual congregation to be part of something that a single congregation could not accomplish on its own. Denominational structures and agencies provide broader accountability, support, shared learning, and shared mission.[2]

Mission and social agencies will connect with and work with sister agencies who may have a different focus but which, together, can potentially mean the accomplishment of something that no one agency could have done on its own. When I was part of a broad discussion about the potential of a new theological college in Hanoi, Vietnam, I was amazed at how so many distinct agencies and associations were involved—church groups, mission groups, funding agencies, and government lobbying groups, each bringing a distinct expertise to the table so that, as noted, through common cause something noteworthy could be accomplished.

Feeder and placement agencies. Academic institutions in particular but other agencies as well have a key network of associations that provide them with either primary beneficiaries—customers—or staff, or alternatively, placement for those who move on, such as graduates. Universities and colleges look to high schools, for example, and seminaries look to local congregations for the necessary linkages that would encourage potential students to enroll. A university in many respects is a hand-to-mouth institution: they only live as others feed them students, and so they very intentionally nurture the relationship with feeder agencies that send those students.

[2]Independent churches may feel they have more latitude on theological and policy matters, but they miss out on the tremendous opportunity to be part of a network of congregations who together support a theological seminary or university and together engage in both local and global ministry. Churches have exponentially more impact when they are part of something—a denomination—that allows them to partner with other congregations in common cause.

But then also, again for the university or the seminary, these institutions form and educate students to a particular end. Some will be going on to graduate studies, and each department of the university will often have a network of connections with potential postgraduate institutions—connections that help smooth the path for graduates who would like to pursue further studies. Seminaries, of course, need to have a strong connection with church and denominational bodies so that their students can make the transition from their studies into ministry assignments. Professional schools—in business or education, for example—typically have a whole range of associations that are in place to smooth the way for their students to find employment. Thus a faculty of education will very intentionally cultivate its connections with the board of education in its region and with teacher associations so that their programs are strengthened but also with the end in view: their students will find placements.

But then also, nonprofit agencies need new and talented staff. Thus they cultivate links to colleges and universities where they provide field experiences for students who one day will be potential staff members. They mark up their calendars with the dates of the hiring fairs at local college and university campus, and they make sure they have a location for their display table. They need qualified staff and so they build the link with the source of those staff.

Service agencies. The larger the institution, the more dependent it is on a whole range of businesses and agencies to meet an essential need. Suppliers, service providers, and support agencies meet particular institutional needs. A university might have a contract with a major food company to manage its cafeteria. Virtually every nonprofit organization will have an accounting firm that does their annual audit. And others will link up with training agencies to develop a particular expertise for their staff. This category might also include funding agencies—foundations to which the institution can make application for project grants.

Consider also the link between universities and service organizations that provide internships, practicums, or co-op opportunities, agencies that provide the field work counterpart vital to academic programs that recognize the critical place of the field experience in the degree program.

Certification, authentication, and convening agencies. Finally, we also need to speak of those agencies and affiliations that in some form or another certify the legitimacy of the work the organization is doing. As often as not, these are also the agencies that provide a measure of institutional accountability. An obvious example of this for academic institutions is the agency or agencies that accredit the degree programs being offered. But denominations function in this capacity as well as those already mentioned, in that they, in effect, certify that such-and-such a congregation is truly "Lutheran" if the congregation purports to worship and do ministry and mission within that tradition. They also function as a means of certifying the qualifications and capacities of prospective ministerial candidates.

Then there are also those agencies that it would be appropriate to speak of as having the authority and capacity to convene. In some cases, denominational and accrediting bodies perform this function as well but here I am thinking of, for example, the Council for Christian Colleges and Universities, which does not accredit but which does have the power to convene and to work with the presidents, for example, of Christian universities and colleges and address matters of shared social, ethical, or academic concern. (The CCCU is also a service agency, in that it provides, for example, a New Presidents Institute for new CEOs of the member universities and colleges, and it also provides study tour options for students within the member institutions. But here I primarily highlight the CCCU as a convening agency.)

Do a taxonomy. Create a visual—perhaps on a large white board—indicating the whole range of associations that the institution currently has in place, and then ask the key and pertinent questions of what you see in that taxonomy.

What is missing? As you consider your mission and your strategic objectives, what key association, partnership, or affiliation is either essential to your mission—or potentially significant, but not as yet in place?

What strategic association needs to be strengthened? A theological seminary might recognize that its affiliation with a particular church or denominational body is vitally important but is either neglected or at least not receiving the attention the association deserves.

What affiliation or partnership might be initiated to address a complex problem creatively? Perhaps you are fulfilling your mission, but a particular association might open up new possibilities for innovation. Thus, for example, the University of Guelph (Ontario) and Humber College have a fascinating joint program in place that enables students to get an undergraduate liberal arts degree but also become certified in a trade. Two institutions with complementary missions enter into a partnership that respects their distinctive mission but also expands the possibilities for each organization as they play into and leverage the strengths and capacities of the other agency.

But then, of course, all of this presumes that institutional intelligence includes the capacity to work inter-institutionally.

CAPACITIES FOR WORKING PARTNERSHIPS

Since these kinds of partnerships are so critical to mission effectiveness it follows that institutional intelligence includes the capacity to work with other agencies in a way that effectively leverages institutional potential.

And yet this crucial capacity does not come easily. Working with other agencies can be thoroughly rewarding, and there is no doubt that institutions need to and do recognize that they are more effective and can exponentially leverage their impact through strategic affiliations. But these affiliations can also be challenging. Indeed, some of the greatest frustrations and headaches for those who work in institutions will come because we believe in these partnerships but find them to be so difficult to manage. And often it is the case that the more critical the affiliation and the potential through the connection with another agency, the more emotionally and intellectually taxing it can be.

There is no doubt that as soon as two institutions come into a form of intentional association, they run up against not only a different mission, but also diversity of history, governance structures, and the 101 assumptions that come with a different institutional culture.

But we stay at it and persist and attend to and develop the capacity to work with other agencies for the simple reason that they are not only necessary but have such potential, for both or all parties, to be a significant factor in missional accomplishment.

It is helpful to think of a set of capacities that are essential for this dimension of institutional intelligence.

Mission clarity. First, an institution needs to be very clear about its own mission. We can only be in partnership with others if we are settled on our own identity, mission, and institutional purpose. Institutional partnerships assume the capacity for missional thinking.

This ability to think clearly about one's own mission incorporates two things. It means that the institution knows what it is trying to accomplish and needs to accomplish; there is clarity about the outcomes for which the agency was created in the first place. There can only be effective synergy if both agencies in a partnership are clear on what they bring to the table in terms of institutional capacity and purpose.

But also, this kind of missional thinking also means a certain humility regarding one's own institutional structures—the institutional identity in its own right. What matters, ironically, is not the institution but the mission. You care more about the outcome that is captured by your institutional purpose than you care about your own institutional identity and brand.

As a denomination, perhaps, you choose to support the work of another denomination that is establishing a congregation in a new city suburb. You conclude that it is the outcome that matters, not whether the new congregation is Lutheran or Baptist or Pentecostal. What counts is a Christian presence in that particular neighborhood.

As a college, you choose to actively pursue a merger with another college for the simple reason that you can accomplish much more together than you can accomplish individually. In the end, it is the mission that matters— by which we mean the specific outcomes that matter to our institutional identity—rather than a false kind of loyalty to the current expression of institutional identity.

The effective partnership or affiliation means that you are able to respond to the following question: How is our mission enhanced or fulfilled by partnership with this sister agency or business? Without any apology, we can be utilitarian: we are in this for a win-win outcome for both agencies; there is a tangible benefit or outcome as the fruit of this partnership. The partnership must foster and not compromise mission. It needs to lead to clear outcomes that are clearly linked to institutional purpose.

Mutual respect. Second, institutional intelligence, when it comes to affiliations and partnerships, requires a fundamental respect for the mission, the governance structures, and the brand of the other agency.

We only work effectively with others if and as we have clarity about their mission—the mission of the agency with which we are in partnership—not just our own. And we have an appreciation of the legitimate requirements of the sister agency. But more, it means respecting the other agency—including an agency that might actually be a competitor for funds or, for a university or seminary, for students. In other words, we attend to and appreciate the mission of the sister agency: we recognize their position within the world of nonprofits and to the degree that we are able, understand what it is that the other agency is being called to be and do. We respect and appreciate the other on their own terms. And we necessarily view a potential partnership as a means by which both agencies are the stronger for the arrangement.

And this also means that we respect not only the mission but also the institutional integrity, including the governance structures of the other agency. Thus, for example, as a president my primary point of connection with another agency would be through the chief executive officer. If we are representing our own institution in some negotiations, then we do so through the proper channels and in full respect for those systems of governance and administration of the potential partner agency.

This necessarily requires that we attend to any potential conflict of interest; one cannot sit on both sides of the negotiating table—literally or figuratively—when a partnership is being negotiated and managed. And on this score, see the section in appendix A on conflict of interest, which stresses that in this regard, optics and perception matter.

All of this also means that we consistently attend to the ways in which our work, within our organization, might affect the quality of the relationship we have with an affiliate agency. I think of the faculty member who says that he teaches New Testament Greek and when controversial questions arise, perhaps even a reading of the text that might challenge the denominational policies and practice of the sponsoring church of the seminary where he teaches, he states that he simply "lets the chips fall where they may." The seminary needs to sustain a commitment to its own academic processes, of course. But still, certainly we can ask that faculty teach with a regard for and even a respect for the church constituencies that the seminary serves and an appreciation of the potential fallout of what is being taught in the class.

When a faculty member of a Christian university is teaching a course on human sexuality, it behooves the faculty member to appreciate that the students in the course come from and may be going back to the church communities that actually send students to this university and may well support it financially. Again, this does not mean that we do not address controversial matters or that we do not provide students with alternative perspectives on the issues being discussed in class. But it does mean that we sustain a respect for a key partner—in this case a church constituency— a partner that is essential in the fulfillment of our institutional mission.

Mutual contributions. Third, if you receive, then it only makes sense that you also give in return. If you have a benefit from the partnership, then find ways to contribute back into the partnership.

Thus, for example, I have been either the dean or the president of three different theological schools accredited with the Association of Theological Schools in the United States and Canada (ATS). With each institution, it was a basic assumption that the ATS added value for us, and so we offered something back—by way of committee involvements or by participation in visiting teams for the accreditation process. We receive and so we give; we get benefit, and so we contribute for the benefit of the greater whole.

When we had a group of denominations working in Ho Chi Minh City on what it would take for us to work together, even if it would mean more than one theological school, it was simply inappropriate for one denomination to come along to see what was emerging with no intention to genuinely contribute to the common causes and the shared partnership that was emerging. Well, it was fine to come to test the waters. But what became clear was that one member of the group was actually not really testing the waters. He was not genuinely interested in partnership. On the contrary, those with institutional intelligence choose not to be parasites. Or consider the example of a newly established seminary that persuades their accrediting association that they do not need to invest in a theological library because their students can use the libraries of other seminaries in the same city. That is fine, but only if they have a formal agreement with those other seminaries and, of course, if they contribute to the rather substantial expense of sustaining a good library. In other words, be a true partner: you receive, but you also contribute.

And perhaps here it would also be worth saying that we should view our partnerships as a point of strength and that we therefore actually profile our partnerships, say "thank you" and affirm our appreciation for the value that comes through the partnership. Here I am reminded of the theological college that I visited in Mostar, Bosnia and Herzegovina. It was a joint venture—a partnership between three different mission and church groups. And it was an effective program. But it was curious to learn later that while two of the groups made it clear in their own communications that they were involved in this joint effort, one of the three made it sound like, in their communications, they were the sole participant. An opportunity was lost for them not only to acknowledge the partnership but actually to celebrate it.

Healthy and vital institutions have strategic partnerships that allow them to accomplish so much more than they could on their own. This fact is not some kind of diminishment of the significance of our work or our mission. Rather, as a matter of institutional integrity, we can profile and celebrate the ways in which our work happens in a synergy partnership with others. We view our partnerships as a form of institutional strength, not weakness. Thus if an agency is at work in a country or region, or a city neighborhood, we should be able to ask the agency how they are partnering with others toward common goals and objectives.

Imagine that you are a donor, supporting the cause of an organization that is working toward the elimination of poverty in a community or a region. And it is completely appropriate if not essential that as a supporter you ask if this agency is in strategic partnership with other agencies so that together they are more effective.

But, more than anything else, institutional intelligence—when it comes to strategic alliances—is evident in this: you know, and your institution knows, that partnerships and alliances are essential to fulfilling your mission. You steward your resources and leverage your capacity, in coordination with another agency, to achieve a greater end. It means you believe this

and you will invest time and energy to make it happen. You will invest in
the partnership on the assumption that it matters. Anyone who works with
you will know that you see yourself as committed not so much to your
own institution as to the mission and that the mission means working with
other agencies in common cause.

When all is said and done, I have stressed the need for institutional
capacities, but something should be made clear: it is not ultimately institutions that make this happen, but people within the institution. Kent John
Chabotar—writing about academic institutions, but in a way that applies
to all—makes the following cogent observation:

> Institutions are not proactive, competition-oriented, and so on. People
> are. An alliance needs a "champion" who is willing to inspire others
> to approve and then push the implementation. If not the president or
> chancellor, the champion needs "air cover" from top officials to in-
> spire others to get onboard and provide [sic] the champion from ad-
> verse consequences from the alliance's opponents.[3]

Presidents need to believe in and model what it means to foster strategic
associations. Nonprofits need boards that fully support the cultivation of
the alliances and partnerships. But, as much as anything, dynamic institutions have individuals in all sectors of leadership—faculty leaders, program
heads, departmental team leaders—who are looking for ways by which
their work and the particular work of their department could be strengthened
through collaboration with an external agency. And thus, ultimately, two
things are needed.

First, as Chabotar suggests, it is not so much institutions that make this
happen, but people—strategically placed individuals who have this resolve
and capacity to forge these partnerships. It is people who have the institutional intelligence—meaning, with reference to the above three points,
it is people who (1) have a clear understanding of the mission of their
own organization; (2) have a deep respect for the mission and institutional

---

[3]Michael K. Thomas, with commentary provided by Kent John Chabotar, "Between Collaboration and Merger: Expanding Alliance Strategies in Higher Education," TIAA-CREF Institute,
November 2015, www.tiaainstitute.org/public/pdf/between_collaboration_and_merger.pdf.

integrity of the other agency; and (3) know how to give and contribute and not merely receive.

And second, institutions that foster effective partnerships have not only champions but specifically champions who receive the support and encouragement from the CEO. Chabotar speaks of "air cover." We might also use the image from American football: the president runs interference for those within the institution who are fostering and developing these associations. A president can insist that associations, partnerships, and affiliations will be part of the institutional culture: this will be one of the institutional strengths of this organization and people at all levels of leadership within the organization will be given support to foster partnerships, affiliations, and alliances with other agencies.

Here's a word to the wise, which I say as a university president: don't get into a partnership with another agency without keeping your president informed all along the way! A running back knows he will not get far down the field without good blocking; he does not run ahead of those who are running interference for him. Similarly, at each stage of the partnership formation process, keep the president informed and be sure that you have the support of the president. Having said that, wise presidents will take risks, will encourage champions to explore possibilities, will give credit where credit is due when a strategic alliance is formed, and will—as needed, as Chabotar observes—help fend off opponents, naysayers, or sceptics who so easily undermine creative initiatives.

MERGERS AND JOINT VENTURES

Sometimes two agencies in a similar industry conclude that the best way forward is not to merely partner to a common end or objective but to actually merge resources and infrastructure.

Why merge? This can be very complicated, but when all is said and done, it comes down to these two reasons. First, agencies merge because the two agencies—two churches, two colleges, two nonprofits, two publishing houses—recognize they can achieve exponentially more by consolidating their resources.

The second reason is viability. One or both or more agencies conclude that they are no longer financially viable and thus sustainable without a formal association with another sister agency. I have served as the president of a university that is the merger of two colleges. While one of those might have been able to have a modicum of success on its own, the other was without doubt facing the very real prospect of having to close its doors. Together they created not only a more viable institution but a university that is significantly stronger—in terms of missional impact—than if either of the two had remained independent, autonomous colleges.

Thus a college with diminishing student enrollment, for example, will explore the possibility of a joint operation with another college—to join and leverage resources and increase the potential for missional impact. Two congregations in a neighborhood will choose to join forces and assets to strengthen substantially their witness within that part of the city.

Others might not choose to merge but rather, for many of the same reasons, choose instead to establish a joint venture—by which a new entity is created that, in effect, is a merger of their resources for a particular objective: two development agencies will function as, in effect, one agency when it comes to an on-the-ground response to a particular crisis.

Institutional thinking—intelligence—at such a point is so very vital and critical. We can so easily develop a kind of false loyalty to the agency as it has always been or to our own brand. The genius of effective organizational thinking is that we always come back to the bottom line: the outcome is what matters. What we want is impact. What we are seeking is that the mission would happen. And so we actively look for ways to leverage our institutional assets with those of another agency to achieve a common objective. This does not for a moment mean that bigger is better; it is often the case that a smaller congregation has a greater impact, in part due to their smaller size—with a more intense and community dynamic. But still, two smaller churches might determine that together they would be able to have a greater impact than if they were one larger congregation.

But when finances make one or both parties no longer viable, then being proactive is the wise course of action. When a college has dropping enrollment and little hope of a viable student body, then it makes sense to explore merger or joint venture options sooner rather than later. When two institutions can share institutional infrastructure, it frees up resources that can be leveraged for the mission of the joint venture.

One of the premier examples of that kind of merger is surely Liverpool Hope University on the outskirts of Liverpool, England. Two colleges established in the nineteenth century—Warrington Training College (Anglican) and Our Lady's Training College (Catholic)—formed an ecumenical federation in 2005 with the blessing of their respective bishops, Archbishop Derek Worlock and Bishop David Shepperd, to found what is now one of the premier private universities in the United Kingdom. This is a classic example of an institution of extraordinary profile and missional strength coming through the leveraging of institutional resources. They are, as their motto states, "better together" thanks to the vision of many and to the blessing of the two bishops. They created something together that has exponentially more mission impact than anything either institution could have done alone.

Institutional thinking always comes back to missional impact and potential. The same is true, for example, of two Anglican parishes in the diocese of Vancouver Island. The bishop, after extended study, concluded that two congregations were no longer viable as stand-alone church communities. They could no longer, given their small size, sustain the cost of supporting the clergy and caring for the repairs on their aging church buildings, let alone find ways to expand their missional impact in their communities. Congregational members were upset and protested vigorously, insisting that they had been faithful members all these years. They wondered how the bishop could act in such a cavalier way against their dear parish. But the bishop was approaching this very thoughtfully and carefully; they were being nostalgic and sentimental. The right thing, missionally, was for two congregations to join forces: sell one of the two buildings to fund the repairs and upgrades to the other building and then leverage their joint efforts and institutional resources to not just survive but actually have an impact in their community.

When a joint effort is made—either through a merger or a joint venture—five key questions need to be asked:

- What is driving this potential merger? What is the motivation that is informing the conversation and the potential outcome? If two agencies are involved, the motivation might be different for each, but this should be clear: we are up front and open about what is motivating us to enter into these negotiations.

- What is the mission of each institution and how can we lay out the implications for mission in the merger? How will the mission change or be re-framed to accommodate the way in which the two agencies leverage their resources?

- Is there a high level of trust, especially between the leaders? If we have the trust, good; if not, then find a way to talk about this and cultivate trust, maybe through extended conversations or meals together, to find the mutual trust essential for negotiating a merger.

- What sunset clauses should be instituted or included in the proposed merger plan from the very beginning? Stage the merger, in other words. It is possible that for the first year or two years of the merger we might put elements in place that are only meant to be temporary? For example, the board of the new entity might be a merger of both boards, even though all parties recognize that the result is a board that is likely larger than ideal—too large to be effective in the long run. They accept this limitation, for the time being, with a view that in time a smaller board will emerge.

- What form of governance will be required for the new merger and who is best suited, whatever the reasons, to fill the key leadership positions in the new entity?

These can all be complicated and politically messy questions. And in some cases, it is difficult for those caught up on the merger negotiations to address the issues openly and constructively, even if they have the very best of intentions. And so another question, a sixth question, is whether the parties would be advised to bring in an external consultant and advisor to be part of process and be close enough to the process to help the parties address these very questions.

CONCLUSION

In conclusion, I need to be explicit about something to which I have alluded thus far in this chapter. Partnerships, affiliations, and joint ventures are all so very important and essential for an effective organization, but they are also labor intensive and, in many cases, emotionally draining. And at some point an institution might well decide that the engagement in the connection or association is no longer worth the investment of the time and energy and financial resources.

There is always sadness when it simply does not work and when a parting of ways is required. And yet there is no reason to sentimentalize these partnerships and associations. If they work, good! But if, even with our best efforts, the connection is not fruitful, then the wise course of action is to part ways in a way that is amicable and, as much as possible, mutually affirming. Parting ways can be done with goodwill, without recrimination but merely a gracious acknowledgment that the partnership is not bearing the fruit needed to justify what is being invested in the effort—no sentimentality, no idealism, no guilt. We gave it our best shot, and with goodwill all around, we move on.

But when they do work—when there is an affiliation or partnership that is truly win-win—collaborative partnerships are one of the most satisfying dimensions of organizational life that we will experience in the good work we do in fostering organizational effectiveness.

CONCLUSION

Institutions matter, and some essential building blocks—elements—for crafting and attending to our institutions will increase an organization's capacity to fulfill its mission. What we long for is institutions that work and that we, as individuals who work within them, would have the institutional intelligence to know how to make a substantive contribution to those institutions of which we are a part.

In response to all of this, I propose that effective institutions do two things. First, they identify their point of we might call "operational drag." And second, they provide an adequate orientation for those who work with and support the institution—an orientation to how these critical building blocks are essential to organizational effectiveness.

IDENTIFYING OPERATIONAL DRAG

Regarding institutions, none of them are perfect, of course. We are always in building and development mode, assessing and attending to how the institution of which we are a part could be more effective—more able to fulfill its mission. And one helpful way to look at an institution is to ask, if there were one thing that was keeping this organization from its potential, what would it be? Sure, most if not all of us are part of organizations where we can think of 101 things that need improvement, adjustment, or substantial change.

But consider this. Could it be that within your organization there is one critical point of constraint or operational drag, something that is weighing or limiting your potential and impeding your capacity to address other problems and opportunities? If, when all is said and done, you actually only have one problem, what would it be? Using the seven elements of an effective organization as a check list, perhaps, ask what is missing or what needs attention or revision or, perhaps, radical change— that one thing that must be addressed if the organization is to make significant progress and development.[1]

Is the operational drag missional clarity—the need, as an organization, to do the due diligence of identifying institutional identity and purpose?

Or is it the lack of governance systems, so that what impedes the organization is the lack of clear terms of reference for the trustees, the executive leadership, and the role of others in the organization? Is governance the issue, where in effect the institution lacks a shared understanding of the role of the board, the role of the senior leadership team, and a culture that allows for and encourages decisions to be made and actions taken for the sake of the institution? Or is there operational drag because people and systems just simply do not work so that problems are addressed and opportunities are embraced in a timely way?

Does the organization have the right people in place—on the board, especially in the role of board chair? In the senior leadership team? And do you have an approach to personnel issues that is attentive to best practices—in hiring the right people, developing their capacity, and, as needed, transitioning those people out who are no longer effective? Does the organization have the capacity to hire well—people of intelligence and ability who are committed to the mission? And does the organization give evidence of the courage and capacity to let people go, graciously and generously but firmly, when this is called for?

Is there an organizational culture that is marked by a hopeful realism— including the capacity to name and address the complex and perhaps difficult situation in which the organization finds itself—but in a way that is creative, innovative, and open to possibilities?

---

[1]The Theory of Constraints (TOC) is a perspective introduced to management theory by Eliyahu M. Goldratt. See Eliyahu M. Goldratt and Jeff Cox, *The Goal: A Process of Ongoing Improvement* (Great Barrington, MA: North River Press, 2004). Goldratt observes, using the metaphor that the chain is only as strong as its weakest link, that there are many constraints but as often as not, one key constraint limits the capacity of the organization to achieve its institutional purpose.

Or is the operational drag found around the lack of adequate resources, or perhaps some aspect of the financial situation? Finances are likely always an issue, and it is easy to say things like "we would have few problems if we simply had more money." But it is not as simple as that. It is possible to have limited finances and to have a flourishing organization. Rather, when it comes to money, ask more specifically if there is some aspect of the financial picture that is creating significant institutional constraint. For some institutions, it is the lack of clarity about their economic engine, or perhaps their over-dependence on one stream of revenue. For others, it will simply be that they are carrying too much debt and much too much of their financial operations are tied up in servicing the debt.

Then also, is it possible that the greatest problem is the lack of adequate facilities, and perhaps website "facilities," to house the organization?

Or the major limitation—the operational drag—could be that the agency or institution lacks the essential and critical partnerships and alliances that are essential to their capacity to fulfill their mission.

Find this. Name the operational drag. Of all the problems and challenges the organization is facing, which is keeping you—more than anything else that is a limitation or a vulnerability—from achieving your organizational effectiveness? And then, of course, it follows that everyone needs to get with the program; that is, this point of constraint will be the focus of institutional energy and creativity. It may be hard work, but if what is causing operational drag is addressed—despite the investment of political and social capacity—the outcome is more than worth the pain; it will be a breakthrough moment for the organization.

For most organizations, the problem that keeps them from flourishing is likely—not always, for sure, but this is the most common constraint—a system of governance and a lack of clear and transparent systems for making decisions and then implementing those decisions. Struggling institutions typically lack good structures or they do not follow them; and, as often as not, there is a minority of individuals who are themselves the operational drag, keeping the organization from its potential. And the only hope is to, quite literally, break the hold that they have on the organization.

But also, there is only one way to address and respond to operational drag, and that is effective institutional leadership. Organizations will not flourish, they will not be effective, without adequate—qualified and capable—leadership. The only hope is an effective board of trustees with a board chair who knows how to moderate the board discussion, fend off inappropriate external influences or internal minority voices and come to a common mind. And the only hope is senior leadership who can partner with the board to address the fundamental challenges and opportunities that present themselves to the organization.

AN ORIENTATION FOR THE NEWLY APPOINTED

Finally, the following needs to be stressed: we need to foster institutional intelligence within the organization by providing an adequate orientation to the organization for new members of the board and newly appointed staff members.

What is the mission? Everyone is working toward the mission, regardless of their particular role. And this means not only knowing the history of the organization but getting a read on where it could be in the years to come. If you are a board member, you are asking, what might this institution look like in five years? How will the mission of this institution find concrete expression in the upcoming years? If you are a department head or director, you are always in conversation with others: What is our mission and what are we doing to foster the fulfillment of that mission?

What is the governance structure and where are key decisions, including the budget, made and how are these decisions made? And what is the role of the newly appointed board or staff person? If you are on the board, then understand what it means to be a board member: know both the limits and the responsibilities of serving on a board. If you are a member of faculty of a college, then get a good read on how institutional governance works and how faculty governance works in your organization. If you are a director or department head, you know where your role fits within the whole. In conversation with others, particularly with those to whom you report, have a clear understanding of what it is that you need to do so that the mission of the organization is happening.

What are the personnel policies of this organization? How do they work and how do they foster personal and institutional effectiveness? And with this, what is the vision that the organization has for its institutional culture so that each person can be aware of and attentive to the critical and essential ways by which a vibrant institutional culture is being nurtured? And with this, we can also talk about the challenges, from our past, that might as yet shape the current institutional culture. We name the past as part of keeping the negative from our past from unduly informing our present.

How do finances work in this institution? What is the economic engine, and what are the other essential streams of revenue that make it possible for the mission to be fulfilled?

And finally, take a walk. Tour the facilities with the newly appointed board member or staff person. Talk frankly about what the facilities mean and how they foster institutional mission and where there are limits, challenges, or potential elements of the facility that impede the capacity of the organization to fulfill its mission.

Everything is done with this in mind: for each person who is part of our organization, we are going to encourage and foster and stress that institutional intelligence is a good thing. It matters that we think about our institutions, and we invest time and energy in understanding how they work and how we can work effectively in them and through them.

Is all of this worth it—given the stress and pain and politics and setbacks that are part of institutional life and work? Well, some days will no doubt be filled with frustration that makes us wonder if it is worth the time and effort. But the principle remains: we invest in institutions because with them and in partnership with others as colleagues in these institutions, we can make a substantially greater contribution to the things that matter to us than we could ever possibly do on our own.

BOARDS AND PRESIDENTS

What becomes clear sooner or later is that if we have healthy organizations nothing—quite literally nothing—is as crucial as the working relationship between the board and the executive, between the trustees of the mission and the president or the executive director.

In what follows, I am making the following critical assumption: the two are distinct, and the board needs to be the board and the president (or the equivalent—the executive director or the senior pastor of a church) needs to be the president. Since both roles are critical to institutional health, then it is vital that the two be not only distinct but in dynamic counterpoint for the effective exercise of wisdom and power and the fulfillment of the mission. This means, as noted in the chapter on governance, that the president is located in the executive side of shared governance and that the board is composed of those who represent the various external constituencies of the organization.

The usual and so very helpful rule of thumb is this: boards govern; presidents and senior executives manage. Boards lead, for sure, but they lead through a practice of governance that in turn empowers and supports the need for the senior executive, notably the president or senior pastor of a church, to actually lead. The distinction between governance and management is crucial. It is not absolute, and we do not need to be inflexible or legalistic on this point. There will be times and situations where the board, through the chair, perhaps, will step in and play a managing role. But this should be the exception, perhaps only in a time of institutional crisis. Thus as a rule, boards don't manage; they govern.

The boards have simple but clear responsibilities:

- Boards confirm the mission and ensure that the institution is on mission and on mission in a way that reinforces the institutional core values.

- Boards appoint a president who will—on behalf of the board and in accountability to the board—implement the mission, and then, in turn, support, encourage, advise, and assure that the mission happens; the board also set the limits and performance standards for the president.

- Boards assure the various constituencies that the institution is financially viable and resilient.

The added value of a board is precisely that it doesn't manage but rather steps back and provides the thirty-thousand-foot view, reflecting the insight and perspective of diverse constituencies and stakeholders, confirming together, collectively, that the institution is on mission and that the president is effective in providing leadership for the institution.

No one has made this point more emphatically and pressed for this in our nonprofit institutions as much as John Carver, who through many publications has beat this drum, insisting that this distinction between the board and the senior executive is one of the keys—if not *the* key—to effective organizations. He insists that boards govern by establishing the policies that will guide the administration in delivering the mission. And then they step back and allow the executive leadership to do what they have been appointed to do.[1]

If the board holds a president responsible for the fulfillment of the mission, then it follows that the person in this role needs to be empowered to do what needs to be done so that the mission happens. I am not suggesting that power is then concentrated in the office of the president. Rather we must insist that the organization needs both the power of

---

[1]See John Carver and Miriam Carver, "Carver's Policy Governance® Model in Nonprofit Organizations," http://policygovernance.com/pg-np.htm, accessed November 17, 2016.

trusteeship and the power of the executive, and both need to be expressed in dynamic tension—a healthy tension—with each other.

Carver presses this point and even suggests that the board give away as much authority as possible to the senior executive without, of course, jeopardizing their own responsibilities as the trustees of the organization.[2]

But all of this only works if a foundational working principle and practice is sustained and affirmed again and again: the board speaks as one. If the board is a board of fifteen, the president is not responsible to fifteen people; he does not have fifteen people who think of themselves as the president's boss. An individual member of the board only has power and influence, only has voice, as a participant in the work of the board and in seeking with colleagues on the board to come to a common voice, a common conviction on the issues that properly come to the board. And a wise president recognizes that the strength of the board comes in its common voice and thus a wise president does not lobby or even appeal to individual board members on the issues on which the board must act or speak. Rather, wise presidents work intentionally with the board chair in the cultivation of this common voice. And further, presidents invest considerable energy in board development—fostering the capacity of the board to be an effective board. Wheeler and Ouellette state it well when they write,

> Executives who hope that their most meaningful accomplishments will have benefits for the school beyond their tenure can best realize this goal by keeping governors at the center of the decision-making process. In so doing chief executives capacitate those who govern to "keep the flame" from one era of presidential leadership to the next.[3]

But then also, boards are only effective if they truly hold the executive leadership accountable and where they are prepared to intervene—hopefully rarely—if the institution is floundering. It is not an overstatement to observe that when an organization is ineffective, it all comes back to the board: their willingness to not be unduly loyal to the executive, but to act,

---

[2]Ibid.

[3]Barbara G. Wheeler and Helen Ouellette, *Governance That Works: Effective Leadership for Theological Schools* (New York: Auburn Theological Seminary, March 2015), 35.

collectively and courageously, out of a prior commitment to the health of the organization.

With all of this in mind, then, here are some "best practices" for board and executive governance.

THE INTEGRITY OF THE BOARD

Boards, to be effective, have to have sufficient authority to do their work without undue interference from external bodies. And it needs to be clear that the president reports to the board. Thus external agencies—perhaps church bodies for a Christian university—only truly support the institution when they respect the work of the board and the necessity that the president recognize only one ultimate accountability, the board of the institution. Similarly with a church pastor, in the end, the accountability is to the board and not to individual congregational members.[4]

THE COMPOSITION AND SIZE OF THE BOARD

Effective boards are built for leveraging wisdom. And this means a number of things when it comes to board composition. First, boards are ideally marked by diversity—diversity of competence, gender, age, and ethnicity, which brings diversity of perspective. Second, term limits for the board—for members and for the board chair—are essential if the board is going to grow and learn and bring in new perspective for new challenges. A good rule of thumb is a maximum of eight years, though a term limit of six years would be more than adequate, with arrangements for overlapping terms so that there is continuity and discontinuity in board transitions.[5]

---

[4]I realize that there are some churches where the denominational polity insists that each congregational member has some measure of authority and that the pastor is responsible to the congregation as a whole. While an ideal, of course, this is simply not practical—either in terms of implementation or when it comes to the psychological health of the pastor! Thus, any such polity needs to affirm that the voice of the congregation is expressed through the elders and that the pastor has a vehicle for genuine accountability in the elder board or church council.

[5]To stress this point, term limits—limited tenure—is imperative. It is not an overstatement to say that long-term board effectiveness is only possible with limited tenure and term limits. The only hope for a board to have new wisdom and insight into new challenges is by bringing new members on to the board. In other words, there is a shelf life to board member effectiveness. Stay on a board for six or eight years, make a contribution, invest time and energy in service on the board, and then step down graciously and pass on the baton to another who will invest in a similar manner and bring different strengths and perspectives to the challenges the organization is facing.

These two crucial points assume a third, that the board takes primary responsibility in recruiting board members to fulfill this very agenda. And it is my observation that this does not happen unless the president takes the lead—working with a nominations committee to assure that the board is as diverse as appropriate for the purposes of the institution.

Finally, on this point, it is easy to make the case that smaller boards are more effective boards. They are able to come to trust in each other and hold each other accountable more effectively. Just as crucially, they are more likely to be able to speak with one voice—particularly when it comes to a difficult decision (such as transitioning the president, which is exponentially more difficult the larger the board). How big? I advise definitely no larger than fifteen, but twelve works, and less than twelve is even better. If you have eleven or fewer you will find that every member of the board is invested in the process; you avoid the problem of fence-sitters, observers, or those who take up space but find it difficult, in a larger group, to genuinely contribute.

BOARDS AND ORGANIZATIONAL SUPPORT

What lies behind this observation is a key principle or two: board members are not just observers and not just critics but are also personally invested. Further, it is difficult for the development team to appeal to a broad constituency for financial support if the board members themselves are not invested in the financial well-being of the institution. They have skin in the game. Effective boards are giving boards.

THE AGENDA FOR THE BOARD MEETING

The agenda for a typical board meeting should, then, reflect the role of the board in governance. They are not debating or making decisions about matters that should be on the desk of the president—or, in a university, on the agenda of the faculty meeting or academic council. They are not managing; they are governing. And this should be patently evident in the agenda and the board packet that is circulated in advance of a board meeting.

And this means no subcommittees. Carver rightly notes that as soon as the board creates subcommittees they inevitably get involved in management.[6]

---

[6]Carver and Carver, "Carver's Policy Governance."

If there is a subcommittee, it is only to help the board do the board's work, not to help the management in the work of administration. We come back again and again to both the role of the board and the need for the board to speak as one voice. And this means that the board, as a rule, meets as a committee of the whole.

And the agenda always comes back to mission: is the mission happening? And here too it needs to be stressed that while the board has a responsibility to assure that the institution is financially healthy, they do not have a bottom line interest in whether the budget is balanced. Their main concern is the mission. When a school has a balanced budget and no students, it should be alarming to a board member rather than reassuring that somehow they are able to balance the budget even though the mission is not happening.

So the agenda for a board meeting can be quite simple. First, it includes a report from the president—as the one employee and the one appointed by the board to assure that the mission of the institution is happening. Then the agenda will include financial reports, nominations of board members, and board development. This development can include and needs to include focused conversation about the mission of the organization—where diverse constituencies on the board have the opportunity to hear from one another.

THE PRESIDENT'S LEADERSHIP AND ACCOUNTABILITY WITH THE BOARD

Presidents lead boards by providing them with the information they need—timely, accessible, and appropriate—for the board to be an effective board. They work to keep the board clear about the mission of the institution so that the board in turn can hold the president accountable for helping the institution stay on mission. Presidents speak often of the core values of the institution with the intent that the board will not only hold these same values but then work with the president to ensure that these are the values being nurtured by the institutional processes.

All of this means that the president is not a board member. It is not uncommon for presidents to assume that as president they have a vote on the board. But the genius of an effective institution is precisely that the board is the board and the president is the president. The president is accountable to the board and thus it follows that the president is not on the board and in effect accountable to herself. Even more obvious, the president should definitely not be the chair, in which case the board is surely not really a board but merely an advisory committee to the president. But more to the point, the president does not need to be a board member to be effective as president. Indeed, at its best, the board will meet *in camera*—without the president—as part of fostering its capacity to be the board, distinct from but also in counterpoint to the role of the president, to be the board. By insisting that the board meet in camera, the president signals that the work of the president needs a strong, informed, engaged, but also independent board that can truly hold the president accountable.

THE VITAL RELATIONSHIP BETWEEN THE BOARD CHAIR AND THE PRESIDENT

In many respects, the most pivotal relationship in an institution is the relationship between the president and the chair of the board. When this relationship works—marked by trust, mutual respect, and mutual accountability—the institution is well served. And when this dynamic is missing, it is only a matter of time that the relationship between the president and the board will suffer and that thus, in due time, the whole institution will struggle.

Both need to let the other be the other. Presidents need board chairs who know that as board chair, they only speak for the board as a whole, that they have no independent authority other than the authority of the board speaking collectively. Presidents in turn know that they are accountable to the board, but that this finds existential expression through focused accountability to the board chair. But the outcome is not that the organization is now led by the chair; rather, the president is still the president. And the president knows that the work of the president requires the backstop and essential role of a board chair.

EFFECTIVE BOARDS AND ESSENTIAL POLICIES

Presidents, to be effective, need to assure that the boards to which they are accountable have in place, at the very least, three kinds of policies.

Terms of reference. Put in writing—ideally in a board handbook—the "terms of reference." What is the work of the board and how will it exercise its responsibilities as moderated by the chair and in support of the president?

Terms of reference include these: What decisions are made where in the institution? Who is responsible for what, and in what ways are they held accountable for the exercise of their role and power? University board members, for example, should have a clear understanding of the work of the faculty and the role of the faculty in governance. They should both believe in and understand what it means to actually protect academic freedom and the authority of the faculty to oversee the curriculum and teach their courses. Church board members should know what it means to be a church board member and how the work of the board happens in complement to the work of the senior pastoral leadership and to the legitimate voice of the congregation as a whole.

The terms of reference should regularly be reviewed so they are up-to-date and relevant, actually informing the work of the board and thus of the whole institution. New board members should receive an orientation so that they are brought into an understanding of how this organization works—how power is shared and what is the character of the power they have within this particular organization, which may be different from a previous board on which they have served.

Conflict of interest. An effective board has in place a policy and a practice on "conflict of interest." The governance system, beginning with the trustees (but for the institution as a whole) should have a clearly outlined policy and practice regarding conflicts of interest. It is imperative for board members that they avoid even the appearance of a conflict of interest (optics matter), including any personal or familial financial benefits and any relationships with organizations that serve overlapping constituencies. We avoid creating the potential for creating a conflict of interest or even the perception of a conflict of interest. There is a duty of loyalty to the organization where you serve.

You do not serve on a board when your sibling or parent or offspring or close relative is the president. Or if an item on the agenda might implicate you in a conflict of interest, you declare a potential conflict of interest and recuse yourself when said topic or issue comes to the table for review and discussion. You are not part of the deliberation. You cannot serve on a church board if a member of the staff is a family member. It simply cannot be done. Any appeal to altruism is misguided. The board cannot objectively review and hold the staff accountable or review a proposed budget with salary implications when a close family member is on the board and sitting at the table with board colleagues. Institutional intelligence requires that we attend to all the ways in which a conflict of interest might undermine effective governance.

Perhaps we need to be doubly clear here and actually spell out what this means. If you are a board member in a local church and your son is a candidate to be the youth pastor? Easy call. You recuse yourself from the search and interview process and you resign from the board if your son is actually appointed to the position.

If you are on the board of a college and your sister is a candidate for a senior position, you recuse yourself from the process and actually step down if she is appointed.

You do not serve on the board of two sister institutions that might in any way be viewed as in competition for students or donor dollars.

If you are on the faculty tenure committee of a theological seminary and your close friend is coming up for tenure, and you know and everyone knows that you will not be able to objectively evaluate whether your colleague should receive tenure, you recuse yourself. Optics matter.

If you are a major donor to an institution or, perhaps, a representative of a key external constituency—perhaps a denominational official of an affiliated denomination—always insist on respecting the integrity of the board as a governing body and, as an external stakeholder, honor and work within the governance structures of the institution. In the long run, this is not a matter of limiting your influence but of strengthening the governance systems of the institution of which you are a part.

In each of these situations, take the lead. Do not wait for others to mention this or assume that if there is a problem, the chair will speak to you about it. Raise the issue; take the initiative; indicate that you will recuse yourself and step down and off the committee or board if this is what the situation requires.

Having said that, if someone is in a conflict-of-interest situation, there is no avoiding that the chair of the committee or the board will need to take the lead and quietly raise the issue and suggest that a recusal would be appropriate. But it is always easier for all involved if we can each take personal responsibility for any situation where we might be in an actual or a perceived conflict of interest.

Board effectiveness. And then, third, effective boards have policies in place that encourage intentional reflection on board effectiveness—the board as a whole and the work and contribution of individual board members. Presidents encourage the board to develop policies that force the board to review not only the work of the president but also their work as a board.

All this matters for a very simple reason. There are no effective organizations without an effective board. Thus board effectiveness is a high and essential priority for everyone—working diligently to function in light of the terms of reference, attending to potential or perceived conflicts of interest, all with an active resolve to work, as a board member, toward making certain that this board functions as effectively as possible.

INSTITUTIONS ARE GOOD FOR THE SOUL

The Spiritual Dynamics of Working Within an Organization

C an we speak of institutions as venues—communal spaces and social structures—for spiritual formation? Can we speak of organizations as good for the soul or say that our active participation in institutions provides us with a range of opportunities, stress points, learnings, and challenges that become for us the very place and means by which we grow in faith, hope, and love?

The Christian believer can always work with an assumption regarding a fundamental call: namely, that God in Christ and through the Spirit calls us to and graces us that we would be maturing in our faith, learning to love, growing in our capacity for generous service. In a way comparable to a church and perhaps, for some, even more intensely than a faith community, an institution is a forum for testing our mettle and moving us toward deeper faith in Christ—the very institutions where we serve as colleagues, employees, and board members.

Yes, of course, the biblical expectation would certainly be that our formation happens within the community of faith, the worshiping congregation of which we are a part (see Ephesians 4:11-16). And not for a moment am I suggesting that our institutions take the place of the church in our lives. Not at all. It is merely that for many, the focus and intensity of our work lives in institutions will be an opportunity for spiritual formation. And more, we need to foster spiritual dispositions and capacities to thrive and grow in the institutions of which we are a part.

What this assumes is that human flourishing can and will happen in and through institutions. Institutions are spheres of human involvement and influence where we can grow in wisdom, learn what it means to love the other, foster a capacity for vocational and personal integrity, and, of course, learn to live with joy and peace in the midst of difficulty and, not infrequently, turmoil. And, perhaps most of all, we can grow ever more deeply in our capacity to live in union with Christ.

I should perhaps nuance all of this a bit and stress that institutions *can* be good for the soul. They will not always be good for us, of course. Organized work life can be deeply debilitating. We have to face the reality that if we do not guard our hearts—or perhaps better, attend to the movement of our hearts—life and work in institutions can easily leave us angry, bitter, and cynical. Nothing is gained by sentimentalizing institutions. Further, sometimes we are wise to recognize that "this is not the cross I am called to bear," that the organization of which we are a part is simply not a place that is conducive to our spiritual well-being. And in those situations, it is best either to leave (resign and find a new job) or to create a psychological wall—perhaps with social and physical distance, where you do the bare minimum as an employee, but keep your heart disengaged. Even churches can be marked by a culture of psychological manipulation and abuse. Some can handle this and create a guard to their hearts and minds. For others, they can only survive and thrive if they can leave—move on and find a community where they can actually be. This has to be an option. It would be an unfortunate outcome, but it has to be an option.

So then, we can affirm that institutions can be spaces and places for human flourishing, but we need to be intentional. And we can, of course, draw on the spiritual wisdom of those who have gone before us. While many voices and sources of wisdom are pertinent here, I will mention three that can give us spiritual wisdom for engaging institutions. First, consider the wisdom of the great monastic administrator, theologian, and spiritual writer St. Bernard of Clairvaux (1090–1153), in many ways the premier representative of the monastic movement in the church. I will lean into his wisdom when it comes to the dynamics of an authoritative community that is learning what it means to live in love.

Second, Ignatius Loyola, the founder of the Society of Jesus (1491–1556), has much wisdom to offer those in institutions, largely because he established an intentionally apostolic order that, in turn, influenced good thinking about what it might mean to speak of a spirituality for the active life.

And then third, consider also the insights of Dietrich Bonhoeffer (1906–1945), whose work includes focused reflection on what it means to live in community in the institution he established—the Finkenwalde school for preachers, established to prepare pastoral leadership for the Confessing Church under the Third Reich. All three of these writers stress the importance of gratitude, but I will reference Bonhoeffer in particular when I speak to this in the comments below.

Leaning into the wisdom of the Christian spiritual heritage, then, I am suggesting that our life and work within institutions can be for the well-being of our souls. I will consider this question under the following four headings or topics: (1) institutions as places where we learn to work within an authoritative community; (2) institutions as social venues where, in a community, we are learning to love our neighbor and learning the humility of interdependence; (3) institutions as venues of human engagement where we can, using the Ignatian phrase, learn to find God in all things; and (4) institutions as entities calling us to a healthy differentiation, reminding us that our true home is with God.

WORKING WITHIN AN AUTHORITATIVE COMMUNITY

Institutions are social structures that by nature are hierarchical. Some might protest that hierarchies are inherently bad and that any exercise of authority—hierarchical authority—is necessarily suspect and an abuse of power. Alternatively, we can view these authoritative structures as vital to the capacity of the organization to achieve its mission. But we can go further. The issue is not just one of pragmatics, as though hierarchy is a necessary evil. Instead we can affirm that authority is fundamental to human life and human flourishing. We are designed, wired, to live under authority. We only flourish when we are not only in community, but more specifically in an authoritative community. Bernard and the entire monastic tradition assumed that persons, individual human souls, could only thrive if we lived not as independent and autonomous persons but within structured, authoritative communities where we actually learn to defer to a hierarchy.

I am a baby boomer and those of my generation do not tend to like the words *submission, authority*, or *hierarchy*. Perhaps we are reacting to the abuse of authority that we saw; perhaps we are simply free spirits. But as a rule we are not inclined to see authority as a good or essential thing. And yet what we have come to learn and need to learn—and what the whole of the Christian spiritual traditions insists—is that the gift of an authoritative community provides us with, at the very least, two things.

First, institutions provide us with mechanisms for accountability. If and as you work within an institution, it is not long before you realize that you are not an independent and autonomous worker; you are not your own boss; your work is not, in the immediate at least, (just) between you and God. To the contrary, you learn that you have a job and that you are accountable to someone for whether you do that job. If as a faculty member you want tenure, then you are accountable to the dean and the tenure committee. And this runs throughout the whole institution. Everyone—literally everyone—is accountable to someone. As a president, I serve the board with real and tangible accountability, and since the board as a whole is not likely going to effectively supervise my work, then the practical outcome is that I see myself as accountable—practically and existentially speaking—to the board chair. But the main point is that I am accountable to someone for the quality and character of my work. I report to the board; I am a man under authority. And it is a matter of personal and spiritual integrity that I take this accountability seriously. I live and work and serve under—that is the right word, *under*—constituted authority.

But even as a writer, working with an editor of a publishing firm, I work with a genuine accountability to the publishing house. I am under contract for a manuscript, and I meet my deadlines—taking them seriously because I am accountable to the editor and the publishing house for the quality of work that I do for them and with them.

And the point is that we all need accountability. It needs to be genuinely empowering accountability if we are going to thrive. But it is still accountability. We need deadlines; we need the spiritual discipline and humility of being accountable and having a boss and submitting our reports on time, when they are due, and with a quality that reflects the commitment and potential we have within the organization.

When students sign up for an academic program, they enter into an authoritative community: they sit in class and defer to this authority—submitting assignments on time, respecting the terms by which they are enrolled in the class and the academic program. This is soul forming; we only know spiritual vitality when we graciously accept these dynamics.

And second, when we speak of institutions as authoritative communities, it means that we will not always get our way. We will get outvoted. We will differ with the boss and, well, just have to accept that what we think is right—the right action, the right decision, the right outcome—will not happen. We may believe very strongly in what is best both for ourselves and for the organization. As part of a denomination, we might speak with much conviction to something that is terribly important to our theological and ethical vision for the church. But we will get outvoted. And we will defer to the majority decision; we will accept that our will—what we had hoped would happen—did not happen.

This is—dare we say it—actually good for the soul. We learn to trust God and the purposes of God. We learn to respect due process and the fact that we are part of an authoritative community that has a system of governance and decision making. And this means we know how to live graciously when we do not get our way, without resentment or anger or residual frustration.

The ideal is that you learn this as a child—a young person at home, perhaps with your siblings. But sooner or later it has to be learned, and we only thrive in institutions if we get this. We lean into this way of being and responding not as though it is a great evil or a problem but rather as something that is crucial to our own spiritual formation.

And the genius of our institutional engagement is precisely in this: How can we learn to defer, to submit, to yield the floor, without losing our soul? Can we be fully engaged but still defer to constituted authority? How can we vote eagerly in an election and perhaps get outvoted and then live graciously with the outcome? Can we engage the deliberative process with conviction, speak our mind and our conscience, and defer to the will of our colleagues?

I wonder if we can thus say that an institution has an almost sacramental quality to it: it becomes to me a means by which I learn to live under the authority of Christ—in obedience to Christ. Of course, they are not one and the same; of course the authority of the president of the organization is not the authority of Christ. Of course not. For Bernard and all the monastic leaders, the voice of the abbot was the voice of Christ; they were one and the same. But we are not prepared to assume as much. And yet what I learn is that in living out my deference to constituted authority in the institution of which I am a part, I learn and grow into the grace of living under the authority of Christ. It becomes the mechanism by which, in my life, I learn to say and know and feel that it is not in the end about my desires and my will but about the will of God that is exercised in tangible and concrete ways in and through the organizations of which I am a part.[1]

For Ignatius Loyola, the religious order he founded—the Society of Jesus (Jesuit)—included a vow of obedience to the pope. Many contemporary Christians recoil at such seeming subservience, insisting that we should only give that level of loyalty to Christ. But for Ignatius, we live and serve in submission to Christ only if and as we learn to live in deference to constituted authority, however that finds expression in our lives.

---

[1]When we say that an organization or institution has an almost sacramental quality to it, we are making a distinction: the organization is not God; the authoritative community is not ultimately "lord" to us. The language of sacrament is a way of making a critical and necessary distinction between the reality and the symbol, between the reality and the means by which that reality is known and experienced. And the distinction is essential. However valuable and essential authoritative communities are to our spiritual health and well-being, they are not God to us. And this becomes the essential basis for any kind of civil disobedience, whether to civic or ecclesial authorities. And it is what lies behind a whistleblower policy and procedure being in place—an essential element in a mature organization, which recognizes that anyone in the organization should be able to call the organization to account when core values are violated or when those in authority are abusing whatever measure of authority has been assigned to them. There have to be mechanisms in place that signal that no one in the institution has absolute and unquestioned authority. And yet it is important to remember this: we only have the right to challenge the system when we have demonstrated the capacity to graciously live within an authoritative community.

LEARNING TO LOVE

Then also, let's face it: institutions are made up of people. And we are called to love people—any people, all people, anyone who comes into our sphere of life, work, and influence. And an institution is a good place to learn what it means to love your neighbor as yourself. Institutions are schools of love. Each day, every working day and sometimes on our off days, we are learning how to love the people in the organization where we work.

This means that we are called to be attentive to the other, deferring to the other, and, of course, kind, generous, patient, and forbearing with one another. Are there limits to our patience and forbearance? Yes, of course, we may have to let a person who is underperforming know that their employment is ending. But even then, love rules the day.

In institutions we learn what it means to love. For Bonhoeffer, the key to love is hospitality and the heart of hospitality is that we learn how to listen to the other. To love is to listen, and we can only thrive in institutions if we regularly learn to talk less and listen more; to speak much less than we might be inclined to speak; and to attend more to our neighbor, our colleagues, the people we are called to serve, our donors and supporters, and indeed all the key stakeholders without whom we would not be in existence.

To love is also to bear with one another and to forgive one another. And we need to stress this: in institutions it is imperative that we keep short accounts. I have a vivid memory of a colleague I had when I was the dean of Regent College in Vancouver, BC, who tended to be rather intense and opinionated and more than willing to differ with me and others in faculty meetings. And differ we did. But what I so appreciated was that if there was any possibility of offense it was only minutes after a faculty meeting that there would be a tap on my office door—and he would open the door just wide enough to stick his head through and ask, "Are we okay?" If I hesitated, he would come in and make sure that the day did not go any further without the two of us being at peace with each other. We will make mistakes. We will say things we should not say; we will do things that are not consistent with our core values and commitments. We can learn to say sorry—to others and to yourself—learn to attend to the quality of the working relationships.

All of this assumes good conversation, where we are growing together, learning together, and actually coming more and more to see our need for the other. We listen. And then we seek to speak the truth in love. We learn, in love, to get past niceties and to get past the fear of hurting feelings to a point where in deep consideration for the other—in kindness—we know the grace of open conversation. We learn to say what needs to be said for the well-being of the other and of the institution of which we are a part. We get beyond the fear of the anger and disappointment of the other and say what needs to be said—graciously and kindly, but still staying what needs to be said.

This is, of course, the love of mutual dependence. Institutions thrive quite simply because we learn to exercise our strengths, capacities, and callings in a way that is mutually dependent on the strengths and capacities of others. Institutions are social constructs where we learn interdependence. We are not independent operators; we are not heroes or lone rangers. Rather, to get anything done—quite literally, anything—requires that, within an authoritative community, we lean into the capacities of others. We learn that no one is self-sufficient, that no one has all the answers, all the skills, all the wisdom. We need one another. We defer to one another as we together seek common cause.

FINDING GOD IN ALL THINGS

It is surely one of the great insights of the Ignatian spiritual tradition that we meet God not only in retreat, in prayer, in the church, but also in the world and specifically in the work to which we are called in the world. For this tradition—an apostolic order—it was revolutionary to recognize that in moving into the world as those who act in the name of Christ, they would actually find that God had gone before them. And surely this disposition needs to shape our approach to our institutions and foster within us a capacity to "see God in all things"—to see all the diverse ways in which God may be acting, quite independent of our efforts, within the institutions of which we are a part.[2]

---

[2]This theme of "finding God in all things" is a thread that runs through the whole of Ignatian spirituality.

It is so easy for us to assume that we build institutions through our efforts. And, of course, our work *does* make a difference. But it is also crucial that we recognize that in all the work we do—yes, quite literally *all* the work we do—we are but participants in the work of God. And in the work of church or institution or agency-building, God is a player and if we are attentive, we can and will see evidence of the diverse ways in which God is present to our organizations.

And we will give thanks, daily, for the ways in which the Creator is good and is present to our organizations. We will be ever grateful.

And we will be patient, for indeed it will often be the case that it seems like God is not as present and active as we would like God to be!

And we will keep ever open and alert to the new possibilities, to the surprising ways in which God may be present to us: a conversation in which an insight emerges that we had not expected, an overture from a sister agency for a partnership that strikes us as sheer genius but was not part of our planning, some good thing that seemed to come out of nowhere.

We will be ever-attentive to the ways in which God is present—before and behind, on the right and on the left—to our work. We will give thanks, and we will respond with courage and joy to the ways in which God is inviting us to be part of something that we know, in the end, is the work of God.

Giving thanks is so crucial; the organization is only effective when a whole range of individuals make a difference and contribute generously. And so we are grateful for those around us. Every day it makes sense to thank at least one colleague or donor or member of the board, as an acknowledgment of the goodness and presence of God in your institution. We learn, as Bonhoeffer stresses, to be grateful for what already is—the good that is already happening—rather than always complaining about what is not given to us, recognizing that unless we are grateful for what God has given us, he can hardly entrust us with more.[3]

As noted, finding God in all things means patience—with God, with people, with systems, and with the pace of institutional change and growth. It means that we graciously accept the quotidian of organizations: the

---

[3]Dietrich Bonhoeffer, *Life Together and Prayer Book of the Bible*, Dietrich Bonhoeffer Works, trans. Daniel W. Bloesch and James H. Burtness (Minneapolis: Fortress, 1996), 5:37.

processes; the meetings; the mundane; the details; the hard labor-intensive work of policy development, of grading papers, and of cleaning tables. Beware of thinking that any of this is below you.

And when we speak of finding God in all things, we are reminded of the scourge of idealism and the temptation or propensity to be continually disappointed that the organization you are part of is so far from ideal and thus to live perpetually in dismay that we are so far short of what we think it would be like to be part of a great institution—with the assumption, of course, that we ourselves deserve a much better institution. We need to have the grace to turn from the ideal and accept, with grace, the less-than-perfect, even the very far from perfect. This is not to accept mediocrity or banality but rather to accept that we are all learning and that our institutional maturity comes oh-so-very slowly. The constant complaint, the perpetual disappointment with all that is not as we had hoped it would be in our institutions may well blind us to what God is actually doing. Bonhoeffer states it so well, when he writes, "if . . . we only keep complaining to God that everything is so miserable and so insignificant and does not at all live up to our expectations—then we hinder God from letting our community grow."[4]

Finding God in all things also means that because all institutions are built, with God, by multiple persons and contributions, our contribution will always be just that: *one* contribution. And this means that our only hope for thriving and for making a contribution is that we learn the grace of accepting good policy statements, good mission statements, and good systems without demanding perfection. We compromise; we accept the slightly less than ideal because we are only one voice in the process. And yes, the policy or mission statement or whatever it might be may not be perfect, but it reflects the best possible with our colleagues' contributions. We know that we do not have the last word and we actually do not want the last word. We want an outcome, a decision, that reflects our best wisdom together.

Wisdom in institutions is found in the details and specifics of institutional life and in the particulars of policy development, contract negotiations,

---

[4]Ibid.

and curriculum revisions. The deep and defining institutional vision and values are embodied in the particulars—the conduct of meetings, the drafting of institutional policies, the daily work of attending to whatever it is that needs to be done. And thus the words of the letter to the Galatians remain ever present to us, "So let us not grow weary in doing what is right" (Galatians 6:9).

Finding God in all things means, further, that we are attentive to the ways in which we might be surprised through an interruption to our day. Some, of course, are so focused on their work responsibilities that they are simply not interruptible. They are on task! They have a to-do list, with deadlines, and pity the soul that dares to knock on their door and ask if perchance they could have two minutes to discuss a small problem.

Others, to the contrary, insist that "interruptions are my ministry." They view each interruption as a God-ordained appointment—a means, precisely, by which they are finding God in all things.

In response, I wonder if neither option actually reflects the best approach to our work. Surely we can recognize that we have to focus if we are going to be able to do good work. We need to be able to close the door and meet a deadline: a lecture for an upcoming class, a revised policy statement for board review and action, a proposal that we are required to submit to a foundation. To be faithful in our work, we need to have times when we are able to focus. And we need to respect this in one another; if someone has their door closed, recognize that they are doing something that requires focus. Therefore, we don't send them communications, such as a text message, that demand an immediate response when an email message is sufficient, so that they can respond at their convenience. And this also means that we do not assume that a person whose door is always open is somehow more engaged, more personal, and more committed to the best values of the organization. We need focus, and we respect the need of our colleagues for focus.

And yet we also need interruptions. We need them because they are part of institutional life and things come up and need a response that could not have been planned or anticipated. We pause in the hallway for a brief exchange; someone drops by the office with a question or a comment for which they would value a response. What we learn is that our day has seasons of focus, but also times in which our door is open and colleagues can drop in. We have a rhythm to our work of focus and interrupt-ability, all with a recognition that many times the interruption will actually be a God-moment in our day—an encounter in which we are reminded that we need to be attentive to how we might be called to see God in all things.

INSTITUTIONS AND DIFFERENTIATION

Our work within institutions can be deeply gratifying: the joy of partici-pating in something bigger than ourselves, the synergy of leveraging our contribution alongside that of others toward a shared vision and outcome. But we also need to acknowledge that institutions can be hurtful. Institu-tions can be deeply affirming places, but they can also be venues where we get roughed up.

As implied, this is not to discount the huge points of satisfaction that often come through our participation in the organizations of which we are a part. Rather it is to stress that we cannot expect it, demand it, or assume that this is where our ego needs will be fulfilled. You cannot thrive let alone survive within institutions until and unless you learn to have multiple sources of external spiritual and emotional support. You cannot expect the institution itself to be the source of your ego needs, your emo-tional well-being, and your spiritual sanity. More to the point, wise women and men know that their fundamental personal and emotional needs are not going to be met by the organization where they work.

This is so for two reasons—at least two: first, the call to obscurity and second, the inevitable institutional rough edges that will be a source of frustration and difficulty for us. Regarding obscurity, one of the grave spiritual dangers within institutions is that in our work we would only function, to use the language of Colossians, to please our [institutional] masters (see Colossians 3:24). That is, our work is done so that we are seen, noticed, appreciated, affirmed, and rewarded, perhaps with more pay or with a promotion or both, or just to get affirmation. Some con-temporary guides to life in the work-world actually encourage this: you are always, it is implied, building your resume and thus always seeking to get noticed for all the ways that would advance your career.

It is a deadly disease. It is not that we are not accountable, and it is not that we do not report on our activities, specifically where and when we have an accountability structure. It is rather that so much of what is essential to our work is done in obscurity. Some of the most important work we do in organizations is done away from the eyes of those whom we serve—quietly, carefully, with due diligence. We do not trumpet our successes or accomplishments or contributions. We just quietly go about our work, which in many situations is behind the scenes, away from the limelight.

My rule of thumb, as I report to the board of my institution, is to ask, what do they need to know so that they can do *their* work—as a board? I do not need to drop small hints about my long hours or difficult decisions or, frankly, anything that is not pertinent to what they need to know to be an effective board. The irony, you might say, is that when we report to those to whom we are accountable, it is not actually about us. I may celebrate the work of others—my colleagues, perhaps—but it is not about me. The main point remains: I give the board the information they need to be able to do their work.

Thus we encounter the wonderful notion that, actually—again, as in Colossians 3:23—we do our work, to use the language of the Authorized Version of the New Testament, "as unto the Lord." It is here that we find our deepest joy, satisfaction, and personal fulfillment: before God, we have done good work. We receive our work, even in institutions, from God, and we offer the work of our hands and minds back to God. And we do so whether we are thanked, affirmed, or, in our minds, adequately appreciated.

Second, the counter-side to obscurity is that we will actually get noticed but not appreciated and perhaps even criticized. It is virtually impossible to be fully engaged in an institution and not experience significant and sometimes crushing personal disappointment and even criticism. You might get significant praise along the way. If you do your job and do it well, you will likely get plenty of affirmation. But you will also have those days when you take a bit of a hit. You did not perform well and you were criticized. Or you did your job, you did what needed to be done, and you did it well, but someone was very still disappointed and let you know; rather than saying "thank you" and appreciating what you did, they instead either misunderstood or simply disagreed with you and they let you know it.

A veteran university president suggested to me that presidents at their very best probably only have 70 percent support in terms of political capital. Federal or national leaders would be thrilled to have 70 percent support. In other words, you will always have those who are not happy with you and your work. It is what it is. And at some point, even if you have done your very best, you may well be asked to resign or forced to leave your position. You might even get fired. Institutions can be delightful places to work; they can be crushing places to work. Both. And thus I often recall a line, attributed to Martin Luther King Jr., that he sought the grace that he would not allow his head to be inflated by praise, or his spirit crushed by criticism. This is a position of freedom and joy. This is the emotional space, to use the language of Ignatius Loyola and the *Spiritual Exercises*, of holy indifference.[5]

But this spiritual disposition—be it the joy of obscurity or the freedom from both praise and criticism—is only possible if our deepest sense of self is found not in the institutions of which we are a part, but in God. Thus we sustain a healthy differentiation from the institution—fully present, even working diligently in obscurity, but with freedom, needing not to be affirmed and not fearing criticism, because one's personal ego needs, one's sense of personal value and worth, is found in God.

Where we feel all of this most keenly, I suspect, is when it is time for us to leave—whether we choose to move on at our own initiative or whether our termination is forced: they have asked for our resignation. Either way, by our own initiative or that of others, a transition is coming.

Some people overstay. They cannot imagine life without this institution, this job, this position that has meant so much to them. They stay when it may well be long overdue for them to move on. They have over-identified themselves with a role or an institution and have stayed beyond their best-by date, neglecting to realize that there is a shelf life to many positions within institutions. The grace we seek, in other words, is to be fully engaged in a role—the role that has been assigned to or given to us—but

---

[5]Ignatius speaks of the most perfect kind of humility in *The Spiritual Exercises of St. Ignatius*, trans. Louis J. Pohl (Chicago: Loyola University Press, 1975), #167.

then, with grace, move on when it is time to move on to a new chapter or a new challenge.

But even when we leave on good terms, or on our own terms, there is something we need to acknowledge. Leaving an institution looks and feels like pulling a finger out of a glass of water. It is rather amazing how quickly the organization heals over. We may think that we were somewhat indispensable and valuable and appreciated, and perhaps we were. But the survival instincts of institutions are remarkable; people move on and oh-so-quickly. And, actually, this is the way that it should be. We did our part; now we move on. And what concerns us most is that the institution thrives, not whether we are sorely missed.

Then also, we need to speak of those times when we are forced out—fired, asked to resign, criticized perhaps from so many angles that we feel no choice but to move on. Institutions can be brutal places. Even though they are indispensable to our lives and to our vocations, they are also places where we will as often as not get hurt. This may include that we have to leave a job under rather unpleasant circumstances. It will happen to many if not most of us. And the huge temptation will be to leave with fire in our eyes—angry, hurt, lashing out at those who have wronged us, and eager to vindicate ourselves and prove that the institution, particularly the authorities that did us in, are in the wrong and need to be either shamed or brought to some form of justice. That is the temptation, and those moments and days when we are in that pain and so angry and hugely disappointed with those who did not defend us are a season of deep spiritual vulnerability. It is imperative to guard our hearts from a "root of bitterness," to use the language of the book of Hebrews. It is so easy—all too easy—to allow the hurt and rejection from one job to poison the well of our hearts, and the result is that we take this toxicity with us to the next job or appointment or season of life. The grace we seek is captured so well by my son, when he went through a rough patch: as he put it, we walk away without villainizing those who have wronged us and without victimizing ourselves. If we can do this, we are the stronger for it and we actually bring grace and strength to our next assignment. We grow in our capacity for magnanimity. It is the grace of a tough skin—we don't take things personally—and a tender heart, evident in gentle eyes.

We need not be tolerant of psychological abuse or any kind of abuse. But we will be wounded along the way and we have to learn how to leave and be on our way and leave a blessing behind us, refusing to allow any pathology or toxicity to remain in our own hearts.

If we know the grace of differentiation, it will surely be because there are external practices—external to the institution—that are for us a source of comfort and inner strength: evensong at the local Anglican cathedral; an evening with friends, not mere acquaintances but friends, over a good meal and grace-filled conversation; an hour in the garden with a rake or hoe or pruning shears; a Sabbath, a day of physical, social, and psychological disengagement; a winter evening by the fire with a superb novel.

CONCLUSION

Institutions are good for the soul, but only if we are attentive and intentional, alert to the ways in which cynicism and impatience can percolate into our spirits, while actively nurturing our personal capacity, within the institution, to grow in faith, hope, and love. And this means, to use the wonderful language and practice commended to us by the *Spiritual Exercises*, the examination of conscience, or typically spoken of as simply the "examen."[6] What is urged is that we be attentive to what is happening in the movements of our hearts—the joys, the sorrows of the day—and considering, before God, what they mean and what we are learning and, most particularly, what the Spirit is signaling to us through the emotional ups and downs of the day. This is ideally a daily exercise so that our joys are actually able to inform and sustain our work and so that our sorrows are considered and moderated so that they do not unduly leave us with the potential to descend into cynicism. We keep short accounts—emotionally aware and knowing that what happens to us emotionally may well be the most significant thing about us.

Yes, as noted, institutions can be good for the soul. But we must be attentive.

---

[6]Ibid, #24–26.

AN INSTITUTIONAL INTELLIGENCE
ESSENTIAL READING LIST

INTRODUCTION—THE MEANING OF INSTITUTIONS

Davison Hunter, James. *To Change the World: The Irony, Tragedy, and Possibility of Christianity in the Late Modern World*. New York: Oxford University Press, 2010.

Heclo, Hugh. *On Thinking Institutionally*. Boulder, CO: Paradigm Publishers, 2008.

Kilmann, Ralph H. *Beyond the Quick Fix*. Washington, DC: Beard Books, 2004.

Lencioni, Patrick. *The Advantage: Why Organizational Health Trumps Everything Else in Business*. San Francisco: Jossey-Bass, 2012.

MISSION

Drucker, Peter F. *The Effective Executive*. New York: Harper and Row, 1966.

———. *Managing the Non-profit Organization: Principles and Practices*. New York: Harper-Business, 1990.

Frame, William V. *The American College Presidency as Vocation: Easing the Burden, Enhancing the Joy*. Abilene, TX: Abilene Christian University Press, 2013.

GOVERNANCE

Bahls, Steven C. *Shared Governance in a Time of Change: A Practical Guide for Universities and Colleges*. Washington, DC: AGB Press, 2014.

Brown, Jim. *The Imperfect Board Member: Discovering the Seven Disciplines of Governance Excellence*. San Francisco: Jossey-Bass, 2006.

Carver, John, and Miriam Mayhew Carver. *Carver Guide: Basic Principles of Policy Governance*. San Francisco: Jossey-Bass, 1996.

———. *Reinventing Your Board*. Rev. ed. San Francisco: Jossey-Bass, 2006.

Chait, Richard P., William P. Ryan, and Barbara E. Taylor. *Governance as Leadership: Reframing the Work of Nonprofit Boards*. Hoboken, NJ: John Wiley, 2005.

Jinkins, Michael, and Deborah Bradshaw Jinkins. *The Character of Leadership: Political Realism and Public Virtue in Non-Profit Organizations*. San Francisco: Jossey-Bass, 1998.

Wheeler, Barbara G., and Helen Ouellette. "Governance That Works: Effective Leadership for Theological Schools." *Auburn Studies*, no. 20 (March 2015). https://auburnseminary.org/wp-content/uploads/2016/04/Governance-That-Works.pdf.

PEOPLE

Bridges, William. *Managing Transitions: Making the Most of Change*. 3rd ed. Philadelphia, PA: Da Capo Press, 2009.

Cloud, Henry. *Necessary Endings: The Employees, Businesses, and Relationships That All of Us Have to Give Up in Order to Move Forward*. New York: HarperBusiness, 2010.

Collins, Jim. *Good to Great: Why Some Companies Make the Leap . . . and Others Don't*. New York: Harper Business, 2001.

CULTURE

Schein, Edgar H. *Organizational Culture and Leadership*. 2nd ed. San Francisco: Jossey-Bass, 1992.

Scott, Susan. *Fierce Conversations: Achieving Success at Work and in Life, One Conversation at a Time*. New York: Berkley, 2004.

FINANCE

Collins, Jim. *Good to Great and the Social Sectors: A Monograph to Accompany Good to Great*. New York: HarperCollins, 2005.

Holmes, Paul A., ed. *The Pastor's Toolbox: Management Skills for Parish Leadership*. Collegeville, MN: Liturgical Press, 2014.

Jeavons, Thomas H., and Rebekah Burch Basinger. *Growing Givers' Hearts: Treating Fundraising as Ministry*. San Francisco: Jossey-Bass, 2000.

McCrea, Jennifer, and Jeffrey C. Walker. *The Generosity Network: New Transformational Tools for Successful Fundraising*. New York: Deepak Chopra Books, 2013.

Nouwen, Henri J. M. *The Spirituality of Fundraising*. Nashville, TN: Upper Room Books, 2010.

Townsley, Michael K. *Small College Guide to Financial Health: Beating the Odds*. Washington, DC: National Association of College and University Business Officers, 2009.

Walker, Julia I. *A Fundraising Guide for Nonprofit Board Members*. Hoboken, NJ: Wiley, 2012.

BUILT SPACE

Alexander, Christopher, Sara Ishikawa, and Murray Silverstein. *A Pattern Language: Towns, Buildings, Construction*. New York: Oxford University Press, 1977.

Bess, Philip. *Till We Have Built Jerusalem: Architecture, Urbanism, and the Sacred*. Wilmington, DE: ISI Books, 2006.

Brand, Stewart. *How Buildings Learn: What Happens After They're Built*. New York: Viking, 1994.

Hjalmarson, Leonard. *No Home Like Place: A Christian Theology of Place*. Skyforest, CA: Urban Loft Publishers, 2014.

Inge, John. *A Christian Theology of Place: Explorations in Practical, Pastoral and Empirical Theology*. Burlington, VT: Ashgate, 2003.

Pohl, Christine. *Making Room: Recovering Hospitality as a Christian Tradition*. Grand Rapids: Eerdmans, 1999.

Rybczynski, Witold. *How Architecture Works: A Humanist's Toolkit*. New York: Farrar, Straus and Giroux, 2013.

Tournier, Paul. *A Place for You: Psychology and Religion*. Translated by Edwin Hudson. New York: Harper and Row, 1968.

Visser, Margaret. *The Geometry of Love: Space, Time, Mystery, and the Meaning of an Ordinary Church*. New York: HarperCollins, 2008.

Wertheim, Margaret. *The Pearly Gates of Cyberspace: A History of Space from Dante to the Internet*. New York: W. W. Norton & Company, 2000.

STRATEGIC ALLIANCES

Arsenault, Jane. *Forging Nonprofit Alliances*. San Francisco: Jossey-Bass, 1998.

Crutchfield, Leslie B., and Heather McLeod Grant. *Forces for Good: The Six Practices of High-Impact Non-Profits*. San Francisco: Jossey-Bass, 2008.

La Piana, David. *The Nonprofit Mergers Workbook*. St. Paul, MN: Fieldstone Alliance, 2000.

ALSO AVAILABLE FROM
GORDON T. SMITH

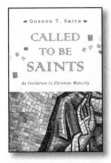

Called to Be Saints

Courage & Calling

Consider Your Calling

Listening to God in Times of Choice

Spiritual Direction

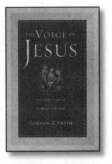

The Voice of Jesus

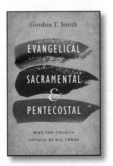

Evangelical, Sacramental, Pentecostal

Finding the Textbook You Need

The IVP Academic Textbook Selector
is an online tool for instantly finding the IVP books
suitable for over 250 courses across 24 disciplines.

ivpacademic.com